Dr. Gary D. German
Emeritus Professor of Linguistics and American Civilization
University of Western Brittany, France

———— ❁ ————

I have known Philip Bigler for 52 years and can attest that the spirit of respect and dedication to America's fighting men that is so clearly manifested in his latest book, *Tomb of the Unknown Soldier: A Century of Honor*, is a reflection of his lifelong, steadfast love of country. As the son of a World War II era U.S. Navy torpedo bomber pilot, the author is all too aware of the sacrifices that have preserved the United States and the ideals for which it stands since the foundation of the Republic.

Bigler knows what he is talking about. As a professional historian at Arlington Cemetery, where he worked for years documenting events and ceremonies at the Tomb of the Unknown Soldier, he knew every nook and cranny of the site and met many dignitaries and came to know many of the Old Guard sentinels who protect the Tomb.

For much of his career, he was also an extremely talented high school teacher in Virginia and Maryland and finally retired as the Director of the James Madison Center for Liberty & Learning at James Madison University. He wrote and taught seminars on the nation's Founding Fathers and instructed pre-service teachers in the art of effectively and honestly teaching history. Little wonder that Bigler was honored in 1998 at the White House by President Clinton with the "National Teacher of the Year" award. This unique experience shines through in the book.

Indeed, the author takes the reader on a fascinating journey providing a step-by-step account of the events and decisions which resulted in the consecration of the Tomb in 1921 and the successive developments that led to the inclusion of the Unknowns who perished during the World War II and the Korean and Vietnam Conflicts.

Tomb is a pleasure to read offering a host of insightful facts which are a testimony to Bigler's erudite scholarship. This is demonstrated not only by his meticulous attention to detail but also the thorough documentation of sources cited in the form of copious endnotes.

The book is written in a clear, elegant prose style and is also beautifully illustrated with a large number of rare photographs from the inception of the Tomb to the present day. As one would expect, his approach is highly pedagogical with every episode enriched by interesting anecdotes that simultaneously enliven the narrative and highlight the many hard decisions made at each critical stage of the expansion of the Tomb. His ability to contextualize events is also admirable.

Written nearly 100 years after the Unknown Soldier of World War I was lain to rest, this book is a wonderful tribute to all those men and women who made the ultimate sacrifice for this nation. It should be required reading for all Americans, young and old alike.

A Narrative History

TOMB
of the
Unknown Soldier

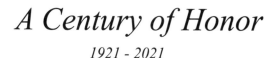

A Century of Honor
1921 - 2021

by

Philip Bigler

Former Arlington National Cemetery Historian
1998 National Teacher of the Year

APPLE**RIDGE**
PUBLISHERS

First Edition: April 1, 2019
Hard Cover Printing: November 11, 2020

Copyright © 2021 by APPLE RIDGE PUBLISHERS

Tomb of the Unknown Soldier:
A Century of Honor, 1921 - 2021

Apple Ridge Publishers
217 Bob White Lane
Quicksburg, Virginia 22847

http://www.appleridgepublishers.com
http://www.tomb2021.com
http://www.tombcentennial.com
Contact: info@appleridgepublishers.com

Soft Cover: ISBN: 978-1-5136-4277-2
Hard Cover/Revised: ISBN: 978-0-578-69126-8

PRINTED IN THE UNITED STATES OF AMERICA

In Loving Memory of My Parents

CDR Charles E. Bigler USN
12 July 1924 - 25 December 2003

&

Bernice R. Bigler
27 October 1920 - 28 February 1989

Sec. 7A, #113

Also by Philip Bigler

IN HONORED GLORY: *Arlington National Cemetery, the Final Post*

HOSTILE FIRE: *The Life and Death of Lt. Sharon A. Lane*

SCANDALOUS SON: *The Elusive Search for Dolley Madison's Son, John Payne Todd*

TEACHING HISTORY IN AN UNCIVILIZED WORLD

TEACHING IS TOUGH! *A Practical Guide to Classroom Success*

REMEMBERING JOHN F. KENNEDY: *The New Frontier and the Nation's Capital*

LIBERTY & LEARNING: *The Essential James Madison*

BE A TEACHER: *You Can Make a Difference*

WASHINGTON IN FOCUS: *A Photographic History of the Nation's Capital*

FAILING GRADES: *A Teacher's Report Card on Education in America*

Cover Photograph

✻

Guard at the Tomb of the Unknown Soldier
21 October 2018
by Philip Bigler.

Table of Contents

Table of Contents (cont.)

Timeline

1915 cont.	Dec. 18: President Woodrow Wilson marries Edith Galt in Washington, D.C.
1916	May 15: Judge Ivory Kimbell, the leading advocate for the construction of the Memorial Amphitheater, dies in Washington, D.C.; he is buried at Arlington National Cemetery in Section 3, #1538.
1917	Jan. 31: The Germans launch a policy of unrestricted submarine warfare in an effort to starve the British into submission; neutral shipping, including American merchant vessels, are targeted.
	Feb. 3: The American cargo vessel, SS *Housatonic*, is sunk by U-53.
	Feb. 25: The Cunard liner, RMS *Laconia*, is sunk while en route from London to New York; two Americans are killed.
	March 1: The Zimmermann telegram is made public.
	March 4: Woodrow Wilson is inaugurated for a second term.
	March 5: Wilson delivers his second inaugural address.
	March 8: Riots in Petrograd mark the beginning of the first Russian Revolution.
	March 15: Tsar Nicholas II abdicates his throne.
	March 16: The *Vigilancia* is sunk without warning; 15 Americans are killed.
	March 21: The American tanker *Healdton* is sunk killing 21.
	April 2: President Wilson delivers his war message to Congress.
	April 4: The Senate passes the war resolution by an 82 to 6 vote.
	April 6: The House passes the war resolution with 373 yeas to 50 nays.
	April 9: Vladimir I. Lenin leaves Zurich, Switzerland for Russia in a sealed train.
	May: The United States initiates a wartime draft.
	Oct. 25: The Bolsheviks seize power in Russia.
	Nov. 3: PVT Thomas Enright, CPL James B. Gresham, and PVT Merle Hay become the first American soldiers killed-in-action.
	Dec.: Only 175,655 American troops are deployed in Europe eight months after President Wilson's declaration of war.

1918	March 13: The Soviets sign the Treaty of Brest-Litovsk ending Russia's involvement in the Great War.

1918

March 13: The Soviets sign the Treaty of Brest-Litovsk ending Russia's involvement in the Great War.

May 28: American forces engage in their first major combat operations at the Battle of Cantigny.

July 17: Tsar Nicholas II and the Empress Alexandra are executed along with their five children in Yekaterinburg.

Nov. 9: Kaiser Wilhelm abdicates the Hohenzollern throne ending 400 years of Prussian rule; he is granted asylum in the Netherlands.

Nov. 11: An armistice is declared at 11:00 AM; American military deaths during the Great War are estimated to be 116,000. Of this number, 63,000 died of illness or disease.

1919

May 30: President Wilson and his wife, Edith, participate in Memorial Day ceremonies at the Suresnes American Cemetery in France.

June 28: The Treaty of Versailles is signed.

Oct. 2: President Wilson suffers a massive stroke while at the White House in Washington, D.C.

Nov. 19: The Senate fails to ratify the Treaty of Versailles by the required two-thirds majority.

1920

The first American war dead from the Great War are repatriated to Arlington.

May 15: The Memorial Amphitheater is dedicated at Arlington National Cemetery on the fourth anniversary of Judge Ivory Kimball's death.

June 20: The Memorial Amphitheater is officially turned over to the Quartermaster Department of the Army.

Nov. 7/8: The British Unknown is selected at St. Pol-sur-Ternoise in France.

Nov. 9: The French Unknown is selected.

Nov. 11: Ceremonies are held for the British and French Unknown Soldiers.

Dec. 21: Congressman Hamilton Fish of New York introduces legislation, HR 426, to authorize the burial of an American Unknown Soldier at Arlington National Cemetery.

1921

March 4: Woodrow Wilson signs Public Resolution #67 authorizing the selection of an American Unknown Soldier.

1921 cont.	Aug. 24: Congress authorizes the awarding of the Medal of Honor to the Unknown Soldier.
	Oct. 23: Four unknown candidates are disinterred from the American cemeteries at Meuse Argonne, St. Mihiel, Somme, and Aisne Marne.
	Oct. 24: SGT Edward F. Younger selects the Unknown Soldier during ceremonies at Châlons-sur-Marne, France.
	Nov. 4: Congress passes HJ Res. 215 declaring Armistice Day a National Holiday in honor of the Unknown.
	Nov. 9: The American Unknown Soldier arrives in Washington, D.C. aboard the USS *Olympia*.
	Nov. 11: The Unknown is interred on the plaza of the Memorial Amphitheater at Arlington National Cemetery with President Warren G. Harding presiding at the interment ceremonies.
1923	The Argonne Cross is dedicated at Arlington "In Memory of Our Men in France 1917-1918;" 5,241 World War I dead are reinterred from Europe for final burial at Arlington.
	March 4: The American Battle Monuments Commission is chartered by Congress to construct permanent cemeteries for American soldiers killed abroad.
	December: Architect Thomas Hastings erects a temporary, 35-foot plaster memorial on the Tomb of the Unknown Soldier to showcase his idea for completing the Tomb.
1924	Feb. 3: President Woodrow Wilson dies at his home in Washington, D.C.; he is later buried at the National Cathedral.
1925	May 11: 6,000 people attend Mother's Day services at the Memorial Amphitheater and at the Tomb of the Unknown Soldier.
1926	March 24: The 3d Cavalry is assigned daylight guard at the Tomb of the Unknown Soldier.
	July 3: Congress approves $50,000 for completion of the Tomb of the Unknown Soldier.
1927	June 12: Aviator Charles Lindbergh places a wreath at the Tomb of the Unknown Soldier shortly after completing the first solo trans-Atlantic flight.
1928	The Quartermaster General begins the process of soliciting ideas for an addition to the Tomb of the Unknown.

1928 cont.	Sculptor Thomas Hudson Jones and Architect Lorimer Rich are selected to enhance and complete the original Tomb of the Unknown Soldier at Arlington National Cemetery.
1929	Congress authorizes the improvement of approaches and landscaping at the Tomb.
1930	Dec. 19: Ground breaking ceremonies are held at Arlington marking the beginning of construction of the new Memorial Plaza.
1932	Feb. 1: The Memorial Bridge linking Arlington with Washington, D.C. is officially opened.
	April 9: The completed Tomb of the Unknown Soldier is unveiled at Arlington without formal ceremony.
1936	Nov. 11: SGT Edward F. Younger, the soldier who selected the Unknown in 1921, places a wreath at the Tomb of the Unknown Soldier.
1937	The Tomb is placed under a 24-hour, 365-day military guard.
1938	Armistice Day becomes a national holiday in the United States.
1939-1945	World War II
1941	Dec. 7: The Japanese attack Pearl Harbor, Hawaii.
1942	April 18: LTC Jimmy Doolittle leads a bombing raid on the island on Honshu.
	June 4-7: The Battle of Midway
	Aug. 2: SGT Edward F. Younger, age 44, dies in Chicago, Illinois; he is interred at Arlington National Cemetery, Section 18, #1918-B.
1944	June 6: Allied forces invade Normandy.
1945	April 12: President Franklin D. Roosevelt dies at age 63.
	May 8: VE Day, Germany surrenders to the Allied forces.
	Aug. 6: The United States drops the atomic bomb on the city of Hiroshima.
	Aug. 9: A second atomic bomb is dropped on Nagasaki.
	Sept. 2: VJ Day, Japan surrenders ending the second World War.
1946	June 24: Congress passes Public Law 429 authorizing the selection of a World War II Unknown Serviceman.

1948	Soldiers from the 3D United States Infantry Regiment, "The Old Guard," assume responsibility for guarding the Tomb of the Unknown Soldier.
	July 15: General of the Armies, John J. Pershing dies at age 87 and is interred at Arlington National Cemetery four days later.
1950-1953	The Korean War
1950	June 25: North Korean troops cross the 38th parallel and invade South Korea.
	Sept. 10: UN forces under the command of General Douglas MacArthur launch an amphibious invasion of Inchon.
1951	Feb.: The military initiates the concurrent return of remains from the Korean War.
1953	Jan. 20: Dwight Eisenhower is inaugurated as President.
	March 5: Josef Stalin dies.
	July 27: An armistice is declared in the Korean War.
1954	April 27: At a press conference, President Dwight Eisenhower first enunciates what becomes known as the "Domino Theory."
	June 1: Congress changes the name of Armistice Day to Veterans Day in order to honor all American veterans.
	July 21: The Geneva Accords temporarily partitions Vietnam into North and South along the 17th parallel.
1956	The remains of 848 unidentified American soldiers from the Korean War are interred at the Punchbowl in Honolulu, Hawaii.
	Aug. 3: Congress passes Public Law 975 authorizing the selection of an American Unknown from the Korean conflict.
1957	Oct. 21: Captain Harry G. Cramer is killed in a training exercise with ARVN forces in South Vietnam.
	Nov. 12: Construction of the two crypts for the World War II and Korean Unknown Servicemen begins at Arlington.
1958-1975	The Vietnam War
1958	Feb. 8: The first Tomb Guard Identification Badge is awarded.
	May 12: U.S. Army Major General Edward O'Neill selects the World War II Trans-Atlantic Unknown at the Epinal American Cemetery, France.

1958 cont.   May 15: Master Sergeant Ned Lyle is given the honor of selecting the Korean War Unknown at the Punchbowl National Memorial Cemetery in Hawaii.

May 16: Colonel Glenn Eagleston, USAF, selects the World War II Trans-Pacific Unknown at Hickam Air Force Base, Hawaii.

May 26: The final selection of the World War II Unknown takes place at sea on the USS *Canberra*. Hospital Corpsman First Class and Medal of Honor recipient, William Charette, makes the selection; the Unknowns are transferred to the USS *Blandy* for the final trip to Washington, D.C.

May 28: The World War II and Korean Unknowns arrive in Washington, D.C. to lie in state at the U.S. Capitol.

May 30: The World War II and Korean Unknown Servicemen are buried on the plaza of the Memorial Amphitheater with President Dwight Eisenhower and Vice President Richard Nixon presiding.

June 2: The graves of the World War II and Korean Unknowns are sealed with marble crypt covers inscribed with the dates of the conflicts: 1941-1945 and 1950-1953.

1959   July 8: MAJ Dale Buis and MSG Chester Ovnand are killed in a Viet Cong attack in Bien Hoa, becoming America's first combat casualties in the Vietnam War.

1961   SP4 Fred Moore becomes the first African-American Tomb Guard.

1963   A detailed study is conducted to chronicle the extent of existing cracks in the Tomb's die block; the first American serviceman is reported to be missing-in-action in Vietnam.

1965   Oct. 25: SSG William Spates (TGIB #033) becomes the first Tomb Guard to be killed-in-action; Spates is buried at Arlington National Cemetery in Section 48, #432 near the Tomb of the Unknown Soldier.

1967   Aug. 31: SGT Marvin L. Franklin (TGIB #056) is killed in Vietnam.

1968   Jan. 17: Lyndon Johnson declares that the "enemy has been defeated in battle after battle" during his State of the Union address.

Jan. 30: Beginning of the Tet Offensive in Vietnam.

March 31: Lyndon Johnson announces that he will not seek reelection.

1968 cont.	Nov. 5: Richard Nixon is elected President on a platform of bringing "peace with honor" to Vietnam.
1971	Jan. 1: The Uniform Monday Holiday Act takes effect moving Veterans Day to the fourth Monday in October.
	Nov.. 11: President Richard M. Nixon orders the construction of a crypt for a potential unknown from the Vietnam War on the 50th anniversary of the burial of the World War I Unknown Soldier.
1972	May 11: 1LT Michael Blassie's A-37B is shot down over An Lộc.
	Oct. 31: An ARVN reconnaissance team discovers a crash site and recovers a few small, human bones as well as some personal items; the remains are classified as BTB Michael Blassie.
1973	Jan. 23: The Joint Casualty Resolution Center (JCRC) is created at Camp Samae San, Thailand, to conduct "field search, excavation, recovery, and repatriation" of American remains in Vietnam; the Secretary of Defense is instructed to find a Vietnam Unknown Serviceman.
	Jan. 27: The Paris Peace Accords are signed, ostensibly ending American combat operations in Vietnam.
	June 18: Public Law No. 93-43 is passed in the United States Senate by an 85-4 margin; it authorizes "the burial of an unknown soldier from the Vietnam Conflict at Arlington National Cemetery after the United States has concluded its participation in hostilities in Southeast Asia."
	Oct. 10: Vice President Spiro Agnew resigns from office.
	Dec. 6: Gerald Ford is confirmed as the new Vice President under provisions of the XXV Amendment to the Constitution.
1974	Aug. 8: Richard Nixon becomes the first president in history to resign from office; he is succeeded by Gerald R. Ford.
1975	March: The crypt for a Vietnam Unknown is finished on the plaza of the Memorial Amphitheater.
	April 30: Saigon falls to Communist forces ending the Vietnam War.
1976	American Bicentennial.
	July 7: Queen Elizabeth places a wreath at the Tomb of the Unknown Soldier.
	Nov. 2: Democrat Jimmy Carter is elected the 39th President of the United States.

1978	A bronze plaque recognizing the service of American soldiers, servicemen, and servicewomen during the Vietnam War is placed in the Trophy Room at the Memorial Amphitheater.
	June 21: Architect Lorimer Rich, the co-designer of the Tomb of the Unknown Soldier is interred at Arlington National Cemetery in Section 48. Rich, who served as a private during the first world war, was granted an exception for inground burial by President Jimmy Carter.
	Nov. 11: The commemoration of Veterans Day returns to its original date.
	Dec. 4: Physical Anthropolgist, Tadao Furue recommends that the remains: "TSN 0673-72 BTB: Blassie be designated unknown."
1979	Jan. 9: Major General Edward O'Neill, the officer who selected the World War II European Theater unknown, dies; he is buried at Arlington National Cemetery, Sec. 30, #1801.
	May 28: The Vietnam Veterans Memorial Fund is established by Jan Scruggs.
	July 18: POW/MIA Recognition day is established by act of Congress.
1980	April 24: After a forensic review, the BTB status is removed from the unidentified remains recovered at An Lộc and are re-designated X-26.
1981	Jan. 20: Ronald Reagan is inaugurated as the nation's 40th President of the United States.
1982	Aug.: The Veterans of Foreign Wars urges the immediate burial of an Unknown Serviceman from the Vietnam War.
	Nov. 13: The Vietnam Memorial is dedicated on the National Mall.
1984	March 21: MAJ Johnie Webb certifies the remains X-26 as unidentifiable.
	May 17: Medal of Honor recipient, Sergeant Major Allan J. Kellogg officially designates the Vietnam Unknown at Pearl Harbor, Hawaii.
	May 23: The dates of American military involvement in the Vietnam War, "1958-1975," are carved into the marble crypt cover in preparation for the Memorial Day funeral.
	May 24: The frigate, USS *Brewton*, arrives at Alameda Naval Air Station in California carrying the body of the Vietnam Unknown.

| **1984 cont.** | May 25: The body of the Vietnam Unknown Serviceman is flown to Andrews Air Force Base onboard a C-141B transport; upon arrival, the remains are taken by hearse to the U.S. Capitol to lie-in-state. |

May 28: The Vietnam Unknown Serviceman is interred at Arlington National Cemetery.

1987   April 10: Master Sergeant Ned Lyle, United States Army, the soldier who made the selection of the Korean Unknown Soldier, dies at age 61; he is interred at Fort Jackson National Cemetery, South Carolina.

1990   May 25: Former Arlington National Cemetery Superintendent, John C. Metzler, Sr. dies.

1991   Jan. 18: Former Congressman Hamilton Fish dies at the age of 102.

June 5: Colonel Glenn T. Eagleston, the officer who chose the trans-Pacific World War II Unknown, is inurned at the Arlington Columbarium, Court 3, Sec. G, Col. 5, Niche 5.

1992   Nov.6: A recovery team visits the crash site of 1LT Michael Blassie's airplane and interviews a former ARVN soldier; they find no additional evidence.

1994   Former Green Beret, Ted Sampley, claims that is possible to identify the Vietnam Unknown Serivceman.

Sept.: A second recovery team visits the village of An Lộc without success.

1995   SGT Heather Johnsen (TGIB #423) becomes the first woman to guard the Tomb of the Unknown Soldier.

1997   Jan. 22: SGT Danyell E. Wilson (TGIB #439) ia the first African American woman to receive a Tomb Guard Identification Badge.

1998   Jan. 19: CBS News airs a story on the possible identity of the Vietnam Unknown Serviceman.

May 13: A plywood privacy fence is erected around the plaza area to prepare for the disinterment of the Vietnam Unknown.

May 14: The Vietnam Unknown is disinterred.

June 30: The Department of Defense announces that the Unknown Serviceman from the Vietnam War has been identified as First Lieutenant Michael Blassie, USAF.

July 11: 1LT Michael Blassie is buried at Jefferson Barracks National Cemetery in St. Louis, Missouri.

1999	Sept. 17: A new inscription: "Honoring and Keeping Faith with America's Missing Servicemen, 1958-1975," is added to the marble cover over the empty crypt of the Vietnam Unknown.
2002	Aug. 19: Former Arlington Superintentdent, Raymond J. Costanzo dies.
2005	A 57-ton replacement block is quarried in Colorado for potential installation at Arlington to replace the cracked die block.
2008	The federal government fails to act on replacing the damaged marble at the Tomb.
2010	Oct. 28: SSG Adam Dickmyer (TGIB #528) is killed during Operation Enduring Freedom in Afghanistan at age 26; he is buried at Arlington National Cemetery in Section 60, #9396.
2012	March 18: Corpsman William Charette, the Medal of Honor recipient who selected the World War II Unknown, dies in Florida and is interred at the Florida National Cemetery in Bushnell, Florida.
2013	June 11: Jean Blassie, the mother of Lt. Michael Blassie, dies at the age of 90.
2014	May 30: The Old Amphitheater near the Arlington House Mansion is renamed for Corporal James Tanner, Section 2, #877, 82nd New York Infantry; Tanner lost both legs during the second battle of Bull Run and later became the stenographer who recorded testimony in the immediate aftermath of President Lincoln's assassination.
2016	SGT Ruth Hanks (TGIB #643), the fourth woman sentinel at the Tomb, becomes assistant relief commander of the 3rd Relief.
2018	Aug. 2: North Korea returns 55 boxes of remains of missing American soldiers who died fighting at the Chosin Reservoir.
	Oct. 3: The Tomb Guard is presented with four, new commemorative M17 Sig Sauer pistols.
2019	Feb. 22: The DPAA reports that 1,057 former MIA's from the Vietnam War have been identified; 1,589 Amrican servicemen are still unaccounted for.
2020	Arlington Cemetery is closed for weeks to public visitation due to the COVID-19 pandemic but the Tomb remains under continual guard; 100th Anniversary of the dedication of the Memorial Amphitheater; the 1915 time capsule is opened.
2021	Nov. 11: National commemorations remembering the 100th anniversary of the interment of the Unknown Soldier from the Great War.

Author's Note

In 1983, I decided to take a sabbatical from teaching. I was fortunate to secure a civil service (GS170) position as a historian at Arlington National Cemetery. My office was located at the Tomb of the Unknown Soldier in the basement of the Memorial Amphitheater, directly adjacent to the building's small chapel and near the Tomb Guard Quarters.

The two years I spent at Arlington were truly memorable. They coincided with the nation's fortieth anniversary commemorations of World War II. Each week, I had the honor to meet some of the remarkable men and women who comprised the "Greatest Generation." These patriotic citizens selflessly put aside their careers and personal ambitions in order to save the world from the dark forces of fascism and fanaticism. I had the rare opportunity to speak with those brave individuals who had shaped American history and its destiny, including Battle of the Bulge veterans, Navajo Code Talkers, Pearl Harbor Survivors, and Iwo Jima marines.

On one particularly memorable January day, I was working alone at the office. Most of the inaugural festivities for President Ronald Reagan's second term had to be cancelled due to the brutally cold weather. I went upstairs to the Trophy Room that day and saw two gentlemen silently watching from inside as the Tomb sentinel walked the mat. I noticed that both men were wearing a sky-blue Medal of Honor, the nation's highest military decoration. I introduced myself and then escorted them downstairs to meet the Tomb Guard. While they were visiting the quarters, I consulted our office's book on MOH citations. One of the men, Master Sergeant Henry "Red" Erwin, still bore the scars from burns he had incurred during a bombing mission over Japan. His citation read, in part:

> He was the radio operator of a B-29 airplane leading a group formation to attack Koriyama, Japan. He was charged with the additional duty of dropping phosphoresce smoke bombs to aid in assembling the group when the launching point was reached. Upon entering the assembly area, aircraft fire and enemy fighter opposition was encountered. Among the phosphoresce bombs launched by S/Sgt. Erwin, 1 proved faulty, exploding in the launching chute, and shot back into the interior of the aircraft, striking him in the face. The burning phospho-

resce obliterated his nose and completely blinded him. Smoke filled the plane, obscuring the vision of the pilot. S/Sgt. Erwin realized that the aircraft and crew would be lost if the burning bomb remained in the plane. Without regard for his own safety, he picked it up and feeling his way, instinctively, crawled around the gun turret and headed for the copilot's window. He found the navigator's table obstructing his passage. Grasping the burning bomb between his forearm and body, he unleashed the spring lock and raised the table. Struggling through the narrow passage he stumbled forward into the smoke-filled pilot's compartment. Groping with his burning hands, he located the window and threw the bomb out. Completely aflame, he fell back upon the floor. The smoke cleared, the pilot, at 300 feet, pulled the plane out of its dive. S/Sgt. Erwin's gallantry and heroism above and beyond the call of duty saved the lives of his comrades.

The other MOH recipient was Corporal Desmond Doss. As a medic and conscientious objector, he earned his medal while serving with the 77th Medical Detachment on Okinawa. Despite being seriously wounded, Doss continued to administer to injured American soldiers and was credited with saving several of their lives. In 2016, his remarkable story was made into a highly successful, Hollywood movie: *Hacksaw Ridge*. Both of these brave and remarkable men were at Arlington that day to pay tribute to the nation's Unknown Soldiers.

In fact, every year, millions of people visit the Tomb. They gather on the plaza and watch in silence as the sentinel maintains his perpetual vigil. They also come to see the impressive Changing of the Guard ceremony which occurs on a regular basis. Foreign dignitaries, likewise, come to Arlington to place a wreath at the Tomb as part of their official visit to Washington, D.C. Indeed, during my last year at the cemetery, the historian's office worked on visits by eleven heads-of-state including those of President François Mitterrand of France and Prime Minister Yitzhak Shamir of Israel.

For all such official state visits, soldiers carrying the flags of all 50 states, positioned in their order of admission to the union, line the mall approaches to the Tomb. Honor guard units representing all five branches of the military services are assembled and stand at attention while a military band plays the visiting nation's national anthem followed by the American "Star Spangled Banner." The visiting dignitary, accompanied by the commander of the Military District of Washington, places a wreath in front of the east façade of the Tomb. He then exits via the Trophy Room and the colonnade. At the west entrance of the Amphitheater, the diplomat's motorcade awaits. It is an impressive and unforgettable sight, one that reminds every spectator of the supreme sacrifice that the Unknowns have paid to secure our nation's values.

These grandiose ceremonies occur with regularity at Arlington, but more routine are the dozens of other daily wreath ceremonies conducted by school children, veterans' organizations, and patriotic groups. These events receive no publicity but are part of the private pilgrimages that so many make to Arlington. Hosted by the Sergeant of the Guard, the wreath is placed in front of the shrine and a bugler concludes the brief service by playing the haunting 24 notes of "Taps."

I was privileged during my tenure at Arlington to work on two visits to the Tomb by President Reagan. On Memorial Day, 1984, the President was there for the burial services conducted for the Vietnam Unknown Serviceman. It was the most important day at Arlington since the burial of President John F. Kennedy some 21 years earlier. As President Reagan so eloquently noted: "Throughout America today, we honor the dead of our wars. We recall their valor and their sacrifices. We remember they gave their lives so that others might live."

The Tomb of the Unknown Soldier is justifiably America's most sacred military shrine. This is its story, this is its history.

(3D U.S. Infantry Regiment "The Old Guard")
Troops line the plaza for full-honor wreath ceremony for a head-of-state visit.

TOMB
of the Unknown Soldier

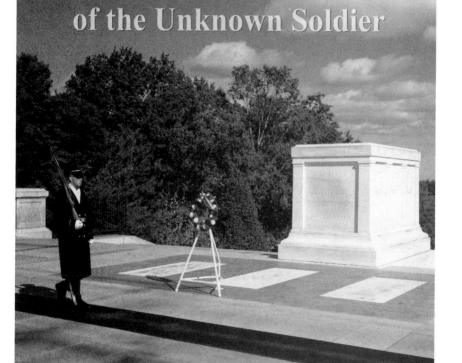

AppleRidge
PUBLISHERS

Memorial Day at Arlington National Cemetery. The holiday was originally known as Decoration Day and was created at Arlington in 1868 as a time to honor fallen Union soldiers.

Chapter I

Memorial Day, 1914

"Nobility exists in America without patent...we have a house of fame to which we elevate those who are the noble men...forgetful of themselves, study and serve the public interest, who have the courage to face any number and any kind of adversary, to speak what in their hearts they believe to be the truth." - Woodrow Wilson

The "Old" Amphitheater at Arlington National Cemetery is located just a short walk from the Arlington House mansion, the antebellum home of General Robert E. Lee.[1] It is immediately adjacent to a stark, grey, granite memorial that marks the common grave of 2,111 unknown Civil War soldiers whose remains were recovered during cleanup operations from area battlefields in 1866.[2] The Amphitheater is a relatively modest structure built from painted wood and brick. It had been initially conceived and designed by the Quartermaster General of the Army, Montgomery Meigs, and was formally dedicated in 1873 just eight years after the surrender of Confederate forces at Appomattox Court House. The Amphitheater's distinctive ionic columns, white trellises, and wooden pergola blend seamlessly into the surrounding landscape, evoking, for some, memories of an ancient Greek temple.

The Amphitheater was originally intended to accommodate the large Memorial Day crowds that made the annual pilgrimage to Arlington National Cemetery each spring, but by 1914, it had become obsolete as the new federal holiday continued to gain in

(Library of Congress)

The "Old" Amphitheater at Arlington National Cemetery. It was the site for Memorial Day Ceremonies at the cemetery for 47 years.

popularity. Initially known as "Decoration Day," Memorial Day had its origins at Arlington when, in 1868, General John Logan issued his famed "Orders #11" declaring that: "the 30th day of May, 1868, is designated for the purpose of strewing with flowers or otherwise decorating the graves of comrades who died in defense of their country during the late rebellion."[3]

So it was that on that Saturday, May 30, 1914, that many aging Union and Confederate veterans once again answered General Logan's call and converged on Arlington and the flag-festooned Amphitheater. Undeterred by the day's bad weather, they proudly wore their old military uniforms, medals, and other patriotic insignia but as the *Evening Star* newspaper somberly noted, they: "were fewer in numbers. Their children and grandchildren had taken the places of many."[4] The President, Woodrow Wilson, had initially declined an invitation to participate in the day's ceremonies, instead opting for a planned leisurely weekend round of golf and an afternoon drive.[5]

His refusal, though, was seen as an affront to the members of the Grand Army of the Republic (GAR). After enduring several days of public criticism and rebuke, Wilson ultimately relented and cancelled his weekend plans with the White House issuing a statement that "evidently a fake construction had been placed on his actions."[6] Wilson was thus present on the dais at Arlington along with an array of other dignitaries although his official participation had been omitted from the day's printed program.[7] The featured speakers for the Memorial Day remembrances were to be Senator Reed Smoot of Utah and the Speaker of the House, Champ Clark.[8]

Shortly after noon, a Marine Corps bugler signaled the assembly which was followed by the singing of the popular hymn, "Nearer, My God, to Thee" and a recitation of the Lord's Prayer. The Reverend N.H. Holmes offered the invocation, subtly referencing the Wilson controversy by noting that: "We pray that the day is far distant when the great leaders of our country will forget as they have not to-day, to join in the service to the memory of those men."[9] The Gettysburg Address and General Logan's Orders #11 were then recited. Dr. J. K. Gleeson, commander of the local chapter of the Grand Army of the Republic and the Master of Ceremonies, offered brief welcoming remarks, noting proudly that Congress had finally appropriated adequate funds for the construction of a much-needed new amphitheater at Arlington. Work was expected to begin that summer with the project to be completed within just twenty months.[10] Gleeson then invited the rain-soaked crowd to stand to observe a silent tribute to the dead before introducing President Wilson.

The 57-year old Wilson had been in office for just over a year, having won the 1912 presidential election with just 41.8% of the popular vote. His landslide win in the Electoral College, though, was due solely to an anomaly—the Republican Party had failed to unite behind its nominee, the incumbent president, William Howard Taft. Indeed, former president Theodore Roosevelt, had launched a powerful third-party challenge which resulted in the Republicans splitting their vote.[11] Coupled with the Socialist Party candidate,

Eugene Debs, siphoning off an additional 6% of the popular vote, Wilson was assured a victory and became only the second Democrat to be elected to the presidency since 1856.[12]

Already, Wilson had earned a reputation for being cerebral and somewhat aloof. He had earned his doctorate in history and government while at Johns Hopkins University, and later had a distinguished academic career both as a professor and as president of Princeton University. During that time Wilson wrote and published extensively, advocating a strong progressive agenda and a robust federal government. In 1911, he was selected as the governor of New Jersey as a reformer before being elected to the presidency the following year.

(Library of Congress)

President Woodrow Wilson arriving at Arlington National Cemetery, 1914. Wilson had initially declined to participate in the May 30th Memorial Day Ceremonies but relented after widespread public criticism.

As Wilson stood to speak, one of the participants held an umbrella in a futile effort to shield the President from the persistent rain that continued to leak through the overhead canvas that covered the rostrum. Wilson readily acknowledged that he had not had the time to prepare a formal speech. As a result, his improvised remarks proved to be neither memorable nor particularly eloquent but still, they were suitable for the solemn occasion.

Wilson first expressed his sincere "gratitude and admiration for the men who perished for the sake of the union"[13] and commended the soldiers for their selflessness. He declared: "They do not need our praise. They do not need that our admiration should sustain them. There is no immortality that is safer than theirs. We come, not for their sakes but for our own, in order that we may drink at the same springs of inspiration from which they themselves drank."[14] The President continued: "I can never speak in praise of war and hoped that their example of self-sacrifice...will make it unnecessary that men should follow war any more," concluding: "It has been a privilege, to come and say these simple words, which I am sure are merely putting your thoughts into language."[15] The President received a warm and polite applause and J. K. Gleason would later acknowledged that: "President Wilson's attendance today will go a great way toward soothing the feeling aroused over the country but it will not do everything. However, he behaved very nicely after he got here."[16]

The formal program at the Amphitheater concluded with the traditional playing of "Taps" in honor of the fallen. The large crowd then slowly dispersed with many of the visitors placing floral tributes on nearby graves while a small contingent of veterans walked over to the front of the Arlington House mansion to place a wreath before the grave of Union cavalry commander, General Philip Sheridan.[17]

A large number of Confederate veterans had participated that day in the Arlington ceremonies.[18] They were collectively anticipating the impending unveiling and dedication of the Confederate Memorial at the cemetery scheduled for just five days later on June 4.[19] President Wilson had agreed to speak on the occasion and to formally receive the monument on behalf of the entire nation.[20]

The passions and divisions of the previous era had been tempered by time and yielded to old age, replaced by a mutual respect by both Union and Confederate veterans. The new memorial was to typify this sense of reconciliation.[21] Located at Jackson Circle just a few hundred yards to the southwest of the Old Amphitheater, the 32-foot, bronze Confederate Memorial had been designed by the

(Library of Congress)

The new Confederate Memorial at Arlington National Cemetery. It was dedicated on June 4, 1914, and was designed by Moses Ezekiel. President Wilson declared: "My privilege ladies and gentlemen: to declare this chapter in the history of the United States closed and ended."

renowned sculptor, Moses Ezekiel. Ezekiel was, himself, a Confederate veteran, having fought at the Battle of New Market in 1864 as part of a contingent of Virginia Military Institute cadets.[22]

The central feature of the memorial is a female figure representing the South in peace. In one hand, she holds a laurel wreath and in the other she clutches a plow share evoking the biblical passage from the book of Isaiah: "They shall beat their swords into plowshares, and their spears into pruning hooks; nation shall not lift up sword against nation neither shall they learn war any more."[23] On the base of the memorial in high relief is the inscription:

Not for fame or reward
Not for place or for rank
Not lured by ambition
Or goaded by necessity
But in simple
Obedience to duty
As they understood it
These men suffered all
Sacrificed all
Dared all – and died.[24]

Some 409 Confederate soldiers, including the remains of 12 unknowns, had been reinterred to the area in previous years. They were buried in concentric circles surrounding the new monument. Another inscription on the Confederate Memorial acknowledged: "An Obedience To Duty As They Understood it; These Men Suffered All; Sacrificed All and Died!"[25]

AS THE FORMAL events at the Amphitheater and at Arlington drew to a close, Memorial Day was still being observed across the nation. At the Antietam battlefield in Maryland, over 5,000 people gathered at the national cemetery to honor the dead while tributes were held at the Soldiers' and Sailors' monument and Grant's Tomb in New York City. In Richmond, Virginia, it was reported that "flowers sent from all over the south are being strewn this morning on the graves of Confederate soldiers...and this afternoon surviving comrades of those heroes escorted by all the militia organizations in the city will parade to the cemeteries for celebration of Memorial Day." [26]

For other Americans, though, the Memorial Day holiday was merely a harbinger of summer and was being used for recreation and relaxation rather than for patriotic commemoration. A capacity crowd watched the annual baseball game at the Naval Academy in Annapolis where the Midshipmen were defeated by the West Point Cadets by a score of 8 to 2; at the Indianapolis Speedway, Rene Thomas won the 500-mile auto race, averaging 82.4 miles per hour; and the Washington Senators split a double header with the Boston Red Sox. On Saturday, May 30, 1914, the United States of America was blissfully a nation at peace.

Endnotes

1 On May 30, 2014, the Old Amphitheater was officially renamed for Corporal James Tanner, 82nd New York Infantry. Tanner was seriously wounded during the Second Battle of Bull Run and had to have both of his legs amputated. He later became a stenographer. On the night of April 14/15, 1865, in the aftermath of Abraham Lincoln's shooting, Tanner recorded witness testimony at the Petersen Boarding House as the President lay dying in an adjacent room. Tanner is buried a short distance away from the Amphitheater in Section 2, #877.

2 Philip Bigler, *In Honored Glory: Arlington National Cemetery, the Final Post*. St. Petersburg: Vandamere Press, 2010, p. 20.

3 John Logan, "General Orders #11." Lane Memorial Library avaiable at: http://www.hampton.lib.nh.us.

4 "President Lauds Heroes of Nation," *The Sunday Star*. 31 May 1914, pp. 1, 15.

5 Woodrow Wilson had missed the previous Memorial Day (1913) ceremonies as well. He instead took a drive in the Virginia countryside with his wife. "Wilson to Follow Saturday Custom," *The Evening Star*, 29 May 1914, p. 1.

6 "Wilson Gives in to GAR's Protest," p. 4.

7 "Wilson to Follow Saturday Custom," p. 1.

8 "President Lauds Heroes of Nation,", p. 1.

9 "Wilson Gives in to GAR's Protest," *The New York Tribune*, p. 4.

10 This prediction proved to be overly optimistic. The Amphitheater was not finished until 1920.

11 In the popular vote, Wilson received 41.8%, Roosevelt 27.4%, Taft 23.2%, and Debs 6.0% In the Electoral College, though, Wilson won by a landslide, receiving 435 electoral votes to Theodore Roosevelt's 88. Taft, the incumbent president, received only 8 electoral votes, carrying just Utah and Vermont. Debs failed to carry a single state.

12 *Presidential Elections 1789 – 2004*. Washington, D.C.: Congressional Quarterly, Inc., 2005, pp. 46-49.

13 Woodrow Wilson, Memorial Day Address. 30 May 1914, available at: http://www.presidency.ucsb.edu.

14 *Ibid*.

15 *Ibid.*

16 Gleason quoted in "Wilson Allays GAR Feelings: His Belated Acceptance to Speak Not Entirely Satisfactory, However," *The Washington Herald*, 31 May 1914, p. 1.

17 General Philip Sheridan was a Union cavalry commander most known for his brutal burning of the Shenandoah Valley in 1864 in an effort to deprive the Confederacy of its food source. After the war, he served on the frontier and was involved in several of the brutal Indian campaigns. Sheridan died at age 57 and was buried in front of the Arlington House Mansion. His grave overlooks a beautiful vista of Washington, D.C. (Section 2, #S-1)

18 "President Lauds Heroes of the Nation," p. 15.

19 June 4th was the birthday of the Confederate President, Jefferson Davis.

20 On the day of the dedication, a huge thunderstorm disrupted the ceremonies. *The Evening Star* reported: "Though the sun shone brightly during the early hours of the exercises, during the last speeches the sky darkened and the air grew chilly. This warning of a storm caused many to leave in haste and prompted the President to be very brief in the speech with which he accepted the monument from the United Daughters of the Confederacy. Scarcely had he finished when the storm broke. The President and his party, including two of his daughters and other women, made a quick run to the White House in an automobile during the heaviest part of the storm.

Hundreds of veterans, women and children, however, were caught far from any protection, beaten by the wind, their umbrellas torn from their grasp and they were drenched to the skin. Without protection of any kind, scores of these men and women huddled together, striving to shelter each other as well as they could by camping on the ground in a group. Many hid behind trees or the stone wall of the cemetery or in the trench along the car tracks while the storm beat down upon them across the drill field of Fort Myer.

The President was much concerned about the danger for these people, particularly, those who, on account of age and weakness, might be most, susceptible to pneumonia." See "Arlington Swept by Terrific Thunderstorm," *The Evening Star*, 5 June 1914, p. 3.

21 In his abbreviated address at the dedication of the Confederate Memorial on June 4, 1914, President Wilson emphasized the reunion of the nation and the reconciliation between the opposing sides. He said: "My privilege ladies and gentlemen: to declare this chapter in the history of the United States closed and ended, I bid that you turn with me your faces to the future, quickened by the memories

of the past, but with nothing to do with the contests of the past, knowing, as we have shed our blood upon opposite sides, we now face and admire one another." "Arlington Swept by Terrific Thunderstorm," *The Evening Star*, 5 June 1914, p. 3.

22 Ezekiel died in 1917 and was buried at the foot of the Confederate Memorial.

23 Isaiah, Chapter 2, verse 4.

24 Bigler, pp. 37-38.

25 Bigler, pp. 37-38. Also see: "Heroism Recalled as Tribute is Paid to Confederate Dead," *The Evening Star*. 4 June 1914, pp. 1-2 and "Confederate Memorial," Arlington National Cemetery available at http://www.arlingtoncemetery.mil.

26 "Honor Confederate Dead," *The Sunday Star*. 31 May 1914, p. 15.

(National Archives)
The newly completed Memorial Amphitheater and the Mast of the Maine *Memorial. The Amphitheater's construction was delayed due to America's entry into World War I.*

Chapter II

The Memorial Amphitheater

"Here is the heart of the Republic."- Josephus Daniels

Just 29 days after the conclusion of the 1914 Memorial Day ceremonies at Arlington National Cemetery, the Archduke and heir to the Hapsburg throne, Franz Ferdinand, and his wife Sofie were assassinated in Sarajevo by a Serbian nationalist.[1] Within weeks, Austria-Hungary declared war against Serbia in retaliation. Other European nations, honoring their various agreements, alliances, and treaties, soon reciprocated with each nation anxious to use the crisis as an excuse to settle old feuds, achieve territorial ambitions, subdue ethnic divisions, establish colonial empires, and gain military supremacy. The so called "Great War" had begun, fulfilling Otto von Bismarck's 19th Century prophecy that: "one day the great European war will come out of some damned foolish thing in the Balkans."[2] On one side of the conflict was the Triple Entente, an alliance consisting of Great Britain, France, and Russia. It was opposed by Germany, Austria-Hungry and the Ottoman Empire, collectively known as the Central Powers. As the warring nations began the process of mobilizing and deploying their massive armies, President

Wilson remained steadfast in his determination to keep the United States out of the European conflagration. In a message to Congress on August 19, he declared that: "the United States must be neutral in fact, as well as in name. We must be impartial in thought, as well as action."[3] Still, no one could anticipate the magnitude of the catastrophe to come.

The German Kaiser, Wilhelm II, immediately faced the dangerous prospect of fighting a two-front war, against Russia in the east as well as a combined Anglo-French force in the west.[4] In August, the Germans launched a surprise, massive offensive against neutral Belgium in an effort to bypass and outflank strong allied defenses and fortifications. The goal of this bold and daring strategy was to swiftly occupy Paris, thereby knocking the French out of the

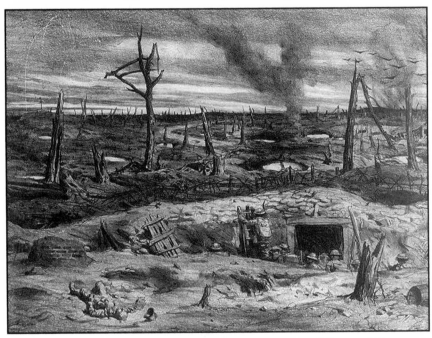

(Library of Congress)

The "Great War" began in August 1914. The major European powers quickly mobilized their massive armies, but the fighting soon degenerated into a bloody stalemate where troops were confined to trenches and where battles were fought on barren land with massive casualties.

war and enabling the Kaiser to redirect and concentrate his forces against the Russian armies massed along the eastern front.[5]

By the end of August, it seemed as if the German objectives were well within reach. The Kaiser's armies had advanced to within just 19 miles of the French capital but at the Battle of Trouée de Charmes (August 24 – 26) and at the First Battle of the Marne (September 6 – 10), the Germans were finally repulsed and forced to retreat. Over two million soldiers were now engaged along a massive front in the west. The resulting casualties were unfathomable. In one week (August 20th through the 27th) the French alone lost over 40,000 men—27,000 killed in a single day (August 22). By the end of 1914, after just five months of combat, British losses were placed at 16,200 killed-in-action with an additional 16,746 missing or captured. Another 47,707 had been wounded in battle. German loses during the same period were put at 142,502 killed.[6] Even more dispiriting was the stark reality that the war had dissolved into a virtual stalemate with the opposing armies stagnant and unable to maneuver. Troops on both sides were confined to muddy trenches and over the ensuing months, thousands of soldiers would perish in meaningless sieges and hopeless battles of attrition that resulted in little tangible gain. By the perverse logic of the time, the more deaths that occurred, the more determined the leadership of the warring countries were to see the war through to final victory in order to justify the massive slaughter on the battlefield.

WHILE THE WAR in Europe continued to rage, the United States attempted to maintain a degree of normality even as the nation's newspapers were filled with horrific stories of distant battles and massive fatalities. President Wilson was dealing with his own personal family tragedy; his wife of 29 years and the mother of their three children, died of kidney failure at the White House on August 6, 1914.[7] The First Lady had been in declining health for several months and her illness had been aggravated by a painful and debilitating fall during the winter months.[8] Yet despite his grief, the President had to confront the pressing international crisis and formulate the nation's response. There was, in fact, no national consensus on the European war. Indeed, fully one-third of the nation was foreign born and this number included over eleven million people of German descent. Another five million were Irish-Americans who collectively held a decisively anti-British attitude. In an effort to reduce ancestral loyalties, Wilson condemned what he referred to as "hyphenism" hopes of keeping public sentiment neutral.[9]

Still, America had strong, historic ties with both Great Britain and France. These nations skillfully attempted to manipulate American public opinion by exploiting the German occupation of Belgium for propaganda purposes. Lurid rumors of German atrocities were widely reported by British intelligence, who claimed

(Library of Congress)

Speaker of the House, Champ Clark, purchasing "Forget-me-nots" in support of Belgian relief efforts. Americans were outraged by the German invasion and occupation of neutral Belgium during the early days of the Great War.

that the German conquerors were perpetrating: "shocking crimes against men, women, and children that human brutality can devise."[10] Drunken soldiers were alleged to have committed all sorts of atrocities against the civilian population. According to one British report: "[In Malines] one witness saw a German soldier cut off a woman's breast after he murdered her."[11] It continued: "In Sempst the corpse of a man with his legs cut off, who was partially bound, was seen by a witness who also saw a girl of 17 dressed only in a chemise…she and other girls had been dragged into a field, stripped naked, and violated, and that some of them had been killed with a bayonet."[12] Another widely disseminated story maintained that an infant had been murdered by the German "Hun" and nailed to a farm

A Christmas cartoon by Clifford K. Berryman from 1915 depicting the stark differences between the holiday in the United States and Europe. Civilian populations on both sides were suffering from food shortages and deprivation.

house door, while in Louvain, 400 civilians were callously massacred with the survivors forced to sing the German anthem, *Deutschland über alles*.[13]

The Belgian countryside had been ravaged by the fighting. Jarvis C. Bell observed on a humanitarian visit in November 1914 that: "Nothing that has been written could exaggerate the misery of Belgium. We drove miles through graveyards...deserted fields are cemeteries."[14] Farms and food supplies had been destroyed and the wartime German government was unable to provide adequate food and supplies to the starving Belgian population. As the winter of 1914 approached, it was estimated that seven million non-combatants were on the verge of starvation.[15]

Because of America's official policy of neutrality, the federal government could not sanction any relief efforts for Belgium, even those intended solely for the civilian population. Instead, the successful business entrepreneur, Herbert Hoover, took the initiative and privately founded the Commission for the Relief of Belgium. Soon hundreds of local relief societies were organized throughout the United States in a massive effort to send food, clothing, and other much-needed supplies to the destitute.[16] In Washington, D.C., school children donated their pennies, while the student orchestra at George Washington University held a charity concert for Belgian relief. Each month, dozens of merchant ships were loaded and crammed full of provisions and dispatched to Antwerp, Rotterdam, and Amsterdam with supplies. One such supply ship, the *Ulriken*, struck a German mine in the North Sea and sank with over 3,000 tons of wheat, further inflaming American public opinion.[17] Yet despite the provocation, President Wilson maintained his policy of neutrality in order to keep the nation out of the war.

IN PEACETIME WASHINGTON, D.C., construction work was progressing on the new Lincoln Memorial, the latest addition to the national mall. The monument, dedicated to the nation's sixteenth president, had been carefully positioned on a direct axis line connecting it to the Capitol and the Washington Monument. It was also strategically situated directly opposite Arlington National Cemetery in anticipation of a new Memorial Bridge that would span the Potomac River in the near future and connect the two landmarks.[18]

Momentum was also increasing on the proposed construction of the Memorial Amphitheater at Arlington National Cemetery. The project had long been a dream of Washington D.C. judge, Ivory Kimball. Kimball was a Union veteran, having briefly served with the 55th Indiana Volunteer Infantry during the Civil War. He later became the head of the Department of the Potomac branch of the Grand Army of the Republic.[19] In this capacity, while attending Memorial Day services at Arlington in 1903, Kimball was outraged by what he perceived to be the inadequate facilities being used to host the ceremonies honoring America's fallen soldiers. In anger, he raged: "[at the] insufficiency of the hole in the ground now at Arlington which is called 'the amphitheater.'"[20]

Judge Kimball began an intensive lobbying effort demanding that the Secretary of War address the issue, and urging Congress to approve and finance the funds needed to build a more suitable facility to house the cemetery's annual Memorial Day commemorations. It was destined to be a long, frustrating, twelve-year endeavor filled with disappointment. Congress ultimately would endorse the concept of building a new amphitheater but then would fail to appropriate the money required for the actual construction. At one point, Kimball movingly appealed to the representatives' sense of patriotism: "We old veterans are dying off and we who are left want to see this amphitheater before we do pass away."[21] Likewise, in the summer of 1913, in a letter addressed to the Secretary of War, L.M. Garrison, Kimball wrote: "They want to see the building dedicated. They are old men; are dying fast, and delay in making the appropriation would mean the death of many comrades before seeing this end accomplished."[22]

On March 4, 1913, the 62nd Congress finally passed an appropriation bill for $750,000 to build the new Amphitheater. In one of his last official acts as president, William Howard Taft signed the legislation into law. Planning for the design and construction of the new Amphitheater at Arlington could now proceed in earnest.

The renowned New York architectural firm of Carrère and Hastings received a commission to provide drawings for the new facility in October 1914.[23] Their initial plans called for the construction of an open-air amphitheater that would incorporate classical Greco-Roman designs and be modeled after the ancient Theater of Dionysius in Athens as well as the Théâtre antique d'Orange in France. It was anticipated that the actual construction of the building could be completed within a two-year timeframe.[24]

The site selected for the new Amphitheater was ideally located in the southern portion of Arlington in close proximity to the Confederate Memorial and the new Mast of the USS *Maine* Monument.[25] The building was to be constructed from quarried white Vermont marble and was to be: "[a] roofless amphitheater, surrounded by a colonnade of white marble columns and arches in likeness of those of ancient Rome."[26] The Amphitheater would include a small interdenominational chapel as well as numerous crypts which would be located and enclosed under the structure's grand colonnade. These burial spaces were to be allotted to the nation's most distinguished military leaders and heroes. According to Colonel W.W. Harts: "There have been provided in the crypt a few places of interment for men who have especially distinguished themselves, and a great many spaces will be left for busts and commemorative tablets to men who have performed especially distinguished service in war."[27] He envisioned that: "[the Memorial Amphitheater] is intended to be to this country in some degree what Westminster Abbey is to Great Britain."[28] No individual, however, would be eligible for interment at the Amphitheater until ten years had elapsed after death, and then only after a recommendation by the armed services with the consent of Congress.[29] This grandiose idea proved unrealistic and was quickly abandoned, running counter to the nation's traditional republican beliefs and democratic instincts which spurned the concept of hierarchical burials. The crypts were des-

(National Archives)

The proposed Memorial Amphitheater as initially envisioned by the architectural firm of Carrère and Hastings. Funding for the structure was not approved until March 1913. The large peace memorial statue on the plaza was never built, due to funding constraints.

tined to forever remain unused and unfinished and would eventually be converted into storage facilities.[30]

A construction contract was formally awarded to the George A. Fuller Construction Company in February 1915. Shortly thereafter, on Monday March 1, at 11:00 AM, a small ground-breaking ceremony took place on the grounds of Arlington Cemetery. It was a cold, blustery, late-winter day with temperatures in the low 40s. The weather limited the size of the crowd to only about two dozen participants and a few spectators. Representing the Memorial Amphitheater Commission was Vice Chairman Ivory Kimball while the Secretary of the Navy, Josephus Daniels, was granted the honor of using a ceremonial shovel to first break ground to mark the beginning of construction for the new Amphitheater. The *Evening Star* reported that: "[the Amphitheater] is intended to supply the long-felt need of a suitable edifice in which to conduct Memorial Day exercises and other patriotic functions which are held at the national cemetery from time to time."[31]

The construction of the Memorial Amphitheater was, in fact, part of a larger plan to bring order, symmetry, and beauty to the cemetery. The Commission of Fine Arts had proposed a restriction of the size, scope, and shape of funeral monuments at the cemetery, noting that the lack of specific regulations had led to: "the present incongruous and inconsistent appearance of the cemetery."[32] Moreover, the commission hoped to: "prevent the erection of inartistic and overelaborate memorials…that are entirely out of proportion to the services of the officers commemorated."[33]

ON MAY 7, 1915, the RMS *Lusitania* was sunk by a German U-boat off of the coast of Ireland. The headline of the *Evening World* exclaimed: "137 AMERICANS LOST LIVES; U.S. DEMANDS EXPLANTION."[34] In fact, the final death toll revealed that 128 of the 188 Americans onboard were killed while the total loss of life onboard the *Lusitania* was placed at 1,198. The Germans quickly issued a public apology, but with the caveat that all of the passengers had been amply warned before departing New York that British-flagged shipping was at risk of being sunk since their vessels were suspected of covertly carrying military supplies and war contraband.[35]

President Wilson was dismayed by the *Lusitania's* sinking, but he refrained from making any immediate public comment. On May 10, however, he delivered a prearranged speech in Philadelphia before a crowd of several thousand newly naturalized citizens.[36] The President took great pride in his oratorical abilities and, despite the seriousness of the ongoing foreign policy crisis, chose to speak extemporaneously utilizing just a few notes. He told the assembled crowd that: "There is such a thing as a man being too proud to fight. There is such a thing as a nation being so right that it does not need to convince others by force that it is right."[37]

It was a careless and foolish statement that did nothing to ameliorate the crisis with Germany or curtail public passions. Indeed, Wilson privately admitted that he had misspoken and, curiously, he informed the press that: "I was expressing a personal attitude, that was all."[38] The Germans continued to perfunctorily express their regrets for the loss of civilian life but accused the British of using the vessel to transport munitions, thereby making the *Lusitania* a viable target of war.

The *Lusitania* incident remained front page news three weeks later when the President visited Arlington National Cemetery on May 31 for its annual Memorial Day services. The ceremonies, conducted once again at the "Old" Amphitheater, took on an added significance since the nation was commemorating the fiftieth anniversary of the end of the Civil War. The *Washington Times* somberly noted that: "the actors in the great war drama of a half century ago are fast receiving their last curtain calls," and counted just 172 surviving Civil War veterans in attendance.[39]

Later that afternoon, President Wilson along with his Secretary of the Navy, Josephus Daniels, attended the scheduled dedication ceremonies for Arlington's newest monument, the Mast of the USS *Maine* Memorial.[40] The *Maine* had exploded and sank in Havana harbor some 17 years earlier on February 15, 1898, killing 260 sailors and marines onboard. The incident inflamed American public opinion and quickly became the *casus belli* for the Spanish-American War. The *Maine* dead, whose bodies could be recovered from the wreckage, were temporarily interred during the hostilities at the Colon Cemetery in Havana, Cuba,.[41] The following year, after a return to peace, 165 of the sailors (63 known and 102 unknown) were disinterred and their remains repatriated to the United States. They were buried as a crew on Hall's Knoll in Section 24 at Arlington National Cemetery.[42]

Several years later, in 1910, the *Maine* was raised and salvaged. At that time, 66 additional remains were recovered; all but one of the sailors were unidentifiable. The bodies were likewise returned to the United States and buried at Arlington in 1912. The wreckage of the ship was finally towed out to sea and scuttled but only after the ship's two "fighting" masts were removed. These relics were transported to Washington where one was to become a focal point for a memorial commemorating the *Maine's* lost crew at Arlington Cemetery.[43]

The recovered mast was mounted on an impressive granite faux battleship gun turret on which were listed the names of the 260 crew members who had perished in the explosion. As the *Evening Star* reported: "No more impressive nor striking design for a monu-

(Library of Congress)

The dedication of the Mast of the USS Maine *Memorial, 31 May 1915. President Woodrow Wilson and Secretary of the Navy, Josephus Daniels, presided over the ceremonies. A construction crane for building the new Memorial Amphitheater is clearly visible in the background.*

ment to these naval martyrs could have been conceived then to take this great mast of a dead ship and have it arise from a pedestal that from a distance seems to be an actual gun turret. Closer view reveals the fact that it is made of granite and marble and contains a chamber that may be utilized as a receiving vault, the entrance [of] which is a heavy bronze door."[44]

A huge, 48-star American flag flew proudly from the ship's mast during the services. The climax of the event occurred when 50 active duty navy sailors climbed and manned the monument's rigging. The ceremonies concluded with the traditional playing of "Taps" and the rendering of a 21-gun salute.[45] To the east of the new memorial, a large construction crane was clearly visible, evidencing the ongoing progress in the construction of the new Amphitheater.

AN ESTIMATED 10,000 veterans and spectators came to Arlington on October 13, 1915 to witness the long-anticipated laying of the cornerstone of the Memorial Amphitheater. A 60-foot square platform had been specially erected for the ceremony at the northeast corner of the foundation. Dozens of plants decorated the stage area which was festooned with flags and other patriotic displays.[46] A large, 35-star Civil War-era American flag was raised to half-mast at the beginning of the program only to be replaced with the current 48-star national flag at the conclusion.[47]

The invocation was delivered by Bishop Earl Cranston and immediately following, Secretary of the Navy Daniels delivered the keynote address. In his lengthy remarks, Daniels noted that the new Amphitheater: "is a recognition of the grand democracy of the dead. Its prime purpose is that the memory of the least of those who lay down their life for love of country may be saved from oblivion."[48] The Secretary explained that the nation fought wars only out of necessity and that: "the American people have never engaged in war except for liberty and justice; they never shrink from war when liberty and justice are at stake."[49] He concluded: "Here is the heart of the republic."[50]

(Library of Congress)

President Wilson using a ceremonial gavel to set the cornerstone of the Memorial Amphitheater. Immediately behind the President is Judge Ivory Kimball, the man most responsible for seeing the Amphitheater project through to completion.

After a musical interlude performed by the Fifth Cavalry Band from Fort Myer, Judge Ivory Kimball was invited to address the audience. Kimball observed that they were gathered on sacred ground which had been consecrated by the graves of the thousands of soldiers who rest nearby. "The necessity for a suitable building in which to hold services at Arlington on Memorial Day has long been evident," Kimball noted, chronicling the long and difficult history in securing Congressional funding for the construction.[51] Moreover, Kimball argued that the Amphitheater would forever be a national treasure and would serve as a lesson in patriotism for future generations:

> This Amphitheater, while it is a memorial for the dead, has its greater use in the lessons of patriotism which it will teach to the many millions who will vis-

it it during the future centuries. How can any American citizen visit Arlington and fail to realize what all these headstones mean, or go away without a higher appreciation of his privileges as an American citizen and of the heritage these lives have left him? A visit here must give him a fuller determination to say and do nothing which will degrade his dignity as an American citizen or lower the value of that priceless heritage for which his ancestors fought and died.

There is one thing more which Arlington and this Amphitheater should teach. Wherever or under whatever circumstances we were born, we should be first and always American citizens with a supreme love for our country and its flag, which we delight to call 'Old Glory.' We should have that love for the flag which should lead us to honor it above everything else.[52]

After Judge Kimball had concluded his speech, President Wilson was invited to set the cornerstone using a ceremonial trowel. A 12"x12"x18" copper box was inserted into a custom cutout in the block. To protect it from moisture, an innovative glass barrier separated the time capsule from the marble to reduce the risk of damage due to moisture, condensation, and corrosion. Among the many items placed inside the time capsule were a Bible, copies of the Declaration of Independence and the Constitution, an autographed photograph of President Wilson, and an official program of the ceremonies. Once the mortar had been applied and set, President Wilson used a specially made gavel to symbolically hammer down the four corners of the stone, thus completing the official services.[53] The only visible inscription would be the engraved date: "Anno Domini MDCCCCXV."

On the very day that the cornerstone of the Memorial Amphitheater was being set, the Germans bombed London using high altitude zeppelins. The air raid indiscriminately targeted the city's civilian population but did little strategic damage. Some 55 people were killed while another 114 injured in the attack, terrorizing the London citizenry. Elsewhere that day, it was reported that the German army had deployed deadly poison gas in an offensive launched against French forces in Belgium.

AS THE YEAR ended, President Wilson was facing a difficult re-election campaign. Although his wife had died just sixteen months earlier, on December 16, Wilson married a prosperous widow, Edith Galt, after a brief courtship. The couple left that evening by train from nearby Alexandria, Virginia for a short honeymoon in Hot Springs as they anticipated the coming new year of 1916.[54]

Wilson had successfully accomplished many of his progressive and economic reforms during his first term. These included the establishment of the Federal Reserve system, the enactment of an 8-hour work day for some industries, the creation of the National Park Service, and the appointment of Louis Brandeis as a justice on the Supreme Court.[55] He had implemented the new XVI Amendment which created the nation's first graduated income tax and, in essence, provided the federal government with a virtually unlimited revenue stream. But Wilson's proudest accomplishment was that he had successfully navigated America away from any military involvement in the Great War in Europe. The nation's neutrality had been successfully preserved despite repeated provocations, and the President's campaign reflected his pride at this accomplishment utilizing such slogans as: "He Kept Us Out of War," "He Proved the Pen Mightier than the Sword," "America First: Wilson and That's All," and "War in Europe; Peace in America; God Bless Wilson."[56]

The reunited Republican Party nominated Associate Supreme Court Justice, Charles Evans Hughes, to run against Wilson. The election was hotly contested and extremely close. Wilson won a narrow majority in the popular vote totals, receiving 49.2% of the vote to Hughes' 46.1%. In the Electoral College, Wilson's margin was even closer: 277 to 254. California's 13 electoral votes proved decisive with Wilson winning the state by a mere 3,800 votes out of 1 million votes cast, thereby guaranteeing his re-election and a second term in office.[57]

ON JANUARY 31, 1917, in a desperate effort to break the stalemate on the western front, the Germans initiated a policy of unrestricted submarine warfare. U-boats began sinking all ships destined for Great Britain or other allied ports in an all-out effort to starve the British into submission. This policy, though, posed a direct threat to American shipping and violated international neutrality rights.

The German submarines were a formable weapon of war but on the surface, they were exposed and vulnerable to enemy guns. Thus, it was decided that all torpedo attacks should be launched underwater and conducted without any forewarning. The submarines, due to their small size and cramped conditions, could not rescue any survivors from sinking ships and this led many American newspapers to accuse the Germans of barbarically committing what amounted to as murder at sea. Each day, the nation's dailies chronicled the names and tonnage of ships sunk by the German U-boats.

In February, two American merchant and cargo vessels (*Housatonic* – Feb. 3 and the *Lyman M. Law* – Feb. 12) were sunk without warning by German U-boats. Public outrage was further inflamed with news of the sinking of the Cunard passenger liner, RMS *Laconia*, which was attacked en route from London to New York. Twelve passengers and crew including two Americans were killed. In one 48-hour period, German U-boats sank an astonishing 21 ships.

In the midst of this foreign policy crisis, President Wilson delivered his second inaugural address on the east steps of the United States Capitol on Monday, March 5.[58] His speech reflected the nation's somber mood: "We are provincials no longer. The tragic events of the thirty months of vital turmoil through which we have just passed have made us citizens of the world. There can be no turning back. Our own fortunes as a nation are involved whether we would have it so or not."[59] He grimly concluded: "The shadows that now lie dark upon our path will so be dispelled, and we shall walk with the light all about us if we be but true to ourselves."[60]

The German U-boat offensive continued unabated with another 36 Americans killed onboard United States' flagged vessels in March. Further exacerbating tensions was the publication of a top secret communique between the German foreign minister, Arthur Zimmermann, and his ambassador to Mexico. The so-called Zimmermann telegram proposed that in the event of war against the United States, Germany and Mexico should enter into a military alliance. In return for Mexico's participation in the conflict, the Germans would ensure a post war return of the territories of Texas, New Mexico, and Arizona ceded to the United States following the Mexican War.[61] By early April, after all diplomatic efforts to resolve the crisis with Germany had failed, President Wilson was prepared to seek a formal Congressional declaration of war.

German provocations notwithstanding, there remained a large anti-war sentiment within the United States. Few people were anxious to send American boys to die needlessly in the trenches of distant European battlefields. As President Wilson prepared to address Congress on April 2, emotions were running high. Some 1,500 peace protestors converged on the East Portico of the Capitol in what was euphemistically referred to as a "pilgrimage of patriotism."[62] They were quickly confronted by a large contingent of policemen who, augmented by 20 mounted officers, forced the demonstrators away from the Capitol steps and onto the plaza. Many of the pacifist marchers were conspicuously wearing armbands reading: "Keep us out of war," intentionally mocking President Wilson's now seemingly mendacious campaign pledge of the previous year. Before conducting a prayer vigil at two o'clock, the corralled marchers repeatedly tried to engage and confront members of Congress intent on attending the impending joint session of Congress.[63]

A separate group of protestors from Massachusetts successfully gained entrance into the Capitol building. There, they con-

(Library of Congress)

Pacifists gather on the steps of the House of Representatives to protest President Wilson's impending request for a Declaration of War against Germany. The crowd was later dispersed by Capitol police and mounted officers.

(National Archives)

President Woodrow Wilson speaking before a joint session of Congress. The President declared that: "The world must be made safe for democracy." For the first time in American history, the United States would send troops to fight in Europe.

fronted Senator Henry Cabot Lodge (R-Mass.) in front of his office. Lodge informed them that he would cast his vote in favor of President Wilson's expected declaration of war and this led to a heated verbal exchange. Alexander Bannwart, a constituent from Dorchester, physically attacked Senator Lodge, striking him in the face, and in the ensuing melee, Bannwart was arrested for assault.[64]

Elsewhere in the nation's capital, though, there was general public support for the forthcoming war. The *Evening Star* reported that patriotic displays were widespread, writing: "Flags floated from nearly every window in downtown Washington, from houses in residential sections, and all automobiles carried red, white, and blue banners or flags."[65] Likewise, telegrams from across the nation deluged the Congress in an effort to sway votes before any deliberations had begun.

President Wilson arrived on Capitol Hill later that day and addressed the Congress seeking a formal declaration of war against Germany. He justified the need for such dramatic action by declaring that: "The world must be made safe for democracy. Its peace must be planted upon the tested foundations of political liberty. We have no selfish ends to serve. We desire no conquest, no dominion. We seek no indemnities for ourselves, no material compensation for the sacrifices we shall freely make. We are but one of the champions of the rights of mankind. We shall be satisfied when those rights have been made as secure as the faith and the freedom of nations can make them."[66] It was an idealistic, albeit naïve, appeal to the nation's innate sense of justice but the President recognized that the war would be a difficult struggle. "It is a fearful thing to lead this great peaceful people into war, into the most terrible and disastrous of all wars," Wilson argued, but "civilization itself seeming to be in the balance."[67] The President proclaimed that the war was directed only against the Kaiser and his imperial government, and that: "We have no quarrel with the German people. We have no feeling towards them but one of sympathy and friendship."[68]

Two days after the President's historic speech, the Senate passed the war resolution by an 82 to 6 vote. The House followed suit on April 6, adopting it by a 373 to 50 margin.[69] For only the fourth time in the nation's history, the United States was officially and constitutionally at war with a foreign nation.[70]

THE UNITED STATES was ill-prepared to wage a major war on the European continent. The nation's peacetime army, including both active duty and reservists, numbered just under 350,000 men. The enlistment and conscription of some four million soldiers would take months as would the full mobilization of the country's industrial resources.[71] Further complicating America's wartime mission was the serious logistical difficulties of transporting thousands of troops safely across the Atlantic Ocean and ensuring that these soldiers were well-equipped, well-supplied, and well-fed.

The commander of the new American Expeditionary Forces (AEF) was John J. "Black Jack" Pershing. A skilled and thoughtful general, Pershing was determined not to sacrifice his troops by rushing them into combat and fighting futile battles with no strategic outcomes. The newly recruited and conscripted American soldiers needed to be adequately trained and prepared for battle and this would take time despite the enormous political pressure and objections from the allied nations. Pershing also insisted that American troops remain independent and under their own commanders rather than be absorbed into existing British and French units. It was admittedly a painfully slow process so that by the end of 1917, eight full months after entering the conflict, just 176,655 American soldiers had arrived in France. They had yet to make any significant difference in breaking the stalemate or altering the ultimate outcome of the war. The Canadian Prime Minster somberly admitted: "The military situation in France is very serious and the issue of the War may depend upon the speed with which the American armies can be organized, trained, and equipped."[72] Still, the AEF sustained its first combat fatalities in November when Private Thomas Enright, Corporal James B. Gresham, and Private Merle D. Hay were killed during a surprise German night raid near Artois, France.[73]

Russia's continued participation in the war against the Central Powers was very much in doubt. The nation had suffered unconscionable casualties, with conservative estimates placing losses at five million dead. Their troops were ill-equipped, starving, and poorly led; widespread mutiny was a distinct possibility. The civilian population, likewise, suffered through food shortages, inflation, strikes, and incompetent government.[74] In March 1917, Tsar Nicholas II had been forced to abdicate the Romanov throne after a popular revolution centered in Petrograd.[75] The new provincial government agreed to abide by its alliances and continued to fight the war, but as one member of the British Intelligence services, Sir Samuel Hoare, astutely observed: "The conditions of life have become so intolerable, the Russian casualties have been so heavy, the ages and classes subject to military service have been so widely extended, the disorganization and untrustworthiness of the Government have been so notorious that it is not a matter of surprise if the majority of ordinary people reach at any peace straw. Personally, I am convinced that Russia will never fight through another winter."[76]

His communique proved prophetic. The Communist revolutionary, Vladimir Lenin, returned from political exile in April 1917 and quickly capitalized on the political chaos. On October 25, his Bolshevik party seized power and began negotiating a separate peace with Germany. The Soviets signed the infamous Treaty of Brest-Litovsk on March 3, 1918. The agreement ended the war for Russia and effectively abrogated the nation's treaty commitments with the British and French. Kaiser Wilhelm was finally free to redirect and concentrate his forces along the western front but by now, the American forces were finally prepared to join the battle.[77] The AEF first major combat occurred at the Battle of Cantigny (May 28, 1918) and the presence of fresh, well-equipped troops had the desired devastating effect.[78] The Americans continually engaged the Germans throughout the summer and fall in such battles as Belleau Woods, the Marne, Amiens, and Meuse-Ardid. The exhausted, battle-weary German army collapsed while political turmoil in Berlin led to Kaiser Wilhelm abdicating the Hohenzollern throne. Finally, on November 11, at 11 AM, the eleventh hour of the eleventh day of the eleventh month, an armistice was declared and fighting in the Great War mercifully came to an end. Over 13 million soldiers had died during the war. The United States lost 116,000 soldiers in just seven months of combat while an additional 202,628 had been wounded. Peace had once again been restored to the European continent.[79]

THE WAR HAD effectively put a stop to non-essential construction projects throughout the United States and thus the work on the Memorial Amphitheater at Arlington had correspondingly slowed. Contractors, subcontractors, and labor had been mobilized to work in the nation's wartime industries while military shipments were given top priority in transportation. Building materials and supplies became increasing difficult to obtain and bad winter weather also conspired to slow construction.[80] By the end of the 1918 fiscal year, the Amphitheater project was well behind schedule even though much of the exterior had already been completed. There still remained months of work on the structure's approaches, roadways, sidewalks, and landscaping. Interior plumbing, painting, and electrical work also had to be finished.[81] But with the return to peace, the Amphitheater project once again became a national focus and priority.

One of the greatest difficulties in finishing the Amphitheater was selecting appropriate inscriptions for its marble façade. Since the building had been conceived, planned, and designed prior to America's entry into the Great War, these engravings necessarily would reflect the nation's history only from the American Revolution through the Spanish-American War. It would not include any of the contemporary battles or leaders from World War I. The Memorial Amphitheater Commission appointed a group of scholars to help devise a list of historical battles, military commanders, and inscriptions to be engraved. The President of Harvard, A. Lawrence Lowell, was selected to chair the panel, which included two other renowned college presidents, Harry B. Hutchins from the University of Michigan, and Edwin Alderman from the University of Virginia.[82]

(Library of Congress)
The Memorial Amphitheater under construction at Arlington National Cemetery.
The new facility would not be finished until May 1920 due to delays caused by
America's entry into the Great War.

In meetings and consultation with other scholars as well as military historians, the General Staff of the Army, and the Department of Navy, the committee decided to recommend that a 1775 quote from George Washington: "When we assumed the soldier we did not lay aside the citizen," be engraved prominently above the apse. Due to space limitations, it was also decided to use a few inspirational words from Lincoln's Gettysburg Address on the archway framing the stage: "We here highly resolve that these dead shall not have died in vain."[83]

In February 1920, Colonel C.S. Ridley gave the architects the go ahead to proceed with all of the remaining engravings. In a letter, he wrote: "It has been definitely settled that the list of battles submitted by Professor Lowell is approved...the drawings for the names of the battles should, therefore, be completed."[84] Forty-four famous battles were to be inscribed on the entablature above the amphitheater's colonnade, while the names of 14 Navy Admirals and 14 Army Generals were to be listed on either side of the building's prominent stage.

When the inscriptions were publicly announced, there was an immediate and predictable controversy. Some people were upset by the omission of various generals and admirals who they deemed worthy of commemoration, but the greatest censure came from southerners who were outraged that not a single Confederate commander had been duly honored. Besides such notables as Stonewall Jackson, James Longstreet and J.E.B. Stuart, the most conspicuous omission was the commander of the Army of Northern Virginia, General Robert E. Lee. Indeed, Arlington National Cemetery had been established on Lee's antebellum estate and his home, Arlington House, remained the visual focal point for the cemetery. An irate Clarence J. Owens wrote to the Secretary of War, Newton Baker: "you failed utterly to make provisions for the South or to urge that the South be included and to arrange for representatives of the South to appear before the Commission to urge that justice be shown the military leaders of the Southland...[as] the son of a Confederate soldier, [I] might have been spared having one of her own turn his hand and his back upon his people, their heroic achievements and their ideals."[85] In another contentious letter, Owens noted the: "...gross injustice with regard to the treatment of the South as to the Arlington Memorial Amphitheater" and that "...there is no act since the War between the States...that has to so great an extent aroused the people of the South and it has done more to engender sectional bitterness and animosity."[86] Alabama Senator Oscar Underwood also wrote to Secretary of War about the failure to include southern commanders: "Our soldiers of the war between the states have become the heroes of the nation, regardless of the side they fought on. The camping ground at Arlington unites them all, and I think it would be most unfortunate if the failure to give recognition there opened the old wounds of the past."[87]

The federal government and the Memorial Amphitheater Commission defended the process for selecting the building's inscriptions. "The names which have been authorized to be included in the Memorial are a part of the architectural design," argued Secretary of War Baker, "and the place for them was approved at the time the design was accepted."[88] The GAR dismissed the southerners' grievances with one member claiming that the: "Memorial Amphitheater was designed to be national, not sectional in character."[89] Such statements did little to appease critics or heal hurt feelings.

THE AMERICAN PUBLIC was eager to make the transition back to a time of peace and domestic prosperity. But immediately after the armistice in Europe had been declared, President Wilson traveled to France determined to play a pivotal role in the negotiations for a permanent peace treaty. Wilson, the professor turned politician, would be absent from the nation's capital for months, returning only once to sign critical bills and pending legislation. The President spent months in France engaged in contentious negotiations which resulted in numerous concessions and accommodations between the allied powers.

In May 1919, Wilson was still in Europe when he and his new wife, Edith, visited the Suresnes American Cemetery to honor the nation's new war dead on Memorial Day. Located just outside Paris, the small, 7.5-acre cemetery had been created out of military necessity and was a tangible reminder of the human toll of war. It contained the graves of hundreds of young American soldiers including those of 24 unknowns.[90] Speaking before a crowd of 7,000 soldiers, Wilson noted that: "These men did not come across the sea merely to defeat Germany and her associated powers in the war. They came to defeat forever the things for which the Central Powers stood for...to see to it that there should never be a war like this again."[91] The President then devoted much of the remainder of his address to advocate for the proposed international peacekeeping organization, the League of Nations. He argued that: "The League of Nations is a covenant of Governments that these men shall not have died in vain...this age is an age which looks forward, not backward, which rejects the standards of national selfishness that once governed the counsels of nations and demands that they shall give way to a new order of things in which the only questions will be, 'Is it right?' 'Is it just?' 'Is it in the interest of mankind?'"[92]

The military newspaper, *Stars and Stripes*, covered President Wilson's visit to the cemetery and reported on other American memorial services being conducted simultaneously throughout Europe, noting that they: "were paralleled on a smaller scale in hundreds of scattered cemeteries in France, England, Belgium, Luxembourg, and Germany" and that: "these cemeteries whose American soldier graves numbered last Friday more than 70,000."[93]

Just weeks after Wilson's visit to Suresnes, the Treaty of Versailles, including the President's cherished League of Nations, was finally agreed upon and formally signed on June 28, 1919. The final document was 226 pages long and consisted of a staggering 440 articles. The controversial Article 231 placed full blame for the Great War squarely upon the German government and required the defeated nation to pay enormous and punitive war reparations.[94] Other provisions literally redrew the map of Europe, creating nine new nations, ostensibly predicated upon ethnic identity or historical precedent. Similarly, the map of the Middle East was transformed, carved out of the corpse of the defeated Ottoman Empire.[95]

President Wilson expected a triumphal return to the United States. He personally delivered a copy of the new treaty to the United States Senate and addressed the body at length, asking for its "advice and consent." The Constitution mandated that a two-thirds majority of the Senate concur for final ratification of any and all treaties.

There was already substantial opposition to Wilson's cherished treaty due mostly to the provisions creating the League of Nations. The Geneva-based international organization was particularly noxious to Republican Senators, who feared that it would embroil the United States in endless world conflicts and countless wars while surrendering America's independence and national sovereignty.[96]

Wilson was incensed by the criticism and launched a personal lobbying campaign to convince Senators to pass the treaty. He decided to take his case directly to the American people, embarking upon a nationwide tour in a concerted effort to sway public opinion and force Senate passage. Traveling exclusively by train, the President delivered dozens of speeches before large crowds, making the case for the treaty's ratification and specifically for American participation in the League of Nations. In Pueblo, Colorado, the President denounced his opponents, claiming: "I have perceived more and more that men have been busy creating an absolutely false impression of what the treaty of peace and the Covenant of the League of Nations contain and mean."[97] He argued that the League's purpose was to ensure that future generations did not have to go to war. Wilson explained: "My clients are the children; my clients are the next generation…they shall not be sent upon a similar errand." He then told the gathered audience that the Gold Star mothers who sent the sons to die in distant battlefields believed that their cause had been just and worthwhile: "They believe, and they rightly believe, that their sons saved the liberty of the world."[98] Wilson ended his speech claiming that the Treaty of Versailles and the League of Nations were essential for world peace, stating: "For nothing less depends upon this decision, nothing less than liberation and salvation of the world."

Shortly after concluding his remarks, an exhausted and weary Wilson took seriously ill and had to suspend the rest of his schedule. He was rushed back to Washington, where he suffered a debilitating stroke at the White House on October 2, 1919. The President would be incapacitated for months and severely diminished for the remainder of his presidency. On November 19, the Senate failed to ratify the Treaty of Versailles by the constitutionally required two-thirds majority.[99] The news would leave President Wilson forever an embittered, disillusioned, and aggrieved man.

———————

AFTER THE FINAL landscaping and road grading had been completed in the spring of 1920, the Memorial Amphitheater was ready to be officially dedicated. The ceremonies were scheduled for Saturday, May 15, 1920. Judge Ivory Kimball, the man whose vision and tenacity, was most responsible for the project's fruition, would not be in attendance. The Judge had died four years earlier, and his grave at Arlington (Section SD, #1538) was specifically chosen so that it would forever be in close proximity to America's new "Temple of Patriotism."[100]

The official dedication program began with military honor guard units assembling on the ellipse near the White House. Notably absent was the participation of any Confederate veterans, who were still miffed over the omission of Southern generals from the amphitheater's entablature.[101] The parade first marched slowly by the south lawn of the White House where President Wilson was able to watch the procession from a distance. His doctor, Rear Admiral Cary Travers Grayson, had refused to allow Wilson to attend the formal ceremonies at Arlington because of his patient's continued fragile health.[102]

Among the many military units was a special honor guard regiment consisting of wounded war veterans, a poignant reminder of the human consequences of war. As the *Evening Star* reported in their coverage of the event: "A gallant…feature, was the color guard…every man in front rank of eight having lost either a leg or an arm in battle."[103] The soldiers made their way to Arlington Cemetery, crossing the Potomac River via the Highway Bridge to the south of the city.[104]

The official program at the Amphitheater began at 2:30 PM. Some 15,000 people had gathered both inside and outside of the

(National Archives)

An honor guard contingent of Navy sailors marching to the new Memorial Amphitheater. Woodrow Wilson was unable to attend the services due to ill health, but the President sent both a wreath and welcoming remarks.

newly finished building. The commander of the victorious American Expeditionary Forces, General John J. Pershing gave an address as did the Secretary of War, Newton D. Baker, who declared that: "We can, therefore, dedicate this memorial as an emblem alike of our grateful pride in what has been done, and in confident assurance of what will be done."[105] Secretary of the Navy Daniels also spoke during the ceremonies: "Today is in a very real sense all-heroes day...On this day we dedicate ourselves afresh to the ideals that these honored dead, one and all, rendered illustrious."[106]

Woodrow Wilson had previously agreed to deliver the primary dedication address and his attendance was included in the official eight-page program. But since he was unable to attend, he instead sent a presidential wreath along with a letter which was to be read by Spanish-American War veteran, Captain Charles Newton. "I cannot attend the ceremony of this dedication, but my heart is there," the President wrote. "I join in grateful recognition of the virtues which the memorial commemorates." He continued: "this great and beautiful building [will] stand like a sentinel on the banks of the Potomac and to view for all time the capital."[107]

One of the lesser known speakers at the dedication was the Army Chief of Staff, Peyton C. Marsh. His remarks, although little noted that day, had profound implications for the United States in the post-war era. Marsh informed the audience that there were currently 593 cemeteries scattered through France and Belgium where American soldiers had been hastily interred during the Great War. These cemeteries were created out of military necessity and most were wholly inadequate for properly honoring the nation's war dead. The military had recently initiated a policy allowing for family members to request the repatriation of their loved one's remains and Arlington had already begun to receive the first of these soldiers. "We have set aside the south-western part of this beautiful cemetery," Marsh said, "…to receive such bodies as are to rest here permanently. Sixty-four have already been interred and hundreds more are on the way."[108] In fact, over the ensuing years, some 70% for all American casualties would ultimately be returned to the United States for burial.[109]

The *Evening Star* concluded its extensive coverage of the dedicatory events noting that: "The Arlington Memorial Amphitheater is said to be the only monument of its kind in the world."[110] Indeed, it suitably honored the contributions of the nation's citizen-soldiers and celebrated the ideals of the American republic. The final cost of the Amphitheater project was $819,289.77.[111] It was a lasting investment in the nation's history.

(Library of Congress)
The opening of the Memorial Amphitheater, 15 May 1920. Some 15,000-people gathered at Arlington for the ceremonies dedicating America's "Temple of Patriotism."

Endnotes

1 The assassination occurred on 28 June 1914. It was part of a series of anarchist and ethnic inspired murders of government officials throughout Russia, Europe and the United States. In 1901, U.S. President William McKinley was assassinated by avowed anarchist Leon Czolgloz.

2 Otto von Bismarck (1 April 1815–30 July 1898), Chancellor of the German Empire. Otto von Bismarck quotes available at https://www.goodreads.com/author/quotes/800128.Otto_von_Bismarck.

3 Woodrow Wilson. President Wilson's Declaration of Neutrality, 19 August 1914. Teaching American History available at: http://teachingamericanhistory.org/library/document/president-wilsons-declaration-of-neutrality/.

4 Kaiser Wilhelm II (27 January 1859–4 June 1941).

5 The German plan was named for General Alfred von Schlieffen. The Germans invaded Belgium on 4 August 1914. Americans were outraged at what was popularly referred to as "the rape of Belgium."

6 David Crane, *Empires of the Dead: How One Man's Vision Led to the Creation of WWI's War Graves*. London: William Collins, 2013, p. 39.

7 Ellen Wilson (15 May 1860–6 August 1914).

8 "Mrs. Wilson Dies at White House," *The Evening Star*, 7 August 1914, p. 1.

9 *Presidential Elections 1789 – 2004*. Washington, D.C.: Congressional Quarterly, Inc., 2005, p. 49.

10 "Murder, Lust, Pillage, Prevailed in Belgium," *The Washington Herald*, 13 May 1915, p. 2.

11 *Ibid.*, p. 2.

12 *Ibid.*, p. 2.

13 *Deutschland über alles* was originally written by Joseph Haydn in 1797. It became the official German national anthem under the Weimar government in 1922 and was later closely associated with the Nazi party.

14 "Stricken Belgians Rejoice over Food," *The Evening Star*, 14 Nov. 1914, p. 4.

15 "Stricken Belgium Again Seeks Aid," *The Evening Star*, 18 Nov. 1914, p. 9.

16 Margaret E. Wagner. *American and the Great War*. New York: Bloomsbury Press, 2017, pp. 50, 51.

17 "Mines Destroy Five Ships; 95 Perish," *The Washington Times*, 18 Nov. 1915, p. 1.

18 The Memorial Bridge became a reality in 1932, the bicentennial of George Washington's birth.

19 "Judge Kimbell is Claimed by Death," *The Evening Star*, 15 May 1916, p. 4.

20 "Omits to Vote Fund," *The Evening Star*, 12 March 1913, p. 5.

21 *Ibid.*, p. 5.

22 Letter from Judge Ivory Kimball to Secretary of War L. M. Garrison, 9 July 1913.

23 Thomas Hastings (11 March 11 1860--22 October 1929).

24 *Ibid.*, p. 5.

25 The Mast of the *Maine* monument was dedicated on 30 May 1915.

26 "New Amphitheater to be America's Westminster Abbey," *The Evening Star*, 27 May 1917, p. 6.

27 Colonial W.W. Harts quoted in "New Amphitheater," p. 6.

28 *Ibid.*, p. 6.

29 "New Amphitheater," p. 6.

30 The crypt areas below the colonnade today are referred to as the "catacombs." They are still used for storage, but the Tomb Guard also utilizes the space for new sentinels to practice away from the public eye.

31 "Ground is Broken for Amphitheater," *The Evening Star*, 1 March 1915, p. 2.

32 "Plan to Preserve Arlington Beauty," *The Evening Star*, 8 January 2015, p. 3.

33 *Ibid.*, p. 3.

34 "137 American Lives Lost; U.S. Demands Explanation," *The Evening World*, 8 May 1915, p. 1.

35 "German Official Note to U.S. To-Day Insists Blame Rests with England; Sorry American Lives were Lost," *The Evening World*, 10 May 1915, p. 1.

36 Eric Larson. *Dead Wake: The Last Crossing of the Lusitania*. New York: Crown Publishers, 2015, p. 350.

37 Woodrow Wilson quoted in Larson, p. 351.

38 Woodrow Wilson quoted in H.W. Brands. *Woodrow Wilson*. New York: Time Books, 2003.

39 "Whole Nation Joins Wilson In His Tribute to Hero Dead," *The Washington Times*, 31 May 2015, p. 1, 3.

40 Several sources indicate that the dedication of the Mast of the *Maine* Memorial took place on May 30. This is incorrect since that day was a Sunday. Instead, all Memorial Day services were moved to Monday, May 31.

41 Philip Bigler. *In Honored Glory: Arlington National Cemetery, the Final Post*. St. Petersburg: Vandamere Press, 2010, p. 36.

42 "USS *Maine* Memorial." Arlington National Cemetery available at: http://www.arlingtoncemetery.mil/Explore/Monuments-and-Memorials/USS-Maine-Mast-Memorial.

43 The other *Maine* mast was taken to the Naval Academy in Annapolis, Maryland. The *Maine* memorial was designed by the architect Nathaniel Wyeth.

44 Three people have been temporarily interred in the base of the *Maine* since its dedication: Lord Lothian, the British Ambassador to the United States, 1940–1945; Manuel Quezon, President of the Philippines, 1944–1946; Ignacy Jan Paderewski, Polish Composer and president of the government in exile, 1941—1992). "Dedication of Maine Monument: A Feature of Memorial Day Celebration at Arlington," *The Evening Star*, 30 May 1915, p. 27.

45 "Tribute is Paid to Sailor Dead at Maine Memorial Services at Arlington Cemetery," *The Evening Star*, 01 June 1915, p. 7.

46 *Report of the Memorial Amphitheater Commission: 67th Congress, 4th Session, Vol. 42*. Washington, D.C.: Government Printing Office, 1923, p.21.

47 "Chief of Nation Aids in Honoring Memory of Dead," *The Evening Star*, 13 Oct. 1915, p. 1.

48 Josephus Daniels quoted in *Report of the Memorial Amphitheater Commission*, p. 27.

49 *Ibid.*, p. 33.

50 "Secretary Daniels Predicts Memorial Bridge Will Join Arlington and the Capital," *The Evening Star*, 13 Oct. 1915, p. 11.

51 Judge Ivory Kimball quoted in *Report of the Memorial Amphitheater Commission*, pp. 41-42.

52 *Ibid.*, pp. 42-43.

53 The following items were placed in the cornerstone: A Bible, a copy of the Declaration of Independence, a copy of the Constitution, a silk United States flag, a copy of the designs and plans of the Memorial Amphitheater, an autograph from the Memorial Amphitheater Commission, one coin and one stamp of each denomination then in circulation, a copy of Pierre L'Enfant's map of the design for the city of Washington, D.C., a copy of the Congressional directory, a copy of Boyd's City Directory of the District of Columbia, an autographed photo of President Woodrow Wilson, a copy of the official program for the cornerstone laying, and a copy of *the Evening Star* newspaper recounting the events and the history of the amphitheater project. *Report of the Memorial Amphitheater Commission*, pp. 24-25.

54 Wilson was 59 years old at the time of his marriage to Edith Galt, age 43. "President and Mrs. Galt Wed in Presence of the Families: Honeymoon at Hot Springs, VA.," *The Evening Star*, 19 Dec. 1915, p. 1.

55 *Presidential Elections 1789–2004*, p. 49.

56 *Ibid.*, p. 50.

57 *Ibid.*, pp. 141, 226.

58 Waldman, Michael, ed. *My Fellow Americans: The Most Important Speeches of America's Presidents from George Washington to George W. Bush*. Naperville, Ill.: Sourcebooks, Inc., 2003, p. 79.

59 The President was sworn in on Sunday, March 4, but he delayed his formal inaugural address until the next day. Woodrow Wilson quoted *in Inaugural Addresses of the Presidents of the United States from George Washington 1789 to George Bush 1989*. Washington, D.C.: United States Government Printing Office, 1989, p. 234.

60 *Ibid.*, p. 235.

61 Margaret E. Wagner. *American and the Great War*. New York: Bloomsbury Press, 2017, p. 156.

62 "Pacifists Besiege Capitol but Fail to Gain Entrance," *The Evening Star*, 2 April 1917, p. 2.

63 "War Congress is Besieged by Pacifists: Wilson May Go to Capitol Late Today; Hostile Constituent Attacks Lodge," *The Washington Times*, 2 April 1917, p. 1.

64 Bannwart apologized to Senator Lodge and was eventually released without going to trial. "Pacifists Attack Senator Lodge in Capitol Corridor," *The Evening Star*, 2 April 1917, p. 1.

65 "Pacifists Besiege Capitol," p. 2.

66 Woodrow Wilson quoted in Waldman, p. 84.

67 *Ibid.*, p. 86.

68 *Ibid.* p. 85.

69 One of the "nay" votes in the House was from Congresswoman Jeanette Rankin of Montana. A confirmed pacifist, she would later become the only member of the House to vote against the declaration of war in 1941 after the Japanese attack on Pearl Harbor.

70 Under the United States Constitution (Article I, Section 8), only Congress has the authority to declare war. It has done so five times: the War of 1812, the Mexican War, the Spanish-American War, World War I, and World War II. There have been, however, numerous undeclared wars particularly after World War II including the Korean War, the Vietnam War, and various military actions in Afghanistan and the Middle East.

71 *World War I Remembered*. Washington, D.C.: The National Park Service, 2017.

72 Robert Borden quoted in Gilbert, Martin. *The First World War: A Complete History*. New York: Henry Holt and Company, 1994, p. 434.

73 Lisa M. Budreau. *Bodies of War: World War I and the Politics of Commemoration in America, 1919 – 1933*. New York: New York University Press, 2010, p.85.

74 Catherine Merridale. *Lenin on the Train*. New York: Metropolitan Books, 2017, p.36, 42, 50.

75 The name of the Russian capital of St. Petersburg had been changed during the war to the more Slavic sounding Petrograd.

76 Sir Samuel Hoare quoted in Merridale, p. 43.

77 Martin Gilbert. *The First World War: A Complete History*. New York: Henry Holt and Company, 1994, pp. 399-400.

78 *Ibid.*, p. 426.

79 Wagner, p. 276.

80 "Conditions Due to War Halt Amphitheater," *The Evening Star*, 10 April 1918, p. 18.

81 *Report of the Memorial Amphitheater Commission*, p. 15.

82 Records of the Memorial Amphitheater Commission are available at the National Archives in Washington, D.C.

83 Memorial Amphitheater. Arlington National Cemetery available at: http://www.arlingtoncemetery.mil/Explore/Memorial-Amphitheater.

84 Letter from Colonel C. S. Ridley to Messrs. Carrère & Hastings, 26 February 1920.

85 Letter from Clarence J. Owens to Secretary of War Newton Baker, 28 June 1920.

86 Letter from Clarence J. Owen to Secretary of War Newton Baker, 3 June 1920.

87 Letter from Senator Oscar Underwood to Secretary of War Newton Baker, 11 May 1920.

88 Letter from Secretary of War Newton Baker to N. J. Gould, 7 May 1920.

89 "Lee Ignored: Dixie Roiled," *The Washington Times*, 9 May 1920, p. 1.

90 The Suresnes American Cemetery currently contains the remains of 1,541 American soldiers including the remains of 24 unknowns. The names of some 974 missing in action are inscribed on the chapel's walls. See the American Battle Monuments Commission's website available at: http://www.abmc.gov.

91 Woodrow Wilson quoted in: "President and General Speak on Memorial Day," *Stars and Stripes*. 6 June 1919, p. 2.

92 *Ibid.*, p. 2.

93 *Ibid.*, p. 2.

94 Brands, p. 116.

95 The nine new European countries were Finland, Austria, Czechoslovakia, Yugoslavia, Poland, Hungary, Latvia, Lithuania, and Estonia. In the Middle East were the British Mandates of Palestine and Mesopotamia (Iraq) and the French Mandates of Syria and Lebanon.

96 *Ibid.*, p. 106.

97 "President Woodrow Wilson's Address in Favor of the League of Nations," delivered at Pueblo, Colorado, 25 September 1919 available at: http://firstworldwar.com.

98 *Ibid.*

99 The vote was 55 to 39 in favor but substantially short of the required 64 needed for ratification.

100 Judge Ivory Kimball (5 May 1843–15 May 1916).

101 "Lee Ignored: Dixie Roiled," p. 1.

102 Rear Admiral Dr. Cary Travers Grayson (11 October 1878–15 February 1938). He is buried at Arlington National Cemetery. (Sec. 30, #S-24)

103 "Wars' Veterans Join in Dedication of Amphitheater," *The Evening Star*, 15 May 1920, pp. 1, 4.

104 The Highway Bridge is now the 14th Street Bridge. The difficulty of reaching Arlington from Washington was apparent and was further impetus for the construction of the Memorial Bridge.

105 "Wars' Veterans," p. 1.

106 "'Is All Heroes Day,' Says Mr. Daniels at Memorial Dedication," *The Evening Star*, 15 May 1920, p. 4.

107 "President's Tribute to Men Who Fought," *The Evening Star*, 15 May 1920, p. 1.

108 "Shrine to Heroes Opened to Nation," *The Evening Star*, 16 May 1920, p. 2.

109 Budreau, p. 75.

110 "Wars' Veterans," p. 1.

111 The massive project required the work of electrical contractors, horticulturists, plumbers, road graders, painters, sewers, iron workers, architects, and stone workers. The major contractors were: George A. Fuller Co. $36,220.99; Carrère and Hastings: $36,422.48; Fred W. Smythe (Plants and planting) $21,200.00; Charles H. Tompkins (Sewers and walks) $20,736.77; L. Morgan Johnston (Road construction) $21,477.72; G. B. Mullen (Grading) $19,436.60. See the Memorial Amphitheater Commission's final report to Congress, 3 March 1921, pp. 61-62.

(Library of Congress)
A grieving woman pays tribute to the American Unknown Soldier at Arlington National Cemetery. The United States buried its Unknown on November 11, 1921, the third anniversary of the armistice.

Chapter III

The Unknown from the
Great War

The Tomb of the Unknown Soldier will be "a Mecca for all mothers of the land whose dead could not be given back to them." – Chaplain Charles Pierce

Stars and Stripes, the official newspaper of the American Expeditionary Forces, reported: "At the eleventh hour on the eleventh day of the eleventh month hostilities came to an end... there followed a strange, unbelievable silence as though the world had died."[1] Later that day, as the certainty of peace became apparent, allied troops began to celebrate the end of the war; bands played and church bells rang, with the revelries continuing throughout the day and night. These lucky troops had somehow survived life in the trenches, a global influenza pandemic, and the horrors of combat.[2] It was now time to celebrate their deliverance.[3]

The signing of the armistice in November 1918 effectively ended the fighting in Europe, but the psychological impact and political consequences of the war would continue to haunt future generations. Millions of soldiers had perished during the conflict and it would be left to the survivors to ultimately bring meaning to this whole-scale mass slaughter of humanity.

World War I had been the first truly technological war, a conflict, according to one contemporary, fought by men and machines. New and terrible armaments had been developed by both sides and were used to great efficiency. These weapons included machine guns, U-boats, poison gas, tanks, long-range artillery, hand grenades, flamethrowers, airplanes, and zeppelins. All had contributed to the terrible carnage and the unprecedented number of war casualties. Individual valor, courage, and heroism seemed meaningless on the new, twentieth century battlefield. Even the bravest of soldiers could be killed instantly by an artillery shell fired from miles away or shot dead by an anonymous sniper's bullet or killed by inhaling toxic fumes from exploding gas canisters.[4] Death was ubiquitous, but it also appeared to be random and meaningless. One British soldier, Captain Llewelyn Griffith, graphically described the slaughter typical on the frontlines: "There were more corpses than men, but there were worse sights than corpses. Limbs and mutilated trunks, here and there a detached head, forming splashes of red against the green leaves, and, as in advertisement of the horror of our way of life and death, and of our crucifixion of youth, one tree held in its branches a leg, with its torn flesh hanging down over a spray of leaf."[5]

During the war, British Commonwealth nations sustained over 1,724,000 casualties—killed, wounded, and missing. On the single bloodiest day of fighting (1 July 1916), 19,240 British soldiers were killed-in-action at the Battle of the Somme.[6] The sheer volume of casualties was unfathomable to the world's civilian populations, while the massive number of deaths posed serious logistical challenges for the warring armies. For both hygienic and psychological reasons, rapid burial of the dead was essential, but this often proved problematic due to the proximity and intensity of the fighting. Dead soldiers were commonly buried at night with few, if any, religious rites or military rituals; their mangled corpses were consigned to hastily dug trenches shrouded only in a crude blanket.[7] By the end of the war, there were over 2,300 allied and enemy cemeteries scattered throughout western Europe.[8] Many of these burial sites were primitive and inadequate, contributing to the stark reality that thousands of soldiers would never be individually identified.[9]

Since most of the fighting on the western front had taken place in northern France, the French government made it a post-war priority to quickly reclaim the dormant battlefields in an effort to restore the old pastures and fields to agricultural use. This required the removal of unexploded ordnance, the clearing out of debris, the filling-in of trenches and bomb craters, the removing of shallow graves, and the recovering of the remaining dead.[10]

The allies simultaneously began a Herculean effort to properly identify, reinter, and consolidate their war dead in newly established "concentration" cemeteries. In order to properly memorialize these deceased soldiers, the new cemeteries mandated uniform, standardized grave markers in order to prevent what one British report warned against: "[the] hideous effigies relatives often have a tendency to erect."[11] The recently created British War Graves Commission helped coordinate these efforts and ordered: "That there should be carved on the headstone the rank, name, regiment and date of death of the man buried beneath it, and that relatives should be allowed at their own cost to add a short inscription to the nature of a text or prayer, subject to the approval of the Commission." [12] Family members in Britain and the other Commonwealth nations were strictly forbidden from making any effort to reclaim and repatriate the remains of their loved ones from the continent. This extremely controversial and unpopular policy was rationalized by the belief that the nation's public morale could not withstand the psychological trauma and emotional impact that would ensue from years of individual memorial services and endless private burials.[13]

Despite the admirable goal of properly identifying all of the war dead, it proved impossible to accurately account for all of the soldiers. As military historian, Patrick O'Donnell, writes: "Artillery vaporized and shredded men on the battlefield, reducing many of their bodies to mere remains—'unknown soldiers.'"[14] The British classified over 517,000 of its soldiers as missing-in-action while more than one million French soldiers were still unaccounted for by the end of the war.[15] The loss of identity in death was a fate greatly feared by all soldiers. Most wore or carried small metal alloy identification disks which listed their name, rank, and regiment but these tokens were easily lost or separated from a soldier during combat, making post-mortem identification difficult.[16] Furthermore, the number of unidentified soldiers increased because, as historian Neil Hanson writes: "Many grave markers [were] destroyed in subsequent fighting, or removed by farmers squatting on their ruined land in primitive shelters and desperate to begin ploughing and re-planting. As a result, all trace of tens of thousands of graves had been obliterated."[17] For countless grieving families, this meant that there would never be a known grave where they could focus their sorrow. In her seminal book, *Bodies of War*, author and historian Lisa Budreau writes: "loss of a loved one in battle [was] magnified by the uncertainty of burial place and the inability to connect a name with a grave or body...[there would be] no funeral service, no head-stone in a local cemetery, nothing left to venerate, and no closure so necessary in the grieving process."[18]

Almost immediately after the cessation of the fighting, small towns, hamlets, villages, and cities throughout Europe began to erect war memorials. These early efforts at commemoration of the local dead attempted to honor hometown soldiers by permanently inscrib-ing in stone the names of their dead and thereby restoring a bit of their lost identity.[19] On a larger scale, the most imposing and somber war memorial to be erected after the armistice was the Menin Gate Memorial to the Missing in Ypres, Belgium. On the monument's massive walls were inscribed the individual names of 54,896 miss-ing British and Commonwealth soldiers who had disappeared during the fighting in Flanders. In the nearby city of Zonnebeck, the Tyne Cot Memorial similarly listed the names of another 35,000 missing soldiers.[20] At Whitehall in England, the renowned architect, Sr. Ed-win Lutyens, erected a large, wood and plaster cenotaph collectively honoring "the Glorious Dead." This temporary pylon became such a popular place of pilgrimage with the grief-stricken public that it was replaced by a permanent stone monument in 1920.[21] In stark contrast to London's bodiless memorial, the French constructed a massive ossuary at Verdun. There, the bones of 130,000 unidentified

(Philip Bigler)

A typical war memorial in the town square of Wellen, Belgium. Hundreds of such monuments were erected after the war to honor the hometown dead.

French and German soldiers were entombed, forever uniting the former enemies in death.[22]

DURING THE GREAT War, the Reverend David Railton served as a military chaplain with British troops.[23] In 1916, during the terrible fighting at the Battle of the Somme, Railton stumbled upon the lone grave of a British soldier who had been killed during the combat. Written on a crude wooden cross was a modest but poignant inscription: "Unknown British Soldier of the Black Watch."[24] The memory of that unidentified soldier haunted Railton for years. He was consumed by the knowledge that literally hundreds of thousands of grieving families would never know the ultimate fate of their loved ones, aware only that they had perished on a distant battlefield fighting for King, Country, and Commonwealth. In truth, many bodies had been obliterated by modern weaponry but there were still thousands of other soldiers who had been anonymously entombed in graves dispersed throughout cemeteries in France and Belgium.

After the armistice, Reverend Railton returned to England and was appointed the vicar of St. John the Baptist's, Margate in Kent. In 1920, still motivated by the painful memory of that unknown Black Watch soldier, Railton contacted Bishop Herbert Ryle, the Dean of Westminster, with a unique idea—a proposal to honor and bury one unidentified British soldier at the Abbey. As the only soldier exempted from the government's strict policy of no repatriation, the Unknown's tomb could function as a symbol of all of the soldiers who had died during the war.[25] Moreover, Railton felt that an honored grave at the Abbey would become a sacred place of national pilgrimage and remembrance serving as a physical grave, a sacred reliquary, for the countless families whose loved ones had never been identified or recovered.[26] As historian Martin Gilbert explains: "the Unknown Soldier [would be] the focus…of the yearning of many of those who would never know where their son's or husband's or father's body had been buried, or ground into the earth."[27]

Bishop Ryle zealously endorsed and championed Railton's idea, noting that: "There are thousands of graves, I am told, of English Tommies who fell at the Front—names not known…one such body (name not known) should be exhumed and interred in Westminster Abbey."[28] He personally appealed to King George V and members of Parliament for the prompt selection and interment of a British Unknown. Prime Minister Lloyd George astutely recognized the symbolic and psychological implications of burying an Unknown at Westminster Abbey, acknowledging that: "Nations must justify mass killings, if only to support the feelings of the bereaved and the sanity of the survivors."[29]

But in a still socially stratified England, burying a "common" soldier at Westminster would be unprecedented. The eleventh century cathedral was indisputably the nation's most known and important religious shrine and it had been the site for all of the coronations of English monarchs since 1066. The church also functioned as a royal crypt, containing the tombs of 17 kings and queens including Henry V, Elizabeth I, and George II. Other British luminaries such as Geoffrey Chaucer, Isaac Newton, Charles Dickens, Charles Darwin, and Alfred Lloyd Tennyson were also granted burial rights in Westminster.[30] The British government, though, had slowly come to the realization that victory in the Great War had not been achieved by politicians or generals or diplomats, but rather through the individual valor of the common soldier. It was their collective sacrifice that finally needed to be nationally acknowledged and commemorated. Lloyd George's secretary noted in a letter: "…it would do honour to the great mass of fighting men; that it would furnish a memorial to them in Westminster Abbey…at present Westminster Abbey has no memorial to the great war."[31]

Despite some initial reluctance by King George V, who felt that too much time had passed since the end of the war, Parliament approved a plan to inter a British Unknown on Armistice Day, 1920.[32] There was no precedent to follow and the nation had just three weeks to organize the selection of an Unknown and to prepare for a state funeral at the Abbey.

ONCE THE FINAL decision had been made to select and bury an Unknown British soldier at Westminster, the ceremonial and logistical planning proceeded with remarkable haste. On November 7, 1920, just days before the scheduled national funeral, the army dispatched covert digging parties to four separate cemeteries (Aisne, the Somme, Arras, and Ypres) located in France and Belgium. These were in areas where the vast majority of combat involving Commonwealth forces in Europe had taken place. The excavating teams, operating independently from one another, were unaware of the overall significance of their mission and had been directed to disinter a random, unknown British body. They were then to confirm its nationality through a thorough examination of uniform remnants and other grave artifacts.[33]

The four bodies that were initially recovered had all been buried for months and each was in an advanced state of decomposition. According to Brigadier General L.J. Wyatt, there was little left, nothing more "than mere bones."[34] The exhumed remains were sewn into individual sacks by the recovery teams and then transported by military ambulances to St. Pol-sur-Ternoise.[35] Arriving separately and at different times, the wrapped bodies were taken into a temporary chapel where they were reexamined by military coroners to ensure that there was absolutely nothing that could lead to the possible identification of the soldiers. Once this was confirmed, the remains were covered with a British Union Jack and the chapel was secured and placed under armed guard.[36]

A few hours later, at precisely midnight, the commander of British forces in the region, Brigadier General L.J. Wyatt, entered the chapel and without any formal ceremony, randomly designated one of the bodies to become the official British Unknown Warrior from the Great War. The selected body was immediately transferred to a plain, pine coffin while the three unselected candidates were removed and reburied at an undisclosed location and without any further acknowledgment.[37] The Reverend Kendall observed later: "All I can say was that he was chosen from the countless unnamed dead in France and Flanders, that the nation might honour him, and this without distinction of rank, birth or service... He may have come from some little village or some city in this land, and he may be the son of a working man or of a rich man, 'Unknown to man, but known to God.'"[38]

The following afternoon, the designated British Unknown was transported to the Castle Citadel at Boulogne, some 60 miles away, for final preparations for his return home. At the castle, the simple, pine coffin was encased inside a much larger and more impressive outer container constructed from the wood of a historic oak tree harvested from the grounds of Hampton Court Castle. The new casket had been designed to resemble an ancient treasure chest and was bound together by wrought iron bands in the shape of a cross. A historic, crusader's broad sword taken from the armament collections at Tower of London was riveted to the top of the casket under a cast iron coffin plate in the shape of a shield, inscribed with the words:

A British Warrior who
fell in the Great War
1914-1918
for King and Country.[39]

On November 10, the British Unknown was solemnly carried from the Citadel by an eight-member British casket team and loaded onto a horse-drawn wagon. The coffin was then shrouded with a large British Union Jack under the silent gaze of a French honor guard contingent standing rigidly at attention nearby. A procession of French troops and Commonwealth soldiers assembled and escorted the carriage through the crowded streets of Boulogne where thousands of area citizens silently paid their respects, many offering floral tributes.[40]

Once at the harbor, the Unknown's casket was carefully carried onto the deck of the British destroyer, HMS *Verdun*. Four sailors, heads bowed and their backs to the casket, maintained the watch.[41] Once under sail, the *Verdun* rendezvoused with six other British destroyers who convoyed the ship across the narrow straits to Dover.[42] Upon arrival at the port, a 19-gun salute was rendered by shore batteries and the ship docked at the Number 3 berth at the Admiralty Pier.[43] A military casket team awaited to convey the Unknown from the ship's deck onto a horse-drawn gun caisson. Hundreds of honor guard troops, all with heads bowed and rifles inverted—barrels facing towards ground—lined the short route to the train station,.[44] A specially decorated train car provided by the South Eastern and Chatham Railway Company awaited to transport the Unknown British Warrior to London's Victoria Station, where the casket would remain under a military vigil overnight.[45]

PRECISELY TWO YEARS after the signing of the Armistice, the British conducted a lavish state funeral for the Unknown Warrior. Mourners lined the streets along the entire 2.5-mile funeral route from Victoria Station to Westminster Abbey. Thousands of troops, military bands, and honor guard regiments joined the parade including 100 gallant veterans who had each received the Victoria Cross, England's highest military decoration. The horse drawn caisson carrying the Unknown's remains paused briefly at Whitehall, directly in front of the newly completed Cenotaph, which remained cloaked under a massive British Union Jack. King George V, wearing his military uniform, placed a wreath in front of the new memorial while prayers were offered and hymns sung. At exactly 11 AM, the bells of Big Ben began to chime, signaling the King to press a special switch which automatically unveiled the finished Cenotaph honoring "The Glorious Dead." A two-minute period of absolute quiet followed, observed throughout England in remembrance of those who had served and those who had fallen. During the so-called "Great Silence," the newspapers reported that: "There was no noise of traffic, no voices; nothing and nobody moved in the whole of that vast imperial capital. The central telephone switchboard later reported that not a single telephone call was made anywhere in London."[46]

The funeral procession then continued on to Westminster Abbey for the final burial rites. A select group of war mothers and widows were given priority seating among the 8,000 mourners in attendance. They "had been selected for the seats of honor because each had lost her husband and all her sons."[47] Special admission was also given to: "A girl [who] wrote she had lost nine brothers killed or missing... [and] also was a 12-year-old boy who wrote, 'the man in the coffin might be my daddy.'"[48]

The open burial crypt inside the Abbey had earlier been filled with 50 bags of French dirt, ensuring that the Unknown would

(Library of Congress)
The Cenotaph Memorial at Whitehall to "The Glorious Dead" circa 1939. The monument was dedicated by King George V as part of the ceremonies surrounding the burial of the British Unknown Warrior.

forever rest on the soil that he had fought and died for. The brief, Anglican committal service was conducted by the Dean of Westminster, Herbert Ryle. The inscription on the new tomb cover on the floor of the church read:

BENEATH THIS STONE RESTS THE BODY
OF A BRITISH WARRIOR
UNKNOWN BY NAME OR RANK
BROUGHT FROM FRANCE TO LIE AMONG
THE MOST ILLUSTRIOUS OF THE LAND
AND BURIED HERE ON ARMISTICE DAY
11 NOV. 1920, IN THE PRESENCE OF
HIS MAJESTY KING GEORGE V
HIS MINISTERS OF STATE
THE CHIEFS OF HIS FORCES
AND A VAST CONCOURSE OF THE NATION
THUS ARE COMMEMORATED THE MANY
MULTITUDES WHO DURING THE GREAT
WAR OF 1914-1918 GAVE THE MOST THAT
MAN CAN GIVE LIFE ITSELF
FOR GOD
FOR KING AND COUNTRY
FOR LOVED ONES HOME AND EMPIRE
FOR THE SACRED CAUSE OF JUSTICE AND
THE FREEDOM OF THE WORLD
THEY BURIED HIM AMONG THE KINGS BECAUSE HE
HAD DONE GOOD TOWARD GOD AND TOWARD
HIS HOUSE

Once the ceremonies at Westminster had concluded, citizens, mothers, widows, and children quietly filed by the Unknown's new crypt to pay their respects while thousands of others patiently waited to place floral tributes at the base of the nearby Cenotaph memorial.[49]

The pomp and ceremony that had surrounded the interment at Westminster Abbey instantly conferred a national legitimacy on the Unknown. This nameless soldier immediately became a power-

(National Archives)

Convalescing American soldiers standing in front of Westminster Abbey, 1919. The Abbey was selected as the final resting place for the British Unknown Warrior.

ful symbol in death, a veritable icon of the nation's determination in a war which, in truth, had been little more than an exercise in mass destruction and death. As historian Neil Hanson explains in his book, *The Unknown Soldier*: "[The Unknown] was not merely a symbol of all the dead. The very anonymity of the body buried in Westminster Abbey allowed every person, if only in the privacy of their own thoughts, to assume a personal link with the Unknown Warrior, and many thousands of grieving people...convinced themselves that their missing loved one really could be buried in the Abbey."[50]

The visual presence of thousands of crippled and mutilated soldiers on the streets of London and, indeed, throughout the British empire, was a stark reminder of the horrible human consequence of the war. Some skeptics saw the new Tomb as an antiseptic version of history, an effort to sanitize and disguise reality.[51] In truth, no one knew anything about the Unknown, either as a man or as a soldier; no one knew his religious beliefs or the circumstances surrounding his death. Yet this anonymous figure would become a perpetual symbol of the nation's sacrifice and valor, a human memorial to the heroism of the soldiers of the British Empire during the Great War.

THE FRENCH HAD also decided to honor and bury their own unknown soldier on Armistice Day 1920. Since most of the fighting along the western front had occurred on French soil, the nation did not face any complicated transportation or logistical challenges in selecting their Unknown Soldier or their *Poilu Inconnu*. Eight unidentified French soldiers were quickly exhumed from nearby cemeteries on November 9 and brought to the Citadel in Verdun. This massive, stone fortification had been originally constructed as part of the extensive French defensive lines and contained miles of subterranean rooms and corridors. The flag-draped coffins of the unknown candidates were conveyed to an underground, candle-lit chamber where they collectively were to lay-in-state. [52] One newspaper account read: "In a low casemate the eight bodies lay in state that night surrounded by a thousand lighted candles, while stern men and weeping women filed silently past."[53] A Breton private, Auguste Taine, whose own father had been killed at Verdun, was given the honor of designating one of the caskets to be the French Unknown.[54]

Although the selection process for the French Unknown was relatively simple and had been completed without difficulty, there was a vigorous and often bitter debate about where to actually inter the body. The magnificent Cathedral of Notre Dame was rejected as a potential burial location because France remained publicly a secular society. The brutal upheavals of the 18th Century during the French Revolution had spawned a widespread anti-Catholic, anti-clerical sentiment throughout the country and contemporary government officials refused to have their nation's Unknown eternally affiliated with the church.[55] The Panthéon initially seemed like a promising alternative since it was the preferred burial site for the greats of French history including Voltaire, Victor Hugo, Alexandre Dumas, Émile Zola, and Jean-Jacques Rousseau. But this location, too, was eventually excluded because, according to one cynic: "The *poilu* whom we are going to glorify is not a great man."[56] He explained further that: "He is the symbol of the immense number of soldiers who sacrificed themselves for the country. He is a symbol of victory."[57]

It was ultimately decided to bury the *Poilu Inconnu* at the base of the neoclassical Arc de Triomphe in central Paris, but the decision was not finalized until just three days before the funeral.[58] There was no existing burial crypt at the location and it would take weeks to construct one. Rather than postpone the funeral, it took place as scheduled on Thursday, November 11, but without a prepared tomb. Field Marshalls Joffre, Foch, and Petain led the procession through the streets of the capital while 100 cannons fired in salute. At the Arc, President Alexandre Millerand read the final eulogy: "Unknown soldier, nameless and triumphant representative of the gallant multitudes of *poilus*, the dead who lie in cold graves in the soil of Flanders, Champagne, Verdun and so many other battlefields, famous or unknown: young heroes who came to us from the other side of the Atlantic, the British Isles and distant dominions, from Italy, Belgium and Serbia, from all points of the earth to offer your lives for the ideal which France once more is representing, sleep in peace! You have fulfilled your destiny."[59]

Once the formal ceremonies were concluded, thousands of French citizens and military veterans quietly passed by the Un-

(Library of Congress)

The Arc de Triomphe in Paris. Commissioned by Napoleon in 1806, it quickly became one of Paris' most notable landmarks and was selected as the burial location for the French Poilu Inconnu.

(National Archives)

General of the Armies, John J. Pershing, places a wreath at the tomb of the French Unknown in Paris, circa 1924. The "flame of remembrance" was added in 1923.

known to pay their respects. Later that night, the *Poilu Inconnu's* casket was removed and stored in a room at the Arc de Triomphe to allow for the construction of a new crypt. The body would remain there for 78 days until it was finally interred in the newly completed grave on January 28, 1921.[60] An eternal "flame of remembrance" would be added to the tomb in 1923.[61]

The impressive funeral rites for the British and French Unknowns led to extensive public pressure in the United States to honor an American soldier in a similar fashion. New York City offered to bury an unknown doughboy on the grounds of the newly christened Pershing Square park in midtown Manhattan, but Secretary of War, Newton Baker, rebuffed these moves as premature. According to newspaper accounts, such a burial: "would set a precedent and that many other cities and towns would 'not be contented to be denied the same opportunity to show reverence and respect.'"[62] Still, American papers editorialized: "Armistice Day seems destined to mean to the whole world what Independence Day means to America. How better express that meaning than through honors to the 'Unknown Dead?'"[63]

The United States, though, had a more important priority—it first had to deal with the contentious issue of repatriation of the nation's war dead. By November 1920, over 9,000 American soldiers had already been disinterred from cemeteries in Europe and returned to the United States for re-burial. An additional 1,800 bodies were awaiting transportation at French ports. On the very same day that the British and French were honoring and burying their Unknown Soldiers in Europe, the *Evening Star* newspaper reported that the: "Bodies of two officers and ten enlisted men of the Navy and Marine Corps, who died overseas were buried this afternoon at Arlington National Cemetery with full military honors."[64]

DURING THE WAR, the United States Army had assigned the Quartermaster Corps the monumental responsibility of transporting, supplying, and equipping the two million man American Expeditionary Force. As American troops slowly began to deploy in Europe, it became apparent that the military needed to establish proper protocols for dealing with the anticipated large number of battlefield casualties and to develop procedures for properly identifying and burying the dead. Just four months after declaring war, the army issued General Orders #104, which created the wartime Graves Registration Service (GRS). Ultimately 18 units would be deployed to Europe and there, GRS troops were tasked with the retrieval, identification, transport, and burying of the dead and ensuring that all soldiers who were killed-in-action would have an identifiable, marked grave.[65]

(National Archives)

American Graves Registration Service troops searching for bodies along the south bank of the Vesle River near the town of Bazoches, France. These troops performed heroically throughout the war. trying to identify all of the nation's dead.

(National Archives)
An example of trench burial at a temporary cemetry established near Fère-en-Tardenois in northern France. Note the wooden crosses used to mark the graves of American soldiers killed-in-action.

Once the AEF commenced combat operations, Graves Registration soldiers were forced to operate in close proximity to the front lines. It was horrific, dangerous, and thankless work as General John J. Pershing noted: "[They] began their work under heavy shell of fire and gas...they gathered many bodies which had been first in the hands of the Germans and were later retaken by American counterattacks." [66] Recovery teams were routinely dispatched to search for corpses and to retrieve any bodies. All of the AEF soldiers wore small aluminum id tags into battle which listed a soldier's name, unit, and rank. These early "dog tags" greatly assisted in identification, as did recovered letters, rings, and other personal effects. But despite the best efforts of the Graves Registration Service, some 4,221 American soldiers, roughly 5% of all U.S. combat casualties, were classified as missing at the end of the war.[67] Of these, 2,148 bodies were physically recovered but were so badly mutilated that they were considered to be unidentifiable. The grave markers of these unknown American soldiers were all inscribed with the same sepulchral epitaph: "Here Rests in Honored Glory An American Soldier Known but to God."[68]

As historian K.S. Inglis notes, there were, in fact, two categories of missing: "either their bodies could not be recovered—blown to pieces, buried in mud, or otherwise eluding burial parties during and after the war; or they could be recovered and interred but not identified."[69] General Pershing described the difficulties inherent in properly identifying the dead during the war, noting that: "Identification was especially difficult, all papers and tags having been removed, and most of the bodies being in a terrible condition and beyond recognition."[70]

Soldiers whose bodies had to be hurriedly interred due to the proximity of the fighting, were buried in long, excavated trenches, shrouded only in a woolen blanket and "just a covering of the body with earth, to get it out of sight for sanitation's sake."[71] Others were interred quickly in existing artillery craters. Those soldiers whose recovered bodies could be collected and safely transported behind the lines fared somewhat better. They were interred in primitive, albeit utilitarian, wooden coffins in individual graves in more traditional cemeteries. None of the bodies of deceased soldiers were embalmed though and all of the American graves were individually marked either by a wooden Christian cross or a Jewish Star of David.

Like the other allies, the remains of American doughboys were dispersed throughout hundreds of burial sites at the end of the war. Many of these rudimentary cemeteries were isolated and inaccessible, making it difficult to adequately care for the nation's war dead.[72] In a post war effort to remedy the chaotic situation, the United States established nine centralized cemeteries in France, Belgium, and England in order to consolidate burials. During the early post-war years, GRS soldiers undertook the gruesome process of exhuming thousands of American soldiers in order to relocate their remains to these large concentration cemeteries. Bodies had decayed rapidly, and even wooden caskets did little to preserve remains. The coffins were invariably water-logged and rotted, forcing retrieval teams to sift the fragmented skeletal remains through wire mesh archaeological trays in order to separate human bone from

(National Archives)

A burial at an American cemetery in Suresne, France. Over 116,000 soldiers died during the war and were buried in hundreds of cemeteries throughout France and Belgium.

(National Archives)

The casket of an American soldier is disinterred at the Aisne-Marne Cemetery after the war. Nine concentration cemeteries were established after the Armistice to properly honor the nation's dead.

the commingled dirt and debris. The recovered remains were then sprayed and disinfected with Cresol, shrouded, and re-casketed for reburial, with the entire process carefully chronicled by soldier-clerks from the Graves Registration Service.[73]

THE UNITED STATES lost over 116,000 men during the world war in just seven months of actual combat. Although the number of dead was small in comparison to those of the British, French, Germans, Russians, and Austro-Hungarians, the casualties still represented the largest loss of American lives during wartime in over half a century. Indeed, from the end of the Civil War in 1865 through 1917, the nation had enjoyed a prolonged period of international peace.[74] This *Pax Americana* was, admittedly, interrupted briefly by the Spanish-American War in 1898, but that conflict was a relatively minor affair, nothing more than, in Theodore Roosevelt's words, a "splendid little war."[75] Hostilities had lasted for just four months with the fighting mostly confined to Cuba and the Philippine Islands. Less than 300 American soldiers were killed in actual combat, but tropical diseases and mosquitoes proved far more deadly than Spanish bullets, costing the lives of an additional 2,000 U.S. troops. With the signing of the peace treaty in Paris that December, the nation began for the first time the process of repatriating all of the nation's war dead back to the United States from foreign shores. This established the precedent of not leaving American soldiers buried abroad on foreign soil.

During the last stages of World War I, Secretary of War Newton Baker publicly pledged to return all of the remains of American doughboys.[76] But after the signing of the armistice, there had been no effort on the part of the federal government to return any of the nation's dead.[77] A year later, Baker seemed to renege on his initial promise, arguing that it was a "wiser and better course to leave those bodies [where they lay]."[78] Many Gold Star Mothers and widows, outraged by what they perceived to be the government's callousness and inertia, formed the "Bring Home the Soldier Dead League," to demand the prompt repatriation of all deceased American soldiers.[79]

The French government opposed any efforts by the United States to repatriate its dead. France's severely damaged infrastructure, they claimed, made it impractical to support such a mission. The nation's domestic priority had to be clearing the now fallow battlefields of unexploded munitions and locating and removing the thousands of corpses that still remained buried in unmarked graves.[80] The French government assured the United States that all American graves would be properly cared for and appropriately memorialized in so-called "Fields of Honor." American army chaplain, Bishop Charles H. Brent, supported leaving the graves undisturbed since it "would preserve as far as may be possible the comradeship of the war among those who met a common fate. It would express to all who are bereaved the undying value of the sacrifice made. It would perpetuate in death that work begun in life to bind together nations of like ideals."[81]

(Library of Congress)
The grave of aviator LT Quentin Roosevelt. His father, former President Theodore Roosevelt, opposed any efforts to repatriate the remains of American soldiers after the war claiming: "...where the tree falls there let it lie."

Former President Theodore Roosevelt concurred with the French policy and opposed any repatriation of American remains. His youngest son, aviator Lieutenant Quentin Roosevelt, had been shot down by German planes while on a mission on July 14, 1918. The *Seattle Star* carried the sensational headline: "Boche Kills Young Roosevelt." LT Roosevelt's body was recovered by the Germans near Chamery, France and was accorded a proper military burial. The former President acknowledged his son's service and sacrifice, writing: "Quentin's mother and I are very glad that he got to the front and had the chance to render some service to his country and to show the stuff that was in him before his fate befell him."[82] But even after the war, President Roosevelt firmly opposed any proposals to move his son's remains, claiming: "We feel that where the tree falls there let it lie."[83]

Colonel Charles Pierce, the Chief of the Graves Registration Service, honored Roosevelt wishes and ordered that the body not be disturbed or moved. In a letter to Mrs. Roosevelt, the Colonel assured her that: "I have taken every precaution to guard the wishes of the family in this matter, and to see that due regard be made of the fact that the body is not to be disturbed under any circumstances."[84] This proscription precluded even the removal of Quentin's body to a concentration cemetery. Theodore Roosevelt would later express his gratitude to Colonel Pierce, writing: "I thank you even more for refusing to have the boy's body disinterred and transferred to one of our established cemeteries. His mother and I greatly prefer to have him lie where he fell and where the Germans buried him."[85]

––––––––––––

THERE WERE SEVERE logistical problems involved in mass repatriation of American remains from Europe. The bodies had been buried for months and were in an advanced state of decomposition. Furthermore, many of the remains had already been exhumed once for reburial in concentration cemeteries, and each disinterment further damaged the bodies. Likewise, the removal from existing graves vastly increased the possibility of the misidentification due to either mishandling or bureaucratic error. Coupled with the diffi-

culties involved in shipping thousands of identical, flag-draped caskets across the Atlantic Ocean to diverse locations throughout the
United States, there was a very real danger of mistakenly delivering
the wrong cadaver to a grieving Gold Star family. Moreover, there
would always be some lingering doubt as to the body's true identity
since the remains were beyond any possible physical recognition
and the caskets could not be opened by family members for viewing.

Then there was the enormous expense involved in returning
thousands of bodies to the United States.[86] Many critics accused un-
ethical funeral directors of extortion, claiming that they were charging the federal government grossly exorbitant prices for the needed
50,000 coffins. It was also feared that unscrupulous and corrupt
undertakers would exploit bereaved families by charging excessive
expenses for domestic funeral services and elaborate private tomb-
stones. As one newspaper reasoned: "Never was there such a chance
for ghoulish graft."[87]

In an article published in the *Washington Times* in 1920,
the magnitude of the task of reinterring the dead was graphically
illustrated. "If all American dead were put in one casket," the *Times*
wrote, "it would require a coffin 300 feet long, about sixty feet high
and would cover a block and a half of Fifth avenue and stretch from
sidewalk to sidewalk."[88]

But regardless of the obstacles and difficulties, the American
people insisted on the right to make their own decision on whether
or not to leave their son or husband buried abroad. Finally yielding
to the intense public pressure, the government relented and sent out
over 70,000 survey cards to solicit the wishes of Gold Star families.
It was assured that all shipping expenses would be paid for by the
federal government, but it still took over two years to process all
of the responses.[89] Fortunately, the French simultaneously withdrew
their objections to the return of American soldiers.[90]

The bodies that were designated to be returned to the U.S.
had to be exhumed and re-examined by teams of Graves Registration soldiers. Their identities were re-verified, and the bodies (or

bones) were placed in new metal coffins. These were then enclosed by a wooden, protective shipping container before being loaded onto trucks and convoyed to a centralized holding area. The caskets were temporarily stored under large canvas tents until transportation via barge, canal boat, or train could be arranged to move the remains to a local shipping port.[91]

Once at the port of debarkation, the crates were rechecked and cataloged by clerks. The wooden shipping containers were then individually draped with an American flag and temporarily stored in nearby warehouses until finally taken to the docks where a local priest or member of the clergy would finally bless the caskets. Then, the flag-draped crates were hoisted two at a time onto American transports ships and carefully lowered into the ship cargo bays for the return voyage to the United States.[92]

Ultimately 45,588 soldiers would be returned to the United States, roughly 70% of all combat causalities at a cost $658 per body.[93] From 1920 through 1923, 273 officers and 4,968 enlisted

(National Archives)
Workers drape a 48-star flag over a shipping casket of an American soldier. The repatriation of remains from Europe took several years to complete, although some 30% of Gold Star families chose to leave their loved one buried in Europe.

(National Archives)

A warehouse full of caskets awaiting shipment back to the United States after the end of World War I. An estimated 5,241 of these remains were buried at Arlington National Cemetery.

would be buried at Arlington National Cemetery. It was decided, though, that none of the hundreds of American unknowns would be returned to the United States.[94]

AFTER THE EXTRAORDINARY success and popularity of the interments of the British and French Unknowns, the American public demanded that the United States should similarly honor one of its soldiers. But the Army Chief of Staff, Peyton Marsh, was reluctant to proceed. The Graves Registration Service was diligently working to positively identify all of the recovered remains. Marsh assured the public, though, that the military would comply with any decision made by Congress and the nation's civilian leadership since they had the ultimate authority over the matter.[95]

Further complicating any hopes for the quick burial of an American Unknown was a general lack of consensus concerning a proper burial location. The nation's great cosmopolitan metropolises of New York, Philadelphia, and Chicago all seemed to be reasonable sites and, undoubtedly, a monumental grave to an American Un-

known in any one of these urban centers would immediately have international stature. The nation's capital, too, had its proponents, despite being scorned by many elitists as little more than a small, provincial, southern town. Despite this unfair disparagement, the U.S. Capitol building already had an existing crypt under the Rotunda. This burial vault had been originally designed to house the remains of General George Washington, but the first president declined the honor and the tomb was never used. Given this precedent, the Capitol location was quickly eliminated from consideration for the burial of an Unknown.[96]

(Library of Congress)

New York Congressman, Hamilton Fish. Fish sponsored legislation to bury an American Unknown at Arlington.

Another D.C. alternative, though, was the newly dedicated Memorial Amphitheater at Arlington National Cemetery. It soon emerged as the most promising burial location after gaining the support of New York Congressman, Hamilton Fish.

The newly elected Fish was a highly decorated World War I veteran, having received the silver star for his "undaunted courage" under enemy fire. He served as a captain with the 369th Infantry Regiment, the renowned "Harlem Hellfighters."[97] Fish's troops consisted primarily of African-American volunteers and the regiment had been rapidly deployed to France in December 1917. Due to the ongoing racial segregation of the American armed forces, though, instead of being absorbed into the AEF, the 369th was assigned to the command of the French Fourth Army. The Harlem Hellfighters fought valiantly during the critical battles of Champagne-Marne and Meuse-Argonne and served continuously on the front lines for 191 days, longer than any other American battalion in the war.[98]

After the war, the Harvard educated Fish returned to civilian life and was elected to the House of Representatives in 1920. There, he became one of the nation's leading advocates for appropriately honoring the country's military veterans, including the under-appreciated service of thousands of African-American troops.[99] Fish also felt that interring an American Unknown at Arlington National Cemetery would pay tribute to all of the nation's heroic troops, noting: "I...had first-hand knowledge of the brave sacrifices made by American forces during the First World War, and I wanted America, as a beacon of freedom and democracy, to have her own memorial to honor the Unknown Soldier."[100] On December 21, 1920, Congressman Fish introduced HJ Res 426, which would authorize the interment of an American Unknown Soldier at Arlington National Cemetery.[101] The resolution read:

> *Resolved by the Senate and House of Representatives of the United States of America in Congress assembled*, That the Secretary of War be, and he is hereby authorized and directed, under regulations to be prescribed by him, to cause to be brought to the United States the body of an American, who was a member of the American Expeditionary Forces who served in Europe, who lost his life during the World War and whose identity has not been established, for burial in the Memorial Amphitheater of Arlington National Cemetery at Arlington, Virginia.

Such sum as may be necessary to carry out the provisions of the joint resolution is hereby authorized to be expended by the Secretary of War.[102]

Later, Congressman Fish testified before the Committee on Military Affairs, explaining: "The whole purpose of this resolution is to bring home the body of an unknown American warrior who in himself represents no section, creed, or race...who typified, moreover, the soul of America and the supreme sacrifice of her heroic dead."[103] He elaborated on his legislative initiative in a letter to the new Secretary of War, John Weeks:

> My purpose in introducing HJ Resolution 426 to bring back the body of an unknown American who was a member of the American Expeditionary Forces in Europe and lost his life during the war, for burial in the Memorial Amphitheat[er] of the National Cemetery at Arlington, is to do honor and pay homage to our unknown dead and to all of their comrades who paid the supreme sacrifice...the body should be so selected that the rank, branch of service and battlefield where the man was killed should be unknown to all...the burial of the unknown warrior should give the whole country an opportunity to express in a National way, their tribute to the glorious dead. It will bring consolation and assuage the grief of the twelve hundred families whose sons died unknown and unidentified, for each and every family will proudly claim this body as that of their own son. It is hoped that the grave of this unidentified warrior will become a shine to patriotism for all ages to come, which will be a source of inspiration, reverence and love of country for future generations.[104]

Still, despite such persuasive reasoning, Fish's resolution languished in Congress and was not passed until the final day of the session as part of a flurry of last-minute legislation. The momentous act received little press attention since that Friday, March 4, 1921, was also the inauguration day for the newly elected president, Warren G. Harding.

The lame duck president, Woodrow Wilson, was still in ill-health and suffering from the lasting effects of a devastating stroke. That morning, the outgoing President made the difficult trip by automobile to Capitol Hill to sign the heavy backlog of bills passed in the waning moments of the 66th Congress. In the mounds of legislation was Hamilton Fish's resolution for entombing an American Unknown. The next day, The *Evening Star* briefly noted that: "The joint resolution of Congress providing for the return from France the body of an unknown American and its burial at Arlington National Cemetery, one of the last measures to be signed by President Wilson, was transmitted today, where arrangements will be made for the return of the body and appropriate ceremonies for interment."[105]

Wilson had rarely been seen in public after his stroke and his frail appearance stunned both legislators and reporters. One newspaper account somberly noted that: "[President Wilson's] hair is very grey—almost white—and thinner. His eyes are not as bright and the lines in the face are deeper. He stoops, and he walks very slowly and with difficulty, leaning heavily on a stout cane."[106]

President-elect Harding visited briefly with Wilson prior to the start of the formal noon swearing in ceremonies. It was a seasonably cold day in Washington with the outside temperature hovering around 38-degrees, and the President-elect graciously excused Wilson from the traditional obligation of appearing at the outdoor inaugural festivities. The ailing Wilson acknowledged that he did not have the physical strength or stamina to attend and with that, a frail and dejected Woodrow Wilson was escorted out of the Capitol building to be driven to his new home located at 2340 S Street, NW. The *Evening Star* somberly reported: "Woodrow Wilson's last hours as President of the United States was a curious commingling of sadness and attempted cheerfulness. For a moment the President appeared as the decrepit figure that he has so often been pictured since his physical collapse two years ago."[107]

CONGRESSMAN FISH HOPED that after the final passage of his resolution that the funeral for an American Unknown could be scheduled for Memorial Day, 1921. This was deemed to be impractical by the War Department due to the short time span and the military was determined not to rush the selection process. There also had to be time allotted for the design and construction of a suitable crypt at the Memorial Amphitheater. The ceremony was thus postponed until November 11, the third anniversary of the armistice.

Initially, the military favored constructing the new tomb on the dais of the Amphitheater just below its magnificent apse. After an inspection tour with War Department officials on September 14, though, Architect Thomas Hastings vetoed the idea, arguing that the enormous weight of a marble tomb would threaten the structural integrity of the stage area. The Commission of Fine Arts noted in

(Library of Congress)

Workmen on the East Plaza preparing the new crypt for the Unknown Soldier. The simple, marble sarcophogus was designed by arhcitect Thomas Hastings and contained no embellishments or inscriptions.

the minutes of their fall meeting that: "The suggestion of the War Department that the memorial be placed in the apse was declared by the architect to be inadvisable, as the foundations at this place are not strong enough for a heavy memorial."[108] Instead, Hastings recommended that the new sarcophagus be built on the east plaza on the location where he had originally hoped to erect a large Peace statue. The proposed site was ideal and quickly approved, but due to time constraints, the original builder of the Amphitheater, the George H. Fuller Company, was commissioned to construct the vault without any competitive bids. Hastings personally designed a simple, marble sarcophagus for the tomb and it was finished in just a matter of weeks at a cost of $4,000. No inscriptions or other adornments were permitted since none had yet been authorized by the Congressional legislation.[109]

WHILE THE PREPERATIONS for the funeral continued in Washington, D.C., four likely candidates and four alternates were designated by the army for consideration to become the American Unknown Soldier. One deceased soldier was chosen from each of the American cemeteries at Meuse Argonne, St. Mihiel, Somme, and Aisne Marne. A completed GRS Form #16A identified the precise grave location for the exhuming teams with the caveat that the graves of the four alternates were not be disturbed unless the primary candidate's body was disqualified. The most important criterion was that the body be indisputably that of an American soldier but was individually unidentifiable and without "the possibility of future identification as to his name, rank, organization, service, or the battlefield which he fell."[110]

After disinterring the four original candidates, it was determined that the alternates would not be needed since: "Each body was that of a member of the American Expeditionary Forces, evinced by uniform and equipment as well as the original burial place. The cause of death was apparent from gun-shot wound on the body. There was absolutely no tangible evidence nor possible clue to identity."[111]

On October 23, the four disinterred remains were transported separately to the City Hall at Châlon-sur-Marne where a small, temporary chapel had been set up. Inside, the caskets were individually draped with an American flag and rearranged to disguise the cemetery of origin. The original #16A forms for all of the candidates and alternates along with any other documents were burned so that the "bodies have no record on file showing from whence they originally came and from which cemetery they were exhumed for shipment to Châlon-sur-Marne."[112]

Six well-respected soldiers from the 15th Infantry, Army of the Occupation, were detailed to serve as body bearers for the unknown candidates. Following the French precedent, it was decided that one of these enlisted men, rather than a commissioned officer, would be granted the honor of choosing America's Unknown Soldier.

SGT Edward F. Younger was one of soldiers assigned to the casket team detail. In many ways, he emblematic of the typical American serviceman.[113] He had served honorably throughout the war, fighting in virtually all of the major AEF offensives. Younger had been wounded twice in combat and although he received no individual decorations for valor, he always performed his duty bravely and without complaint. At Châlon-sur-Marne, the commander in charge of the funeral detachment, Major Harbold, questioned Younger and the other five pall bearers about their background and military service. On the morning of the selection ceremony, October 24, the Major abruptly announced: "the selection has been made. Younger, you will have the honor of placing a bouquet of roses on the casket which [you] will choose from the four assembled here, and by that act, America's Unknown Soldier will be designated."[114]

Younger was understandably overwhelmed and humbled by this incredible honor and keenly aware of his enormous responsibility. At 10 AM, he entered the darkened room in the City Hall alone and stood silently before the four, flagged-draped caskets. Outside, a French military band could be heard playing the hauntingly beautiful "Dead March" from Handel's oratorio, *Saul*.[115] Younger later recalled:

> I began a slow march around the caskets. Which should it be? Thoughts poured like torrents through my mind. Maybe these buddies had once been my pals! Perhaps one of them had fought with me, had befriended me, had possibly shielded me from a bullet that might have put me in his place. Who would ever know?
>
> I was numb. I couldn't choose. From four American cemeteries in France these lads now still in death had been brought. One was to be immortalized as far as humanity could do it. And to me, an unknown doughboy, was given the selection!
>
> Three times I walked around the casket; then something drew me to the coffin second to my right on entering. I couldn't walk another step. It seemed as if God raised my hand and guided me as I placed the roses on that casket. This, then, was to be America's Unknown Soldier, and by that simple act I had started him on his journey of destiny[116]

After the selection, America's designated Unknown Soldier was moved to an adjacent transfer room where the body was placed in a new casket. The coffin plate was inscribed: "An Unknown American who gave his life in the World War."[117] The Mayor of Châlon was invited to deliver brief remarks: "There is not a single Frenchmen who is unaware of what he owes to America, the land of freedom. You brought us the help of your army, the priceless support of your friendship."[118]A short while later, the three unselected candidates were quietly taken by truck to the Romagne American Cemetery for reburial.[119]

America's Unknown Soldier was then taken by train to the French port of Le Havre via Paris, arriving in the early afternoon of October 25. There, the casket was placed on a horse-drawn caisson and escorted with great pomp and ceremony through the crowded streets to the Pier d'Escale where the responsibility for the Unknown was officially transferred to the United States Navy. The coffin was carried onboard the aft deck of the cruiser USS *Olympia* under the command of Rear Admiral Lloyd H. Chandler for final transport back to the United States.[120] The American destroyer, *Rueben James*, accompanied by several French warships, served as honor escort vessels.[121]

THE USS *OLYMPIA* WAS the pride of the American fleet and the logical choice to bring the remains of the nation's Unknown Soldier back from Europe. Indeed, during the early planning for the funeral, Secretary of the Navy, Josephus Daniels, wrote: "it would be most fitting and appropriate that the body of this unidentified soldier or marine should be brought to America in this ship which holds a unique place in American history and was the flagship of Admiral Dewey at the time he won the battle of Manila."[122]

On the *Olympia's* two week return voyage back to America, the Unknown's casket remained battened down on the stern of the ship under its massive guns. Because of its awkward size and shape, it was deemed impractical to remove the coffin to below deck despite the persistent storms and rough ocean seas on the autumn trans-Atlantic crossing. Near the Azores, the weather conditions were so bad that Admiral Chandler feared that the Unknown's casket might catastrophically be swept overboard and lost at sea.[123]

The bad weather, fortuitously, did not delay the *Olympia's* arrival off the Virginia Capes. On Monday, November 7, the ship entered the tranquil and welcomed waters of the Chesapeake Bay where it received an escort by the Navy destroyer, USS *Bernadou*.

(Library of Congress)
The casket containing the remains of the American Unknown Soldier on the aft deck of the USS Olympia. *The ship arrived at the Washington Navy Yard on 9 November 1921.*

The *Olympia* was, in many ways, on a voyage into the annals of American history. The ship's planned route took the Unknown up the Bay past the mouth of the James River, mirroring the epic voyage of the Jamestown settlers on-board the *Godspeed, Susan Constant,* and *Discovery* some 314 years earlier. As the *Olympia* continued its progress northward, the ship passed near Virginia's famed York River, the scene of the great French naval victory over the British navy in 1781, a battle that helped secure George Washington's victory at Yorktown and American independence. Later that day, the ship cruised by Gwynn's Island and the Rappahannock River before the captain ordered it onto a NW compass heading and into the Potomac River, where the *Olympia* overnighted.[124]

(National Archives)
A Clifford Berryman drawing from the Evening Star *depicting the arrival of the USS* Olympia. *Thousands of spectators lined the banks of the Potomac to witness the historic event.*

The next morning, the *Olympia* once again got underway, making slow progress up the Potomac due to the river's notoriously shallow and narrow channel. Just a short distance up-river, at Piney Point, Maryland, the dreadnought USS *North Dakota* (BB-29) awaited at anchor, dipping her ensign in honor of America's Unknown doughboy. Various military installations all along the way fired the traditional 21-gun salute to welcome the Unknown Soldier back home.[125]

The *Olympia* was not due to arrive at the Washington Navy Yard until the afternoon of November 9, so the ship dropped anchor at the Navy Proving Grounds at Indian Head, Maryland, just 30 miles south of the nation's capital.[126] The following day, the weather dawned rainy and cold, appropriate for the Unknown's somber final journey to Washington, D.C.[127] At 12:38 PM, the *Olympia* raised anchor and set sail for the capital while a flotilla of private boats assembled to form an unofficial accompanying procession. Spectators lined the Virginia and Maryland shorelines, anxious to catch a glimpse of the ship and its precious cargo. As the vessel approached Mount Vernon, the ancestral home of George Washington, the ship's bugler rendered the customary naval salute to the nation's first president while the crew stood at rigid attention. Across the river, the coastal batteries at Fort Washington commenced firing.[128]

Despite the inclement autumn weather, thousands of people were gathered at Hains Point to witness the historic return of the Unknown Soldier from France. As the *Olympia* passed by the mourn-

(Library of Congress)
A joint service body bearer team removes the casket of the Unknown Soldier from the USS Olympia. *General John J. Pershing and other dignitaries salute the remains at the Washington Navy Yard.*

ers, the ship veered to starboard in order to enter the Potomac's tributary, the Anacostia River. Just a few minutes later, at precisely 3:01 PM, the ship docked at the Washington Navy Yard.

The mooring of the ship and the final preparations for the arrival ceremonies took another hour. At 4 o'clock, the ship's minute guns fired while the *Olympia's* band played an appropriate funeral dirge as the Unknown's casket was piped ashore and carried down the ship's gangplank. Two squadrons of cavalry and a large reception party including General of the Armies, John J. Pershing, Secretary of War John W. Weeks, and Marine Commandant Major General John A. Lejeune, waited stoically on the dock.[129] After the national anthem was played, responsibility for the Unknown was officially transferred from the United States Navy to the Army. A new contingent of body bearers, consisting of five Army soldiers, two Navy sailors, and a Medal of Honor recipient from the United States Marine Corps, took charge of the casket. Each of the new body bearers had served heroically during the war and had been personally selected for this important assignment by General Pershing.[130] They carefully conveyed the Unknown's coffin to an awaiting gun caisson drawn by six black horses.[131]

The march to the United States Capitol began just as the mid-November sun was setting. It was led by a cavalry band playing "Onward, Christian Soldiers" while a squadron of troopers dispatched from Fort Myer followed in close order. Then came the caisson and a trailing motorcade of dignitaries and government officials.[132] The procession left the Navy Yard's 6th Street entrance and turned left onto M Street SE, where large crowds had gathered along the planned route. The New York *Herald* reported: "At the Navy Yard entrance there was a tremendous crowd, one that had been waiting for an hour or more despite the rain. All along the line of march of twenty blocks men, women, and children lined the sidewalks. It was a silent throng, the people baring their heads, but they did not speak."[133] The procession turned right onto New Jersey Avenue and proceeded ten blocks to East Capitol Plaza.

(National Archives)
President Warren G. Harding places a wreath on the casket of the World War I Unknown Soldier during ceremonies at the Rotunda of the U.S. Capitol. The body would lie-in-state until the funeral ceremonies on November 11.

There, the body bearers carefully removed the coffin from the caisson and carried it up the East Front steps of Capitol, passing through an Army honor cordon. They entered a darkened Rotunda and gently placed the Unknown's casket upon the Lincoln catafalque directly under the building's dome and the magnificent Constantino Brumidi fresco, "The Apotheosis of Washington." At that time, only ten American citizens had been accorded this supreme tribute. Three had been the nation's assassinated Presidents—Lincoln, Garfield, McKinley—while the others who had laid-in-state were either renowned members of Congress or distinguished military commanders.[134] Appropriately, the last person to lay-in-state was the *Olympia's* flag officer, Commodore George Dewey.[135] America's Unknown Soldier was the first citizen/soldier to be conferred with this high honor.[136]

The Capitol had been closed to public visitation to allow various dignitaries to pay their respects to the Unknown. President Warren G. Harding and his wife arrived shortly, and the President placed a wreath of red roses on the casket. He was followed by Vice President, Calvin Coolidge, and the Speaker of the House, Frederick Gillette, who also placed separate floral tributes at the bier. The Chief Justice of the Supreme Court, former President William Howard Taft, did the same.[137] But the most poignant moment of the Rotunda ceremonies came when General John J. Pershing, the former commander of the American Expeditionary Forces, placed his wreath before the casket, honoring one of his soldiers for his loyalty and supreme sacrifice.[138] A five-man, joint service honor guard was positioned around the bier. These men would maintain their stoic vigil on a rotating basis throughout the night and day.[139]

The next morning at 8 AM, the Capitol building was reopened to the public. During the next 18 hours, over 100,000 people paid their private and individual respects to the nation's Unknown Solider. As the people slowly passed by the catafalque, many left behind their own modest floral remembrances as well as countless tears. The Associated Press reported: "A river of humanity, American men, women and children…flowed all day today and far into the night past the bier of the unknown soldier, under the great dome of the Capitol."[140] The press noted the long lines of patient citizens quietly waiting hours to pay their respects: "Every class and every age were represented in the line of march. There were many pathetic scenes as men and women whose sons had not come back from the front lines halted at the bier."[141] The Republic of China sent a beautiful, three-foot bronze statue of the "Angel of Peace" to the Rotunda to honor the Unknown, while other allied nations sent tributes as did dozens of patriotic groups and fraternal organizations. The crowds at the Capitol were so great that the viewing period had to be extended until midnight, after which the building was closed for the night to allow for final preparations for the next day's state funeral.

CONGRESS HAD EARLIER passed a formal resolution to officially declare Armistice Day as a national holiday in honor of the interment of the Unknown. HJ Res. 215 read in part: "Whereas the unknown soldier represents the manhood of America who gave their lives to defend its integrity, honor, and tranquility against an enemy...resolved...[that] November 11, 1921, [be observed as a holiday] as a mark of respect to the memory of those who gave their lives in the late World War, as typified by the unknown and unidentified American soldier who is to be buried at Arlington National Cemetery."[142] School children, government workers, and thousands of other area citizens used their day off to line the entire parade route from the Capitol to Arlington to witness the historic funeral of America's Unknown.

(National Archives)
The caisson carrying the casket of the Unknown Soldier at the U.S. Capitol. The march to Arlington Cemetery would travel down Pennsylvania Avenue and through Georgetown before finally arriving at the Memorial Amphitheater.

At 8:00 AM, the casket was taken from the Rotunda and carried by the eight body bearers down the steps of the Capitol through a cordon of troops at present arms. It was placed on the awaiting horse-drawn gun caisson. Nine generals and three flag officers had been designated as honorary pall-bearers and would accompany the casket on foot to Arlington National Cemetery. The United States Army Band from the Washington Barracks and its drum corps led the large procession, which included contingents of soldiers and sailors from Fort Washington, the Navy Yard, Fort Myer, and Quantico as well as a mounted unit, the 2nd Squadron, 3rd Cavalry. President Warren G. Harding, General John J. Pershing, and several other government officials elected to walk behind the caisson as the funeral march left the Capitol grounds and moved slowly down Pennsylvania Avenue.[143] All of the buildings along the route were decorated with flags and patriotic bunting, while the streets were packed with

(National Archives)

Former President Woodrow Wilson and his wife, Edith, in the procession for the Unknown.

crowds of patriotic citizens who watched in a collective hushed silence. The newspapers reported: "There was no laughter before the cortege appeared, and during the passage of the bier every head was bared...Men and women watching the parade along Pennsylvania avenue gave a remarkable demonstration of respect for the flag and for the casket."[144] Some 44 other patriotic, fraternal, and veterans organizations joined the procession at various points along the route. These included the Grand Army of the Republic, the National War

(National Archives)
Thousands of citizens lining Pennsylvania Avenue to pay their respects to America's Unknown Soldier. Armistice Day had earlier been declared a national holiday by Congress in honor of the Unknown.

Mothers, the Colored Veterans of the War, the Red Cross, the Rotary Club, and the Society of Cincinnati.[145] Former President, Woodrow Wilson and his wife, Edith, rode behind the Unknown in a horse-drawn carriage. The sight of the seriously ill former chief executive elicited spontaneous applause and cheers from the previously silent crowds. The *Evening Star* reported: "The reverent silence all along the line had only been broken by handclapping and some cheers as the former President passed by...It was Mr. Wilson's first public appearance since March 4, when he rode up Pennsylvania Avenue with President Harding. The comment was heard in the crowd that the former President, long a sick man, looked better than many folks expected."[146] Still, Wilson's fragile health prevented him from attending the funeral rites at Arlington, so his carriage left the procession near 16th Street, NW, to return to his S Street home.

President Harding and many of the other government officials decided to abandon the main funeral procession at the White House, intending to travel the remaining four miles to Arlington by automobile via an alternative route. General Pershing, though, was determined to proceed on foot despite his age (61 years old) and followed the Unknown's caisson as the procession proceeded down Pennsylvania Avenue to Washington Circle and then onto M Street and through Georgetown. The parade crossed over the Potomac River by way of the Aqueduct Bridge and entered Arlington through the Fort Myer gate as the sounds of distant minute guns were heard, fired by a field artillery battery positioned on the Washington Monument grounds.[147] The caisson pulled up to the west entrance of the Amphitheater at exactly 11:40 AM, some three hours after it had left the Capitol grounds. Inside, over 3,000 people awaited the arrival while an overflow crowd had gathered on the grounds below the east plaza.

Harding's entourage had planned to arrive at the Amphitheater before the caisson, but the motorcade ran into what the Washington *Times* described as an "unprecedented jam on the roads."[148] A touring car had earlier run out of gas and stalled on the Highway Bridge causing a major road block. Many dignitaries were stuck in traffic, some delayed for over two hours, while others "did not reach the cemetery at all."[149] Other infuriated and frustrated drivers simply abandoned their vehicles while forty District policemen desperately tried to alleviate the traffic delays. A few resourceful motorists even tried to commandeer small boats to convey them across the Potomac River. Anxious Secret Service agents, augmented by several uniformed motorcycle police, tried in vain to clear a path for the President's motorcade.[150] Finally, the President's car was forced to abandon the main roadways and drove through open fields and farms in a frantic effort to bypass the colossal traffic jam. Yet despite these valiant efforts, the President still arrived at Arlington late.[151]

Once President Harding and his entourage took their positions in the Amphitheater, the body bearers removed the casket from the caisson and carried it around the north colonnade to the stage area of the Amphitheater. The entire front of the dais was filled with floral tributes and wreaths in honor of the Unknown. The official ceremonies commenced with the playing of the National Anthem followed by a brief invocation. At precisely 12 o'clock noon, trumpets sounded the beginning of a two-minute national period of observed silence. At its conclusion, President Harding was invited to deliver the eulogy.[152] He began his impassioned speech: "We are met today to pay the impersonal tribute. The name of him whose body lies before us took flight with his imperishable soul. We know not whence he came, but only that his death marks him with the everlasting glory of an American dying for his country. He might have come from any one of millions of American homes."[153] The President talked about the horrors of modern war, concluding that: "It is no longer a conflict in chivalry, no more a test of militant manhood. It is only cruel, deliberate, scientific destruction."[154] He finished with a recitation of the Lord's Prayer.

(National Archives)

The arrival of the Unknown at the west steps of the Amphitheater. President Harding delivered the eulogy during the formal ceremonies inside.

(National Archives)

The East Plaza commital ceremonies for the Unknown Soldier. Thousands of people gathered below the new sarcophogus to pay their respects to America's Unknown Soldier.

Harding then presented the Unknown Soldier with the Distinguished Service Cross and the Medal of Honor (MOH). The Congressionally approved citation read in part: "the Medal of Honor, emblem of highest ideals and virtues is bestowed...upon the unknown American, typifying the gallantry and intrepidity, at the risk of life above and beyond the call of duty, of our beloved heroes who made the supreme sacrifice in the World War. They died in order that others might live."[155] Foreign delegations awarded their own military decorations to the Unknown. Admiral of the Fleet, Earl Beatty, conferred the Victoria Cross on behalf of King George V, while Marshall Ferdinand Foch presented both the French Medaille Militaire and the Croix de Guerre.[156]

Several hymns and scripture readings followed the formal presentation of medals. The Amphitheater rites concluded with the collective singing of "Nearer My God, to Thee." The body of the Unknown was then carried out through the southeast entrance and taken to the newly completed sarcophagus on the plaza. After the President and the other dignitaries had assembled, the committal service was read by Bishop Brent. Congressman Hamilton Fish was appropriately granted the honor of placing the very first wreath

(National Archives)

The casket of the Unknown Soldier is lowered into the burial crypt at the Memorial Amphitheater. The new Tomb had been designed by architect Thomas Hastings without any inscriptions or adornments.

at the Tomb of the Unknown Soldier. Wreaths were also presented by the American and British War mothers. Then, the Crow Indian Chief, Plenty Coups, laid his eagle feathered war bonnet and coups sticks on the Unknown's sarcophagus. Three salvos fired by nearby artillery and the traditional playing of "Taps" concluded the interment.[157]

Later that day, the Tomb of the Unknown Soldier at Arlington National Cemetery was sealed for perpetuity. The new Memorial Amphitheater had, in an instant, been transformed from a place of patriotic gathering into a national shine of pilgrimage. John Dickinson Sherman's wrote an apt tribute to the Unknown Soldier: "For 'Unknown Dead' is merely a symbol...read 'Man in the Ranks'— the common man who did his duty, offered his all, won his fight or gave up his life and is unknown...This is the man who won the war...".[158]

(Library of Congress)
A group of Gold Star Mothers place a wreath at the Tomb of the Unknown Soldier at Arlington National Cemetery. The Tomb became the nation's most sacred shrine honoring the nation's veterans.

Endnotes

1 "Guns along the Meuse Roar Grand Finale of Eleventh Hour," *Stars and Stripes*, 15 September 1918, p. 1.

2 The world-wide flu epidemic killed an estimated 60 million people. Some 59,119 American soldiers died of the disease, more than those who were killed in combat.

3 *Ibid.*, p. 1.

4 Some 70% of all combat casualties during World War I were caused by artillery fire.

5 Captain Llewelyn Griffith quoted in Richard Holmes. *Tommy: The British Soldier on the Western Front 1914-1918*. London: Harper/Collins Publishers, 2014, p. 151.

6 Holmes, p. 40.

7 *Ibid.*, p. 299.

8 Lisa M. Budreau. *Bodies of War: World War I and the Politics of Commemoration in America, 1919 – 1933*. New York: New York University Press, 2010, p. 22.

9 Michael J. Allen. *Until the Last Man Comes Home: POWs, MIAs, and the Unending Vietnam War*. Chapel Hill: University of North Carolina Press, 2009, p. 102.

10 Astonishingly, the bones of World War I soldiers are still being recovered 100 years later. Lisa M. Budreau. *Bodies of War: World War I and the Politics of Commemoration in America, 1919 – 1933*. New York: New York University Press, 2010, p. 39.

11 Neil Hanson. *The Unknown Soldier: The Story of the Missing of the Great War*. London: Transworld Publishers, 2005, p 293.

12 David Crane. *Empires of the Dead: How One Man's Vision Led to the Creation of WWI's War Graves*. London: William Collins, 2013, p 129.

13 Holmes, p. 628.

14 Patrick K. O'Donnell. *The Unknowns: The Untold Story of America's Unknown Soldier and WWI's Most Decorated Heroes Who Brought Him Home*. New York: Atlantic Monthly Press, 2018, p. 142.

15 Allen, p. 120.

16 Hanson, pp. 318, 319.

17 *Ibid.*, p. 320.

18 Budreau, pp. 15, 89.

19 *Long Shadow: Remembering and Understanding.* Directed by Russell Barnes, historian David Reynolds, Clearstory, 2014. *Netflix,* https://www.netflix.com/bro wse?jbv=80109639&jbp=0&jbr=1. Also see Holmes, p. 14.

20 See the Commonwealth Graves Commission available at: https://www.cwgc. org/.

21 Hanson, p. 343.

22 The famed journalist and author, Rudyard Kipling, lost his son in battle in 1915. His remains were never recovered, and Kipling was credited with originating the inscription: "Known but to God" on the graves of unidentified soldiers.

23 Reverend David Railton (13 November 1884–13 June 1955).

24 Crane, pp. 247-248.

25 The Right Reverend Herbert Ryle (25 May 1856–20 August 1925).

26 Hanson, p. 329.

27 Martin Gilbert. *The First World War: A Complete History.* New York: Henry Holt and Company, 1994, pp. 528-529.

28 Ryle quoted in Hanson, p. 332.

29 Lloyd George quoted in Hanson, p. 332.

30 There are also eight Prime Ministers buried at Westminster Abbey including William Pitt, William Gladstone, Neville Chamberlain, and Clement Atlee.

31 Hanson, p. 349.

32 Michael Gavaghan. *The Story of the Unknown Warrior: 11 November 1920.* London: M. and L. Publications, 1995, p. 11.

33 The goal was to discover "proof of nationality yet offer[ed] no trace of individuality." See, Michael J. Allen. "Sacrilege of a Strange, Contemporary Kind:" *The Unknown Soldier and the Imagined Community after the Vietnam War." History and Memory*, vol. 23, no. 2, 2011, pp. 90–131. *JSTOR,* JSTOR, www.jstor. org/stable/10.2979/histmemo.23.2.90, p. 100.

34 Brigadier General L. J. Wyatt quoted in Hanson, p. 356.

35 Hanson, p. 355.

36 "Story of the Tomb of the Unknown Warrior," *YouTube*, 13 June 2018, https://youtube/tN-6NctDdTa; also see Hanson, p. 357.

37 Hanson, p. 357; It was rumored that the three unselected bodies were buried in a shell hole rather than in a cemetery. See Gavaghan, p. 23.

38 "Army Chaplain who took the Unknown Warrior's Secret to his Grave," available at: https://www.theguardian.com/world/2014/nov/11/tomb-unknown-warrior-army-chaplain-secret.

39 "Unknown Warrior," available at https://www.westminster-abbey.org/abbey-commemorations/commemorations/unknown-warrior/.

40 "The Actual Unknown Soldier—Remembrance Day, World War I," *YouTube*, 13 June 2018, https://youtu.be/v=cvOI4RPe8v0.

41 *Ibid.*

42 The six British escort destroyers were HMS *Witherington*, HMS *Wanderer*, HMS *Whitshed*, HMS *Wivern*, HMS *Wolverine*, HMS *Veteran*. Gavaghan, p. 35.

43 *Ibid.*, p. 35.

44 "Funeral of the Unknown Soldier," YouTube, 14 June 2018, https://youtu.be/C9O0U-g2VSk.

45 Hanson, pp. 363-364.

46 *Ibid.*, pp. 369-370.

47 "King is Chief Mourner When Unknown Tommy Given Marshall's Burial," *Great Falls Daily Tribune*, 12 November 1920, p. 2.

48 *Ibid.*, p. 2.

49 "Funeral of the Unknown Soldier."

50 Hanson, pp. 381-382.

51 The so-called Lost Generation (a term coined by Gertrude Stein) of writers and artists were disillusioned about the world war and its impact on society, humanity, and Western Civilization. Among this illustrious group were Ernest Hemingway, F. Scott Fitzgerald, Sinclair Lewis, William Faulkner, and John Dos Passos. Dos Passos wrote a brutal, vivid, and cynical account of death and destruction and the selection of an unknown soldier in his misanthropic essay: "The Body of an American." Available at: http://producer.csi.edu/cdraney/archive-courses/fall09/175/etexts/passos-body-acrobat.pdf.

52 Hanson, p. 360.

53 "To the Unknown Dead," *Essex County Herald*, 30 December 1920, p 6.

54 K.S. Inglis. "Entombing Unknown Soldiers from London and Paris to Baghdad," *History and Memory*, vol. 5, no. 2, 1993, pp. 7-31. *JSTOR*, JSTOR, www.jstor.org/stable/256-18650, p. 11.

55 During the French Revolution, King Louis XVI and his wife, Marie Antoinette, were guillotined as were thousands of Catholic priests. Churches were vandalized, and the graves of saints were desecrated. Ironically, in all likelihood, the French Unknown would probably have been a Catholic.

56 Inglis, p. 13.

57 *Ibid.*, p. 13.

58 8 November 1920.

59 President Alexandre Millerand quoted in "French Pay Homage," *The Evening Star*, 12 November 1920, p. 3.

60 *Ibid.*, p. 14.

61 *Ibid.*, p. 17.

62 Secretary Newton Baker quoted in: "To the Unknown Dead," p. 6.

63 *Ibid.*, p. 6.

64 "Twelve Bodies Buried," *The Evening Star*, 11 November 1920, p. 2. All of the soldiers and sailors who were buried at Arlington that day were interred in Section 18 with one exception. Charley Morris, a Mess Attendant from Mississippi was buried in Sec. 19, #140. The other soldiers and sailors were: Walter Austin, Sec.

18 #601, Silas Ballard, Sec. 18 #599, Vaughn Carson, Sec. 18 #634, James Christensen, Sec. 18 #631, Arthur Corson, Sec. 18 #600, Blake Cuthbert, Sec. 18 #598, William Mitchell, Sec. 18 #633, and Russell Ritchie, Sec. 18 #632.

65 *Report of the Quartermaster General, U.S. Army to the Secretary of War.* Washington, D.C.: Government Printing Office, 1919, p. 37; also see Joseph Shoman. *Crosses in the Wind: Graves Registration Service in the Second World War.* New York: Standford House, Inc. 1947, p. 209.

66 General John J. Pershing quoted in Steven E. Anders: "With All Due Honors: A History of the Quartermaster Graves Registration Mission" available at: http://old.qmfound.com/grave.htm.

67 The number of American soldiers that were missing-in-action was small when compared to the other major warring powers: Britain—191,652; France—537,000; Germany—1,152,800; Russia—2,500,000.

68 "Commemorative Sites Booklet." Washington, D.C.: American Battle and Monuments Commission, p. 2.

69 Inglis, p. 8.

70 Pershing quoted in Anders.

71 "The Distressing Truth Revealed Why It is Not Possible to Properly Bury the Soldier Dead from the Torn Battlefields and How the Undertakers are Pressing the Scheme for Business Reasons," *The Washington Times,* 8 February 1920, p. 2.

72 Report of the Quartermaster General, p. 37.

73 "Activities of the Graves Registration Service in France, 1919-1920." National Archives and Records Service. RG-111, available online at: https://catalog.archives.gov/id/24713; also see Jeremy Gordon Smith. *Photographing the Fallen: A War Graves Photographer on the Western Front, 1915-1919.* East Yorkshire: Pen and Sword Ltd., 2017, pp. 145-153.

74 This admittedly does not include the domestic fighting against the American Indians in the west.

75 John Bethell. "A Splendid Little War; Harvard and the Commencement of a New World Order", *Harvard magazine.* (November–December 1998).

76 "Doughboy" was a nickname given to American soldiers due to the doughnut shape of their uniform buttons. General Pershing felt that the term gave his troops a unique sense of identity and readily embraced it.

77 "50,000 of American Dead to be Returned," *The Evening Star*, 14 March 1920, p. 55, also see Budreau, pp 21, 22.

78 *Ibid.*, p. 48.

79 Budreau, p. 70.

80 It took until 1922 to remove the dead from French and Belgian battlefields. Hanson, p. 319.

81 "Brent Champions 'Fields of Honor,'" *The Evening Star*, 15 January 1920, p. 20.

82 "T.R. Glad Son Could Help," *Seattle Star*, 17 July 1918, p. 1.

83 Theodore Roosevelt quoted in Budreau, p. 70.

84 Letter from Lt. Colonel Charles Pierce to Mrs. Edith Roosevelt, 20 August 1919, National Archives and Records Service available at: https://catalog.archives.gov/id/6706671.

85 Letter from Theodore Roosevelt to Lt. Colonel Charles Pierce, 2 November 1918, National Archives and Records Service available at: https://catalog.archives.gov/id/6706623/2.

86 Budreau, p. 69.

87 "The Distressing Truth Revealed." p. 2.

88 *Ibid.*, p. 2.

89 Budreau, pp. 43, 44.

90 "All U.S. Dead Eligible to be Returned Home," *The Evening Star*, 24 March 1920, p. 9.

91 "Activities of the Graves Registration Service in France, 1919-1920," National Archives.

92 *Ibid.*

93 Budreau, p. 80.

94 Enoch A. Chase, "Fame's Eternal Camping Ground: Beautiful Arlington, Burial Place of America's Illustrious Dead," *National Geographic Magazine*, 1928, p. 626; Poole, pp. 146-147.

95 B.C. Mossman and M.W. Stark. *The Last Salute: Civil and Military Funerals 1921-1969*. Washington, D.C.: Department of the Army, 1971, p. 4.

96 O'Donnell, p. 279.

97 Hamilton Fish. *Hamilton Fish: Memoir of an American Patriot*. Washington, D.C.: Regnery Gateway, 1991, pp. 26-30.

98 *Ibid.*, p. 31.

99 During the Meuse-Argonne campaign, the 369th sustained over 30% casualties. By the end of the war, the Harlem Hellfighters had been in combat for 191 days, longer than any other American regiment. Fish, p. 31.

100 Fish, p. 31.

101 Congressman Hamilton Fish (7 December 1888 –18 January 1991).

102 *The Statutes at Large of the United States of America from May, 1919, to March, 1921*. Washington, D.C.: Government Printing Office, p. 1447 available at: http://www.loc.gov/law/help/statutes-at-large/66th-congress/c66.pdf.

103 Hamilton Fish, "Return of Body of Unknown American Who Lost His Life during the World War," Hearings before the Committee on Military Affairs, House of Representatives, Sixty-sixty Congress, 3rd Session, 1 February 1921.

104 Letter from Congressman Hamilton Fish to Secretary of War John W. Weeks, 9 March 1921, Record Group 407 Entry (PI17) 37A *Records of the Adjutant General's Office*. Central Decimal Files, 1917-1925. Box 563 (Location 370/79/9/3).

105 "Honors to Unknown: American Soldier will be Buried at Arlington," *The Evening Star*, 5 March 1921, p. 2.

106 "Wilson Retires as Cheering Messages Come from Nation," *The Evening Star*, 4 March 1921, p. 17.

107 "Woodrow Wilson's Last Hours as President of the United States," *The Evening Star*, 4 March 1921, p. 1.

108 Minutes of the Meeting of the Commission of Fine Arts, 22/23 September 1921.

109 National Archives, RG 407.

110 *The Unknown Dead, History of the AGRS, QMC, in Europe*, Vol. 2; Also see House Resolution 426 quoted in "Plan for Selection, Transportation and Burial of an Unidentified American," War Department Press Release, 23 September 1921, Record Group 407 Enter (PI 17) 39 *Records of the Adjutant General's Office. Central Files, 1926-1939.* Box 1271 (Location 370/81/1/2).

111 Letter from Major General Robert O. David to Reverend Homer W. Henderson, 23 May 1926. National Archives Record Group 407 Enter (PI 17) 39 *Records of the Adjutant General's Office.* Central Files, 1926-1939. Box 1271 (Location 370/81/1/2).

112 *The Unknown Dead.*

113 SGT Edward F. Younger (circa 1898-6 August 1942) Sec. 18, #1918B.

114 Major Harbold quoted in Edward F Younger. "I Chose the Unknown Soldier," *The Evening Star: This Week*, 8 November 1936, p. 2.

115 "Unknown U.S. Hero Chosen in France," *The Evening Star*, 24 October 1921, p. 1.

116 Edward F Younger. "I Chose the Unknown Soldier," *The Evening Star: This Week*, 8 November 1936, p. 2.

117 *The Unknown Dead.*

118 Mayor M. Servas, National Archives, RG 497.

119 Now the Meuse-Argonne American Cemetery. Mossman, p. 8.

120 Benjamin Franklin Cooling. *USS Olympia*. Annapolis: Naval Institute Press, 2000, p. 212.

121 Mossman, p. 9.

122 Letter from Secretary of the Navy Josephus Daniels to the Secretary of War Newton D. Baker, 31 January 1921, National Archives, RG 407.

123 Cooling, p. 213.

124 *Ibid.*, p. 213.

125 "Capitol Like Tomb for Unknown, Home in Nation's Embrace," *New York Herald*, 10 November 1921, p. 1.

126 "Guns Roar Salute as Olympia Bears Hero Up the Potomac," *The Evening Star*, 9 November 1921, p. 1.

127 The high temperature for the day was just 51°.

128 "Guns Roar," p. 1.

129 Kirke Larue Simpson. *The Unknown Soldier*. New York: Service Bulletin of the Associated Press, December 1921, p. 4; Mossman, p. 11.

130 The body bearers were: Army: Color Sergeant James W. Dell, Sergeant Samuel Woodfill, Sergeant Thomas Saunders, First Sergeant Louis Razga, First Sergeant Harry Taylor; Navy: Chief Water Tender Charles Leo O'Connor, Chief Torpedoman James Delaney; Marine Corps: Gunnery Sergeant Ernest Janson. The story of these men is skillfully told in Patrick O'Donnell's book: *The Unknowns*: see p. 281.

131 Mossman, p. 11.

132 Simpson, p. 4.

133 "Capitol Like Tomb," p. 1.

134 The one exception to this was Pierre L'Enfant, the designer of the city of Washington, D.C. and a Revolutionary War veteran. L'Enfant had initially been buried in Maryland, but his body was disinterred in 1909 and later buried in front of the Lee Mansion at Arlington, overlooking the capital city that he had once envisioned.

135 January 20, 1917.

136 See "Those Who Have Lain in State or in Honor in the Rotunda," Architect of the Capitol, available at: https://www.aoc.gov/sites/default/files/documents/basic-page/lain_state_honor_2018.pdf.

137 William Howard Taft is the only man to have ever been the head of both the executive and judicial branches of government.

138 Mossman, pp. 11-12.

139 Simpson, p. 5.

140 *Ibid.*, p. 8.

141 *Ibid.*, p. 8.

142 HJ Res. 215, Records of the Sixty-Seventh Congress, Sess. I, p. 211. Armistice Day did not become an annual holiday in the United States until 1938. It was changed to Veterans Day after the Korean War in 1954.

143 Mossman, pp. 13-14.

144 "Caisson from the Capitol Passes through Lane of Reverent Throngs," *The Evening Star*, 11 November 1921, p. 2.

145 Mossman, p. 15.

146 "Caisson from the Capitol," p. 2.

147 Mossman, p. 13.

148 "Unknown Hero Laid to Rest," *Washington Times*, 11 November 1921, p. 1.

149 Constance McLaughlin Green. *Washington: Capital City 1879-1950*. Princeton: Princeton University Press, 1963, p. 282.

150 "Auto Causes Huge Tangle in Traffic," *The Evening Star*, 11 November 1921, p. 2.

151 Mossman, p. 16; Philip Bigler. *In Honored Glory: Arlington National Cemetery, the Final Post*. St. Petersburg, Fl.: Vandamere Press, 2010, p. 50.

152 "Program of Ceremonies attending the burial of an unknown and unidentified American soldier who lost his life during the world war," p. 5. Library of Congress. Available at: https://catalog.loc.gov/vwebv/search?searchCode=LCCN&searchArg=22000493&searchType=1&permalink=y.

153 Warren G. Harding. "The Unknown American Soldier." Washington, D.C.: Government Printing Office, 1921, p. 3. Available at: https://archive.org/details/unknownamericans00hard.

154 *Ibid.*, p. 5.

155 Congress passed the resolution authorizing the bestowing of the Medal of Honor on August 24, 1921. *The Congressional Medal of Honor: The Names, the Deeds*. Forest Ranch, CA.: Sharp & Dunnigan, 1984, p. 493.

156 "Program of Ceremonies, pp. 4-5. The other awards presented that day were

the Italian Gold Medal for Bravery, the Romanian Virtutea Miliitara, the Czechoslovakian War Cross, and the Polish Virtuti Militari.

157 *Ibid.*, p. 6.

158 John Dickinson Sherman. "The Unknown Dead," *Fulton County Tribune*, 31 Dec. 1920, p. 2.

(Library of Congress)
Aviator Charles Lindbergh at the Tomb of the Unknown Soldier, 12 June 1927. Lindbergh had recently completed his heroic, solo trans-Atlantic flight and chose to honor America's Unknown on his official visit to Washington, D.C.

(Lorimer Rich Papers, Syracuse University Libraries)
The die block for the Tomb of the Unknown Soldier is loaded onto a rail car in Yule, Colorado circa February 1931. The marble stone was covered by a wooden shipping crate before being shipped back east.

Chapter IV

Completing the Tomb

"[The] completion of the tomb of America's unknown war hero should be pushed as rapidly as possible." – The *Evening Star*

T he Commission of Fine Arts in Washington, D.C. was established at the turn of the century (1910) to help coordinate, design, and organize the architectural and monumental legacy of the nation's capital. Comprised of some of the nation's foremost architects, artists, and sculptors, the Commission considered Arlington National Cemetery to be the western terminus of the National Mall. As such, the agency became intimately involved with the cemetery's expansion and development and, in particular, with the construction of both the Memorial Amphitheater and the proposed addition of the Tomb of the Unknown Soldier.[1]

In the haste to inter an American Unknown by Armistice Day 1921, the chief architect of the Amphitheater, Thomas Hastings, had been commissioned to design a simple but elegant marble sarcophagus on the East Plaza. It was tacitly understood that a more suitable monument would be added at some later date when additional Congressional funding became available. Two years after the burial of the Unknown, the Commission of Fine Arts advocated that any new addition to the Tomb: "should be large in scale and rich in outline and shadows, because it comes against an open and distant view. It should also command attention and make appeal to the higher emotions of the public."[2]

The Amphitheater building was officially turned over to the federal government shortly after its completion. It was placed under the direct administration and supervision of the Quartermaster General of the Army who was also responsible for the day-to-day operations of Arlington National Cemetery. Hastings reluctantly forfeited all creative control of the building, but he remained understandably protective of the integrity of his artistic vision. Moreover, he felt entitled to oversee any future construction for a completed Tomb since the current shrine had displaced his intended "Peace" monument on the Amphitheater's plaza. Hastings explained: "In the original designs of the Arlington Amphitheater which we prepared under the direction of the Arlington Memorial Amphitheater Commission, there was included in the general plan at the point where the Unknown Soldier is now buried a vertical shaft, which was then discussed as a Peace monument, and we felt then that this feature was an essential part of the scheme of the Amphitheater. This work... was omitted in order to save expense. The erection of the monument to the Unknown Soldier which we now propose would be, in effect, merely the execution of the original plan as an integral part of the design."[3]

Despite the ongoing failure of Congress to appropriate any funds to complete the Tomb, Hastings nevertheless received permission from Secretary of War, John W. Weeks, to construct "a full size completed model...made of plaster" on the Unknown's actual sarcophagus at Arlington in order to properly showcase his creative vision for the project.[4] This was accomplished in December 1922 when Hastings erected a scale model on the existing Tomb. The model was allowed to remain in place for a short period of time to allow members of the military and of the Fine Arts Commission adequate time to view and assess the design on its intended location. Hastings' proposed memorial was described as an: "ornamental sarcophagus supported at each corner by a crouching nude figure and

(Commission of Fine Arts)
Hastings full scale plaster model for the Tomb, December 1923. The plinth was temporarily erected on the sarcophogus to be assessed on location. Despite unanimous support from the Commission of Fine Arts, the monument was widely criticized and ultimately rejected by the Secretary of War, John W. Weeks.

placed at the top of a tall shaft; the ensemble would have been twenty-eight feet high in addition to the five feet or the original tomb, which would serve as a base."[5] On the vertical, plaster pillar was the verbose inscription:

WE DO NOT KNOW THE
EMINENCE OF HIS BIRTH
BUT WE DO KNOW THE
GLORY OF HIS DEATH
HE DIED FOR HIS
COUNTRY
AND GREATER DEVOTION
HATH NO MAN THAN THIS
HE DIED UNQUESTIONING
UNCOMPLAINING WITH
FAITH IN HIS HEART AND
HOPE ON HIS LIPS
THAT HIS COUNTRY
SHOULD TRIUMPH
AND ITS CIVILIZATION
SURVIVE

Hastings' design for the Tomb received an enthusiastic endorsement from the Chairman of the Commission of Fine Arts, Charles Moore. In a glowing letter to the Secretary of War, Moore noted that: "the nature of the site and the character of the monument have been met in Hastings' design in a very distinguished manner... The scale of the monument is right and has an appropriate majestic quality...the design is impressive in its mass and fine in its general form and proportions. The monument as designed is in harmony with the Amphitheater. It gives assurance of being in every way a notable work."[6]

The military, however, was far less enthusiastic about Hastings' proposed monument. The Secretary of War rejected the design as too gaudy and ostentatious for the Tomb. Indeed, after just two years, many Americans had already grown fond of the existing monument's simplicity and understated beauty. Many felt that no alterations or changes should ever be made including District Judge, Walter McCoy, who echoed these sentiments in a letter to the *Evening Star*: "It was a great pleasure to read the announcement that you had rejected the design for the proposed monument or shaft at the grave of the unknown. No monument can be as suitable as the tomb itself. The amphitheater is there, the tomb is there, eloquent in their simplicity, add a brief inscription on the slab on the tomb itself seems to me all that may now be appropriately added."[7] District of Columbia resident, Burt Wagner, concurred in a subsequent letter-to-the-editor: "Why all the discussion about the 'unfinished' tomb of our Unknown Comrade?" He continued: "What is there missing and why is it called the pedestal for a monument? Most of those whom I have asked think it has been left in its present shape so as to form an altar for the floral offerings of those who wish to pay tribute to his sacrifice." Wagner concluded his passionate letter noting: "Simply and bravely he went forth, simply and bravely he died, simply and fittingly has he been honored. Let it so remain."[8]

Hastings was distressed by the adverse public reaction to his proposal. He attempted to mollify the military's objections by offering to radically alter his design and submit new architectural drawings which would dramatically reduce the addition's overall profile. His efforts, though, were to no avail and with Congress stubbornly failing to authorize any funds for the project, all planning for a Tomb addition was suspended. An embittered Hastings lobbied the Secretary of War for appropriate financial compensation for his completed work, but his appeals were rebuffed, and the architect was never properly reimbursed for his efforts.

AFTER THE BURIAL of the Unknown Soldier, Arlington National Cemetery became a revered, national place of pilgrimage for patriotic citizens, veterans' organizations, and Gold Star Mothers. Every week throughout the calendar year, various groups would solemnly assemble on the plaza to place a floral wreath on the Tomb in tribute to the Unknown as well as to all of the American soldiers who had died during the fighting in the first world war.

The shrine simultaneously became a major sightseeing attraction for visitors to the nation's capital. Automobiles were permitted unrestricted access to the cemetery grounds and this allowed for insouciant tourists to drive up the slopping hill on Farragut Avenue directly to the Memorial Amphitheater via an oblong access road. There, they could park their cars on the plaza immediately adjacent to the Unknown's grave, Many were oblivious to the site's significance and soon irreverent and rowdy gawkers began to pose for snapshots using the Tomb as a prop while enjoying the spectacular panoramic vista of Washington, D.C. As army Colonel James Pemrose observed in frustration: "automobiles would drive right up before the grave, the passengers laughing and talking, utterly indifferent to the sacredness of the spot."[9]

In an early effort to deter discourteous visitors, the Quartermaster General's office roped off the roadway directly in front of the Tomb in order to restrict automotive traffic. Likewise, a small sign was erected near the Tomb to alert tourists to the fact that they were present at an actual gravesite and should thus behave accordingly. In a subsequent memo to the Quartermaster General's office, Colonel H. C. Bonnycastle explained: "This sign owes its existence to the fact that visitors, upon being accused of sitting on the Tomb, became indignant and claimed immunity from blame because there was nothing to indicate where the remains of the Unknown Soldier had been placed."[10]

Several civilian watchmen were stationed throughout the cemetery during the daylight hours. Two were specifically assigned to the vicinity of the Memorial Amphitheater. One of their official duties was to enforce proper decorum at the Tomb, but these look-outs did so with only modest success, and sporadic problems persisted. The War Department was appalled by the "apparent lack of appreciation of the reverence and respect due the memorial to the unknown dead of the world war" shown by a few sightseers.[11] There were additional reports and rumors that: "some persons sit on this great tomb, strike matches or use it to light their 'smokes'" while others "lounge on the steps…smoke, chat merrily, laugh, make noise and otherwise conduct themselves in a way that it out of harmony with the associations of the place."[12] This led to a group of representatives from the American Legion to personally inform President Calvin Coolidge: "that it is not uncommon for visitors to sit upon this shrine and sometimes eat their lunches on it and throw paper and debris carelessly about."[13]

One potential solution to the problems at the Tomb of the Unknown Soldier was to post an armed military guard there during visitation hours in order to enforce solemnity. It was widely assumed that the mere physical presence of a soldier would deter aberrant behavior and protect the monument from any potential desecration or disrespect. This idea, though, was constantly vetoed by the army leadership who felt that posting a guard detail at Arlington would further deplete its precious manpower which was already under staffed in a post-war, demobilized military. Furthermore, army commanders were convinced that "crowd-control" duty was demeaning and monotonous and that the troops would resent such a posting. Brigadier General H.H. Bandholtz contended that guarding the Tomb would be: "…a real hardship on the soldier required to do sentry duty there, and in time this feeling of irritation, transmitted from sentry to sentry, would unquestionably detract from the respect and veneration in which the shrine in now held."[14] He also rejected the deployment of uniformed soldiers to Arlington for logistical reasons, arguing that there were no suitable facilities to bivouac military sentries near the Tomb.[15]

Instead of posting a military guard, it was decided instead to enclose the Tomb with a picket fence barrier.[16] The unsightly barri-

(Library of Congress)
The picket fence barrier surrounding the Tomb circa 1923. The fence detracted from the shrine's understated beauty and proved so unpopular that it was quickly dismantled.

cade was justified on the grounds that: "The tomb in its present condition does not lend itself to patriotic inspiration. Those visiting it do not experience that feeling of respect and reverence so marked at Washington's tomb and the Lincoln memorial. This is clearly shown by the many acts of desecration which necessitated the erection of a fence."[17] The fence, however, detracted from the Tomb's simple aesthetics and proved so unpopular with the American people that it was quickly dismantled.

Problems with insolent visitors to the Tomb were always well-publicized and often sensationalized by the newspapers. The situation became intolerable after the Washington *Herald* published an article in March 1926 detailing purported abuses. In the column, it was alleged that: "The tomb has become a rendezvous for picnickers who leave refuse there. Souvenir hunters have chipped the marble base. Boys have been shooting craps on top of the tomb."[18] The lurid, albeit grossly exaggerated, story aroused and inflamed public opinion, forcing the military to launch a formal inquiry into the newspaper's startling allegations. After concluding its investigation, army Brigadier General S. D. Rockenback dismissed the *Herald's* story as a complete fabrication. In his report, the General noted that the cemetery was closed at night and that "there is a watchman on duty at the Tomb" during opening hours. "Such comments," he insisted, "...are vilification of the public who visit the Tomb. At no time has there been observed any desecration of the Tomb or lack of veneration on the part of the public who visit it."[19] Indeed, the military review confirmed that although there had been isolated examples of disrespect at the Tomb, there had never been any documented cases of overt, physical desecration. Such accounts to the contrary were dismissed as mere gossip and innuendo.[20]

Still, the years of unremitting negative publicity concerning vulgar behavior at the Tomb of the Unknown Soldier had a cumulative effect. There was a popular consensus that something dramatic must be done to finally solve the perceived problem. Congress responded to the growing public pressure by introducing a joint resolution to mandate a daylight military guard at the Tomb.[21] The proposal, introduced by Representative Allen J. Furlow of Minnesota, stated: "Whereas the Tomb of the Unknown Soldier at Arlington is America's shrine emblematic of our heroic dead who gave their lives for their country during the World War; and Whereas among the thousands of persons constantly visiting this shrine there are some who fail to conduct themselves with the proper reverence... Resolved...that the War Department shall maintain a special guard armed and equipped...whose duty it shall be to guard the Tomb of the Unknown Soldier at Arlington from sunrise to sunset; and be it Resolved further, that as a part of this detail, a bugler shall sound taps each evening just prior to the dismissal of the guard."[22]

Faced with the pending Congressional legislation, widespread public support for a military guard, and persistent lobbying by the American Legion, Secretary of War Dwight F. Davis finally relented and unilaterally directed the army to immediately post an armed sentry at the Tomb. Major General Fox Conner relayed the orders: "One sentinel is to be posted at the tomb from the hour of opening the gates to the Cemetery in the morning until closing of the gates in the evening." The duty was initially assigned to members of the 3rd Cavalry and the 12th Infantry, existing units that were already stationed at nearby Fort Myer.[23]

The somber presence of an armed military guard immediately transformed the atmosphere at the Tomb. The memorial was now approached by visitors with a new sense of reverence and seriousness. The assigned sentinel's stoic vigil, likewise, symbolically represented the nation's gratitude for the ultimate sacrifice paid by the Unknown and, indeed, that of all American soldiers who had died during the first world war. Far from the tedious duty feared by commanders, guarding the Tomb of the Unknown Soldier quickly became an honor and a privilege, and soldiers volunteered for the coveted posting. Major General James McKinley wrote: "Soldiers assigned to this duty suffer no hardship, thereby, as sentinels are relieved every two hours and always have at least four hours rest between tours of duty. It may be stated further that assignments for this important detail are in demand among the enlisted men eligible and that they are justly proud of being assigned this duty."[24]

Decorum at the Tomb was further enhanced by the installation of a temporary chain barrier around the Tomb to prevent visitors from getting too close to the monument. It was decreed that: "No one, except the sentinel on duty at the Tomb, the civilian watchman and the guard of honor, be allowed in the area enclosed by the barrier unaccompanied by an escort…this plan…will result in keeping the general public at a reasonable distance from the Tomb, but close enough to view the Tomb and all ceremonies held there."[25]

(Library of Congress)
A lone sentinel guards the Tomb of the Unknown Soldier. The first military guard was assigned to the Tomb in 1926 during daylight hours. The vigil was extended to a 24-hour, 365 day posting in 1937.

THE MEMORIAL AMPHITHEATER'S impressive reception room was largely an unused, empty space prior to 1921. It was most commonly entered from the plaza area through two massive bronze doors. Inside, eight marble, Ionic columns created an open corridor atrium leading to a semi-circular hallway which provided indirect access to the main stage area of the Amphitheater. On either side of the interior columns, were two spacious, open rooms (north and south) with large, east facing windows overlooking the Tomb plaza. The walls were adorned with brass, electric candle wall-sconces.

Foreign dignitaries, high ranking military officials, and patriotic groups routinely visited the Tomb as part of their official visits to the nation's capital. There were, on average, three formal wreath ceremonies per week during the 1920s. As the *Sunday Star* reported: "No official of any rank or organization of any size, no matter what its purpose, now considers a visit to Washington complete without paying homage at the Tomb of the Unknown Soldier."[26]

Many of the official visitors desired to leave a permanent memento at the Tomb to commemorate their visit to the cemetery. Dozens of plaques, medals, commemorations, and other artifacts were gifted to the cemetery in honor of the Unknown. These items quickly accumulated and posed a serious logistical problem. Initially, "six special wall cases and four glass tables" were placed throughout the Amphitheater's main reception area (now popularly referred to as the "Trophy Room") in an effort to exhibit these objects, but the

(Library of Congress)
The "Trophy Room" at the Memorial Amphitheater. The space was used as an exhibit area including the statue of "The Angel of Peace" given by the Chinese government.

(Library of Congress)
French Prime Minister, Georges Clemenceau, places a wreath on the Tomb of the Unknown Soldier.

sheer volume of gifts necessitated that many items had to be transferred and stored at the nearby Arlington House mansion.[27]

On permanent display in the "Trophy Room" was the original interment flag from the unknown's casket as well as his awarded Congressional Medal of Honor. Also on exhibit were the various military decorations presented to the Unknown by foreign governments including the Victoria Cross (British), the Croix de Guerre (Belgium), and the Cross of the Legion of Honor (French) as well as medals from Italy, Czechoslovakia, Romania, and Poland.[28] The Chinese government had donated a magnificent bronze figurine by the renowned sculptor, Augustus Saint-Gaudens, entitled "The Angel of Peace." This statue was prominently displayed on a six- foot, marble pedestal located under an archway in the main reception area (the statue was later placed on display in the basement chapel of the

Memorial Amphitheater). Among the more eclectic items given to the Unknown was a palm leaf that had been fashioned from "a piece of aluminum taken from the first zeppelin brought down in France soon after the start of the war."[29]

One of the most popular exhibits with visitors was the war bonnet of the Crow Chief, Plenty Coups. The *Sunday Star* reported: "...none more novel than the resplendent war-bonnet, made of eagle feathers...the tail of this bonnet is nearly five feet long, and takes up nearly all of the space in one of the big wall cases."[30] Plenty Coups had served as a representative of all American Indian tribes during the interment ceremonies for the Unknown in 1921 and in a supreme tribute, removed his headdress and placed it on the casket along with his coup sticks. The Associate Press reported: "For the Indians of America, Chief Plenty [Coups] came to call upon the Great Spirit of the Red Man, with gesture and chant and tribal tongue that the dead should not have died in vain, that war might end, peace be purchased by such blood as this. Upon this casket he laid the coup sticks of his tribal office and the feathered war bonnet from his own head."[31]

(Library of Congress)

Chief Plenty Coups (center). During the interment of the Unknown Soldier, he left his war bonnet on the grave. It was placed on display at the Memorial Amphitheater.

IN THE SPRING of 1927, a delegation from the Commission of Fine Arts once again visited Arlington National Cemetery on an inspection tour to survey the conditions at the Tomb of the Unknown Soldier as well as that of the Memorial Amphitheater complex. It was reported in the newspapers that the delegation: "inspected the tomb and declared in their view that completion of the tomb of America's unknown war hero should be pushed as rapidly as possible."[32]

The Tomb's minimalist, pedestal base was never intended to serve as a permanent monument and now, six years after the interment, the Commission felt that it was finally time to expedite the completion of the gravesite and to hold a public architectural competition to solicit prospective ideas, designs, and drawings for finishing the monument. The Commission readily acknowledged that even though there: "[is] no money available; every step should be taken to push for completion the living symbol of America's war dead."[33]

The ceremonial posting of a military guard at the Tomb the previous year had focused the public's attention on Arlington and served as a catalyst to spur Congressional action on funding. There was a growing consensus among many federal officials that in its current condition, the Tomb did not suitably honor the supreme sacrifice of the Unknown and that of the thousands of other American war dead. This was especially apparent when the humble American monument was compared and contrasted to the majestic graves for the unknowns from the other allied nations, most notably those of the British at Westminster Abbey and the French at the Arc de Triomphe. Charles Moore, the Chairman of the Commission of Fine Arts, acknowledged this reality in a letter to Congressman Hamilton Fish, writing: "The treatment we have accorded—or failed to accord—to this monument is in striking contrast to the honor and dignity with which the Unknown Soldier has been treated in other countries."[34] He continued: "the Tomb of the Unknown Soldier at Arlington is the base for a monument to be designed in the future. By no possibility can it be made into an adequate monument in itself."[35] The Quartermaster General, B.F. Cheatham, was more candid, laconically disparaging the current Tomb as "an unfinished block."[36]

The War Department became the leading advocate for Congressional funding. Secretary of War, Dwight F. Davis, in a letter to President Coolidge, cited the previous problems with irreverent visitors at the grave as well as the overwhelming public support for adequately funding the monument project. He wrote: "There has been considerable adverse newspaper c[ri]ticism of the Tomb of the Unknown Soldier at the Memorial Amphitheater, on account of its unfinished condition. These criticisms have been widely disseminated throughout the country and as a result a number of letters have been received relative to this matter. At the time the body was interred, the lower part of the Memorial was constructed and the casket placed therein, with the idea of completing the memorial when Congress should make provisions thereafter."[37]

President Coolidge publicly supported legislative action, but he insisted that any subsequent appropriation mandate that the Tomb's integrity and its unassuming beauty be maintained while preserving the shrine's artistic and intimate relationship to the Memorial Amphitheater. The *Evening Star* reported: "[President Coolidge] believes the sepulcher is generally regarded as incomplete...[and] would welcome one which would give the grave a more finished appearance without destroying its simplicity."[38]

On July 3, 1926, Congress passed Public Bill No. 297 which appropriated $50,000 for the completion of the Tomb of the Unknown Soldier. A small portion of these funds, some $6,000, was to be allotted to finance the proposed national architectural competition. In its prospectus, the War Department insisted that: "the completed Tomb should be comparatively low in size; should be as simple, dignified and beautiful as it can possibly be made and should harmonize with the amphitheat[er] and its surroundings...the most important thing is to get the most beautiful work of art that can be conceived symbolical of the sacrifice which the Tomb itself represents."[39] Massachusetts' Congressman, Robert Luce, reiterated the need for simplicity in a letter to the Commission of Fine Arts noting that: "No design with any ornament whatever will fail to arouse hostility from some source or the other. For that reason, I have come to the conclusion that we might be driven to a perfectly plain cube, massive and symmetrical, with nothing on it but the lettering—'To the Unknown Soldier,' or, 'To an Unknown Soldier.'"[40]

Architect Thomas Hastings was justifiably insulted and felt slighted by the government's actions. Despite his widely scorned earlier model, Hastings insisted that he was still the most qualified architect to fulfill the original conception for the Tomb/Amphitheater complex at Arlington. He was incensed that Congress and the War Department would submit such an important project to the venality of a public contest and pleaded with Secretary of War Davis to stop what he maintained was an ill-advised quest. "As regards the competition which Congress proposes," Hastings wrote, "I do hope and pray that something can be done to arrest this way of obtaining a design. No self-respecting architect would go into such a competition and, therefore, no design is likely to be obtained either worthy of the purpose or place in which it is located. More important than any question of our being remunerated, which of course should be considered, is the importance of having a design which will compose and be in character with the Amphitheater."[41] Hastings remained extremely protective of his artistic creation, claiming: "It would be a great disappointment to me to see something put there with which the public would credit me and with which I had in no way been connected."[42]

Hastings' opposition to the Tomb competition received additional support from the flamboyant New York Congressman, Fiorello LaGuardia. LaGuardia contacted Secretary Davis to denounce the competition as well as its meager financial incentives.[43] He wrote that: "…no artist worthy of the name would enter a competition with a prize of $500 and if he did so for purely patriotic reasons $500 would not pay for the model."[44] LaGuardia then alleged that: "More than that, however, is that according to my information, after the model has been accepted the artist is entirely severed from the work in that your Department would then place the execution of the work, which would be carried on without the direct supervision of the artist. I cannot imagine anything more unmethodical, clumsy and sloppy than such a plan. As you know, an artist may conceive a delicate, beautiful piece of work which can be entirely ruined by improper execution, if the work is not carried on under his direct supervision and by persons competent to do such work."[45]

Secretary Davis respectfully but firmly informed LaGuardia that: "The information you have received…is incorrect in every respect."[46] He assured the Congressman that any architectural firm that was eventually selected for the Tomb's completion would remain intimately involved in overseeing and completing the project. The planned architectural competition would proceed unimpeded.

THE AMERICAN BATTLE MONUMENTS Commission, the Fine Arts Commission, and the Arlington Cemetery Commission were selected to organize and manage the Tomb design competition. They appointed an independent, distinguished, five-member selection committee in 1928 to assess all of the anticipated submissions. Three illustrious architects were selected to serve on this elite panel: Charles A. Coolidge, D. H. Burnham, and Paul Philippe Cret.[47] Cret had already earned a reputation as one of the nation's foremost memorial architects. His distinguished work included the Pennsylvania Memorial (1927) at the Meuse-Argonne Battlefield in France as well as the magnificent Pan American Union (1910) building on 17th Street, NW in Washington, D.C.[48] He would eventually design the Gettysburg Eternal Light Peace Memorial in 1938. Also serving on the judging committee were Colonial Hanford MacNider, the Assistant Secretary of War, and Mrs. William D. Rock, the Chairwoman of the American War Mothers. Mrs. Rock's son, LT William Rock, had received the Distinguished Service Cross while serving with the Tank Corps of the 301st Battalion in France before being killed in action on October 17, 1918. He was buried at Suresnes American Cemetery in France.

Despite Thomas Hastings ominous warnings, the Tomb competition received 73 entrees from prestigious architectural firms from throughout the United States. These various and diverse design concepts were displayed at the Munitions Building in Washington, D.C., without attribution, in order to preserve the integrity and objectivity of the judging process. After a careful and critical review of each of the submissions, the panel selected five of the most promising designs as finalists. The eliminated entries were subsequently returned to the various losing firms by the federal government.

The identity of the remaining five contenders remained a strictly guarded secret and the firms' submissions were now identified solely by the letters "A" through "E." Each of the finalists was given instructions to submit a scale, plaster model of their design drawings for further consideration later that fall.[49]

That November, the evaluation panel reconvened on two separate occasions to assess and analyze the newly submitted plaster models and drawings. On November 14, the committee selected submission "D" as the official winner of the Tomb competition. Major General B. F. Cheatham wrote: "...the Jury of Award in the Competition for the Completion of the Tomb of the Unknown Soldier at Arlington National Cemetery held a meeting and unanimously recommended to the Secretary of War an anonymous design. After their decision a sealed envelope was opened."[50] It was then revealed that the architectural firm of Lorimer Rich and Thomas Hudson Jones

(Library of Congress)
Secretary of War, Dwight F. Davis, and Major General B. F. Cheatham with the winning entry for the Tomb competition. The plaster model was submitted by New York sulptor, Thomas Hudson Jones, and architect, Lorimer Rich.

of New York had submitted the winning entry.[51] According to the judges, the Rich/Jones design: "[was] in keeping with the scale and character of the Amphitheater, which serves as a background to the Tomb of the Unknown Soldier." Furthermore, "the design provides a single space for the inscription. This inscription, in the opinion of the Jury, should be as short and forceful as possible."[52]

(Library of Congress)

The east facade of the proposed Tomb. The three alegorical figures represented "Peace, Victory, and the American Soldier." The wings on the center Victory figure were never carved on the finished Tomb.

The approved design for the Tomb of the Unknown Soldier was widely lauded. It perfectly maintained the shrine's delicate relationship to the Memorial Amphitheater while preserving its minimalist beauty. The central feature of the new monument was to be a white, rectangular, marble die stone erected over the Unknown's existing sarcophagus. Three allegorical, classical figures—Peace, Victory, and the American Soldier (later referred to as "Valor")—would adorn the eastern facing facade.[53] The north and south portions of the marble block were divided into three smaller panels by carved, low relief Doric columns. Each of the panels would be engraved with an inverted wreath, symbolically representing each of the six major American offensives (Ardennes, Bellau Wood, Chateau-Thierry, Meuse-Argonne, Aisne-Marne, Somme) during the Great War. The western panel on the Tomb, the one closest to the amphitheater, was initially left blank but was intended to accommodate an appropriate epitaph that would be determined at a later date. The *Evening Star* reported: "The winning design is a sarcophagus with Doric columns in alto-relief dividing the sides in three panels, each adorned by a wreath. The front panel in bas-relief three figures, symbolizing Peace, Victory, and the American Soldier."[54]

To preserve the existing panoramic vista of Washington, D.C. and to provide an unobstructed view of the Tomb, separate landscaping plans were independently approved for a new, eastern approach. This required major renovations to the existing plaza as well as the construction of new roads, parking areas, and walkways.[55] It would also require the building of a massive, granite memorial staircase to access the east facing front of the completed Tomb.

Another government appropriation for an additional $355,000 was awarded to Hegeman-Harris Company for the Memorial Plaza project.[56] This massive government contract had the added benefit of creating dozens of well-paying federal jobs during the onset of the Great Depression. As the *Evening Star* reported: "[the project had the] special purpose of giving immediate relief to unemployment conditions in the city."[57]

The military had previously imposed strict limitations on the size and scope of gravestones and monuments at Arlington in an effort to curb the use of the elaborate and unrestrained funeral architecture that was characteristic of the older burial sections in the cemetery. This was particularly important now in order to maintain the prominence of the Tomb and enforce a degree of symmetry. Existing cemetery sections 6 and 7, though, were located directly below the Tomb and several burials had already taken place. The War Department immediately ordered the: "discontinuing interments in the Section[s] in front of the Tomb of the Unknown Soldier...[since] interments being made in th[ese] section[s] interfered with the view from the Tomb and the approach which it was proposed to make leading up to the Tomb in connection with its completion."[58] But eventually 169 graves would have to be removed and relocated in order to clear the area for construction. This cost the government an additional $10,140 in expenses.[59]

At 4 PM, December 19, 1930, a small, public ground-breaking ceremony for the Memorial Plaza was held. Secretary of War, Patrick J. Hurley, was given the honor of shoveling the first layer of dirt to mark the beginning of construction. General Douglas MacArthur, the Chief of Staff of the Army, and Major General J. L. DeWitt, the Quartermaster General, participated in the modest ceremonies. Shortly thereafter, the Tomb area was closed to public visitation while construction was ongoing.[60]

———————

ONCE THE DESIGN for the Tomb had been formally approved and finalized, the search began in earnest to locate a suitable block of marble to bring Lorimer Rich's and Thomas Hudson Jones' artistic vision into reality. The Vermont Marble Company, located in the small town of Proctor near the juncture of the Green Mountains and the Taconic Range of the Appalachians, received the coveted government commission for the Tomb project.[61] The company's Danbury quarries had previously supplied the high-quality marble that had been used for the construction of the Memorial Amphitheater as well as for the existing sarcophagus of the current Tomb. Likewise, the Vermont Marble Company had continually produced the thousands of individual marble headstones needed to mark the graves of America's war dead that had been repatriated from the battlefields of Europe during the post war period.

The Rich/Jones plan for the Tomb required a massive block of marble. Such a large and rare stone could only be obtained from the company's Yule quarry in west-central Colorado. The mine was renowned for its 99.5% pure white, calcite marble, considered to be the finest in the world.[62] But locating and extracting such a huge block of marble intact from the mountain proved challenging. There was a persistent danger of mud slides and from falling stones, while the mine workers faced the daily hazards inherent in operating heavy machinery, chisels, saws, cables, cranes, and pulleys.

After months of meticulous searching and weeks of intense work, a 56-ton die stone ideally suited for the main Tomb was finally separated and cut out from the quarry walls in February 1931. Earlier, two smaller pieces had been harvested and these stones would comprise the base and cap for the monument.[63]

Workers, using a derrick and pully system, carefully hoisted the massive die block some 125-feet vertically from the quarry's floor to the mine's surface.[64] There, a rail trolley awaited to convey the heavy stone slowly down the steep mountain slope some 3.5 miles to the main railway. The die block was then loaded onto a flatbed train carriage for transportation back to Proctor, Vermont where the stone would be precisely cut, shaped, and polished in the company's workshops.[65] A wooden shipping crate was erected around the marble to protect it from damage during its transcontinental journey. Painted prominently on the outside of the shipping container was the inscription:

Monument to Unknown Soldier
Arlington Cemetery *Washington*
-From-
Colorado Quarries
Of
Vermont Marble Co.

During the marble block's long trip across the country, the sign simulatenously served as an act of patriotism as well as a powerful billboard advertisement for the sale of high-quality stone from the Vermont Marble Company.[66]

Once the Tomb block arrived at the Proctor workshops, skilled Italian artisans carefully dissected the Yule stones into seven smaller sections and smoothed, shaped, and hand polished the pieces.[67] Four of the cut sections were to serve as a sub-base for the Tomb, while a sixteen ton base, or plinth, would support the main stone. The die marble, now reduced in size to thirty-six tons, would serve as the central artistic element of the Tomb. It would finally be topped by a twelve ton capstone with all of the pieces assembled and joined on site at Arlington.[68]

The final sculpting of the Tomb was to be completed on the plaza under the close supervision of Thomas Hudson Jones. The famed Piccirilli brothers, the finest stone carvers in the nation, were contracted to do the actual carving and finishing of the monument.[69] However, once the Yule pieces finally arrived at Arlington and were inspected, a serious imperfection was discovered in one of the base stones and the piece had to be rejected. This caused a frustrating three-month delay in the project while a replacement stone was located and quarried. In the interim, all construction equipment, derricks, and screens were removed from the plaza to restore the Tomb to its original appearance.[70]

AS WORK WAS slowly progressing at the Tomb, the need to finalize the inscription for the blank west facing panel became a priority. The military decided that: "In order to secure the best possible inscription to be placed on the Tomb of the Unknown Soldier at Arlington Cemetery, it is suggested that persons skilled in the expression of patriotic sentiment be requested to suggest inscriptions. The sentiment should be the most lofty but should be expressed in the simple terms."[71] The Quartermaster General's office was autho-

(Library of Congress)

Workers at Arlington carefully lower the Tomb's die stone onto its base at Arlington National Cemetery.

(Library of Congress)

Joining the Tomb pieces on site at Arlington. Sculptor Thomas Hudson Jones closely supervised the final carving done by the Piccirilli brothers.

rized to make the final determination concerning the appropriate phraseology for the Unknown's epigraph, but due to the relatively small space allotted for the inscription, the engraving was strictly limited to just 20 words and eight lines to avoid overcrowding. In an effort to avoid the public criticism and censure that had occurred during the finalizing of the inscriptions for the Memorial Amphitheater, all deliberations were to be kept secret from the public. In a confidential memorandum in February 1932, Major General J. L. DeWitt confided: "The wording of this inscription has been kept strictly confidential up to this time to avoid the embarrassment of having to consider and act on a number of unsuitable inscriptions voluntarily submitted to the department."[72] The final decision on the Tomb's engraving would be announced as a *fait accompli* without any public input or debate.

After considerable haggling over the grammatical correctness and concise wording for an inscription, the military recommended, with Thomas Hudson Jones concurring, an epitaph that included the dates of American involvement in the Great War. It read:

Here Rests
In Glory
An Unknown
Soldier
Of the
United States
1917 – 1918

This recommendation, though, was eventually overruled and it was decided instead to inscribe the Tomb with the identical wording that marked the graves of all American unknowns still buried in Europe:

Here Rests in
Honored Glory
An American
Soldier
Known But to God[73]

With a decision finally reached on the inscription, the finishing work on the Tomb proceeded quickly. The completed Tomb of the Unknown Soldier was opened to the public on Saturday, April 9, 1932 without any formal dedication ceremonies. The *Evening Star* newspaper featured a picture of the finished monument on the front page of its "Society and General" section, noting: "Finally completed, the Tomb of the Unknown Soldier was opened to the public…the main section of the monument is the largest single piece of marble every quarried in this country."[74] Shortly thereafter, members of the Commission of Fine Arts visited the cemetery to see the completed memorial and were: "greatly pleased with it. The massiveness of the Tomb of the Unknown Solder and the approach providing for it makes the Tomb outstandingly distinctive among the monuments of the world."[75]

Thomas Hudson Jones, as the primary artist for the Tomb, requested permission to sign his work by discretely engraving his name under the foot of the "Peace" figure on the eastern facade of the monument. His request was rejected as inappropriate since the monument was, in fact, the grave of a nameless American soldier. Two decades later, though, both Lorimer Rich's and Thomas Hudson Jones' names were allowed to be inconspicuously inscribed on the top step of the eastern approach to the Tomb to properly acknowledge their artistic contributions to the monument.[76]

Just two weeks after the unveiling of the newly completed Tomb, the military contacted Lorimer Rich about the possibility of adding a protective railing around the monument: "Despite everything the guard can do, people, especially children will insist on putting their dirty hands over the carving and there is danger of souvenir hunters chipping off pieces of the sculpture, etc. Would like suggestion as to some suitable guard rail to keep spectators at a distance."[77] But the most significant military decision came a few years later in 1937, when the honor guard at the Tomb was extended to a perpetual 24-hour, 365-day vigil.

(Library of Congress)
A bugler plays "Taps" in front of the newly completed Tomb of the Unknown Soldier and the finished Memorial Plaza, 1932.

Endnotes

1 Thomas E. Luebke, ed. Civic Art. *A Centennial History of the U.S. Commission of Fine Arts*. Washington, D.C.: U.S. Commission of Fine Arts, 2013, p. 104.

2 Statement Accompanying the Report Made to the Honorable the Secretary of War by the Commission of Fine Arts on the Location and Design of the Monument to the Unknown Soldier available at the Commission of Fine Arts, Washington, D.C.

3 Thomas Hastings letter to Colonel Wainwright, 18 July 1922. Records Regarding the Design and Construction of the Tomb of the Unknown Solder 1926-1933. National Archives and Records Administration: RG 92 (20761665), Location NM81 1894-C.

4 Minutes of Meeting of Commission of Fine Arts, Washington, D.C.: 19/20 December 1922.

5 Luebke, p. 104. *The Evening Star* described the monument as follows: "A full sized model of the original design was placed on the tomb and carefully studied by the members of the commission. It consisted of a shaft about thirty-five feet high rising from the top of the tomb. It was decorated with several carved symbolic figures near the apex and inscribed with tributes to the unknown hero on the sides." "Weeks Rejects Unknown Soldier Monument Design," *The Evening Star*, 1 February 1924, p. 12.

6 Charles Moore letter to Secretary of War John Weeks, 19 December 1923.

7 "Rejection of Design for Monument Praised," *The Evening Star*, 11 February 1924, p. 17.

8 Burt Wagner. "Opposes Any Addition to Tomb of Unknown," *The Evening Star*, 29 April 1927, p. 8.

9 Colonial George Pemrose quoted in "War Mothers Urge Sentry at New Tomb," *The Evening Star*, 11 Nov. 1922, p. 19.

10 Letter from Colonel H. C. Bonnycastle to the Quartermaster General, 31 July 1923. National Archives, RG 92.

11 "Tomb of the Unknown," *The Evening Star*, 29 July 1923, p. 2.

12 *Ibid*., p. 2.

13 "Coolidge Favors Armed Guard at Tomb of the Unknown Soldier when Told of Disrespect," *The Evening Star*, 8 March 1926, p. 1.

14 Brigadier General H.H. Bandholtz quoted in Robert M. Poole. *On Hallowed*

Ground: The Story of Arlington National Cemetery. New York: Walker & Company, 2009, pp. 168-169.

15 Poole, pp. 168.

16 The fence was erected in 1923.

17 Memorandum for the Chief of Staff, 11 December 1923. National Archives, RG92.

18 *Washington Herald*, 9 March 1926.

19 Record Group 407 Entry (PI 17) 39 *Records of the Adjutant General's Office. Central Files, 1926 -1939:* http://catalog.archives.gov/id/7513377 Box 1271 [Location 370/81/1/2].

20 "Reports of Desecration Lead Davis to Order Guard," *The Evening Star*, 24 March 1926, p. 2.

21 HJ Res 185 was introduced on 2 March 1926.

22 National Archives, RG 407.

23 *Ibid*. The orders were sent to the Army on 24 March 1926 effective immediately.

24 Letter from Major General James McKinley to Florence Sullivan, circa January 1935, National Archives, RG 407.

25 Memorandum to the Adjutant General, 27 June 1927, National Archives, RG 407.

26 "Collection of Trophies at Unknown's Soldiers Tomb is Growing," *The Sunday Star*, 6 Nov. 1927, p. 85.

27 *Ibid.*, p. 85.

28 *Ibid.*, p. 85.

29 *Ibid.*, p. 85.

30 *Ibid.*, p. 85.

31 Kirke Larue Simpson. *The Unknown Soldier*. New York: Service Bulletin of the Associate Press, December 1921.

32 "Unknown's Tomb Finishing Urged," *The Evening Star*, 15 April 1927, p. 1.

33 *Ibid.*, p. 1.

34 Letter from Charles Moore, Chairman of the Commission of Fine Arts to Congressman Hamilton Fish, 19 January 1925.

35 *Ibid.*

36 "Designs for Tomb Competition Asked," *The Evening Star*, 12 Jan. 1928, p. 38.

37 Letter from Secretary of War Dwight F. Davis to President Calvin Coolidge, 12 November 1925, National Archives, RG 92.

38 "Guard Disapproved at Unknown's Tomb," *The Evening Star*, 24 Oct. 1925, p. 26.

39 Records Regarding the Design and Construction of the Tomb of the Unknown Soldier 1926-1933 RG 92: Records of the Office of the Quartermaster General 1774-1985: NARA 20761665/HMS Record 19796, Entry #NM81 1894-C.

40 Letter from Congressman Robert Luce to Charles Moore, 20 September 1927.

41 Letter from Thomas Hastings to Secretary of War Dwight F. Davis, 1 February 1928, National Archives, RG 92.

42 *Ibid.*

43 Fiorello LaGuardia (11 December 1882—20 September 1947).

44 Letter from Congressman Fiorello LaGuardia to Secretary of War Dwight F. Davis, 15 May 1928, National Archives, RG 92.

45 *Ibid.*

46 Letter from Secretary of War Dwight F. Davis to Congressman Fiorello LaGuardia, 7 June 1928, National Archives, RG 92.

47 Paul Philippe Cret (24 October 1876—8 September 1945).

48 Cret would eventually go on to complete several other war memorials including the Château-Thierry American Monument (1930) and the Flanders Field American Cemetery and Memorial (1937). His most memorable monument would be the Eternal Light Peace Memorial which was dedicated at the Gettysburg battlefield in 1938.

49 "Jury Soon to Pick Memorial Design," *The Evening Star*, 1 November 1928, p. 28.

50 Letter from Major General B. F. Cheatham to Thomas Hudson Jones and Lorimer Rich, 13 December 1928. National Archives, RG 92. The Commission

of Fine Arts approved on December 6; the Arlington Cemetery Commission approved it on December 7; and the American Battle Monuments Commission approved it on December 8.

51 The finalists in the Tomb competition were later revealed to be: Submission A: Sculptor Gaetano Cecere; Architects Harry Sternfeld and Boris Riaboff of Philadelphia; Submission B: Schweinfurth, Ripley & LeBoutillier of Boston; Submission C: James Earl Fraser; Architect Egerton Swartwout of New York; Submission D: Sculptor Thomas Hudson Jones; Architect Lorimer Rich of New York; Submission E: Sculptor Carl Mose; Architect Horace W. Peaslee; Landscape Architect Charles Eliot of Washington, D.C.

52 National Archives, RG 92.

53 The east façade of the Tomb is actually considered to be its front although today visitors can no longer approach the shrine from that direction.

54 "Unknown Soldier Design Selected," *The Evening Star*, 11 December 1928, p. 16.

55 The two parking areas would be located on opposite sites of the Memorial Plaza. They were named Wheaton Place and Otis Place. In the 1970s, Otis Place was reclaimed for grave space and became Section 7A. It is considered to be one of the most prestigious areas at Arlington due to its proximity to the Tomb. Among those buried in the section are such notables as General Jimmy Doolittle, heavyweight boxer Joe Louis, Actor (and Silver Star recipient) Lee Marvin, and Medal of Honor recipient Colonel Pappy Boyington.

56 National Archives, RG 92. The final cost of the completed project was $450,000.

57 "Work Is Ordered at Arlington to Give Jobless Immediate aid," *The Evening Star*, 18 December 1930, p. 1.

58 War Department Memo, 13 January 1929. National Archives, RG 92.

59 National Archives, RG 92.

60 The Tomb was closed on 5 February 1931.

61 The Vermont Mable Company remained in business until 1976. Its stone was used for such important public buildings as the U.S. Supreme Court, the American Red Cross building, the Senate Office Building, and the Lincoln and Jefferson Memorials. Catherine Miglorie, *Vermont's Marble Industry: Images of America*. Charleston, S.C.: Arcadia Publishing, 2013, pp.8, 122, 127.

62 *Ibid.*, p. 52.

63 *Ibid.*, p. 52. Also see Poole, p. 170.

64 Ron Bailey. *The Colorado Yule Marble Quarry: Our National Treasure*, DVD, 2009.

65 *Ibid.*, pp. 53, 54.

66 *Ibid.*, p. 113.

67 *Ibid.*, p. 82.

68 The die stone is 6'4" in width, 12'3.5" in length, and 5'5" high. It weighs thirty-six tons while the base/plinth is sixteen tons and the capstone twelve tons.

69 The Piccirilli brothers were the primary stone carvers of the Daniel Chester French magnificent statue of Lincoln in the newly completed Lincoln Memorial.

70 Records of the Office of the Quartermaster General, National Archives, RG 92.

71 War Department Memo, 18 May 1929. Records of the Office of the Quartermaster General, National Archives, RG 92.

72 War Department Memorandum from Major General J. L. Dewitt, 16 February 1932. Records of the Office of the Quartermaster General, National Archives, RG 92.

73 Records of the Office of the Quartermaster General, National Archives, RG 92.

74 *The Evening Star*, 11 April 1932, p. B-1.

75 Minutes of Meeting of Commission of Fine Arts, Washington, D.C.: 26 April 1932.

76 See https://tombguard.org/column/2014/06/thomas-hudson-jones/.

77 Memo to Lorimer Rich, 20 April 1932. Records of the Office of the Quartermaster General, National Archives, RG 92.

(Library of Congress)

The Tomb of the Unknown Soldier.

Chapter V

The World War II &
Korean Unknowns

"He gave his life for his country and we take this sacrifice to stand for all the unseen, unrecorded deeds of courage and compassion performed in these conflicts by the obscure many." - Beverley M. Bowie

erman forces launched a massive, surprise blitzkrieg against Poland on September 1, 1939. Honoring their pledge to assist Poland in the event of war, England and France declared war against Germany. Just two weeks later, the Soviet Union attacked the beleaguered country from the east and within days, the nation of Poland had once again been erased from the map of modern Europe. The "peace" negotiated at Versailles had lasted a scant 21 years and was, in reality, little more than a momentary interlude between the two global conflicts of the twentieth century.

President Franklin D. Roosevelt publicly asserted America's neutrality in the war, but the nation's sympathies clearly were with the British and French. In his first State of the Union Address to Congress since the renewal of hostilities in Europe, the President explained: "I can understand the feeling of those who warn the nation that they will never again consent to the sending of American youth to fight on the soil of Europe. But, as I remember, nobody has asked them to consent—for nobody expects such an undertaking."[1] Roosevelt argued that: "there is a vast difference between keeping out of war and pretending that this war is none of our business."[2] In fact, the President had already lifted the restrictions on crucial raw materials and other vital supplies in an effort to assist Britain and France in their war effort against the fascist powers. The President concluded his remarks to the joint session by declaring that: "We must as a united people keep ablaze on this continent the flames of human liberty, of reason, of democracy and of fair play as living things to be preserved for the better world that is to come."[3]

Of more immediate foreign policy concern to the United States, though, was the unimpeded military expansion by Japan throughout the Far East. The Imperial army had already seized the Korean peninsula and annexed large parts of China in an insatiable quest to secure much needed rubber and oil resources to fuel the small, island nation's war machine. The Japanese onslaught in Asia appeared to be unstoppable while their military offensives became notorious for their ruthlessness and brutality. Indeed, the Japanese army's "Three All" policy: loot all, kill all, burn all, sanctioned the murder of hundreds of thousands of innocent civilians. During the siege and subsequent occupation of the Chinese city of Nanking, an estimated 377,000 people perished during a six-week period of unrestrained rampage and pillage.[4]

By 1940, the Dutch, French, and British Pacific colonies were being directly threatened by Japan. Also in jeopardy were the American-controlled Philippine Islands. In an effort to deter further Japanese expansion, the Roosevelt administration unilaterally imposed a strict economic embargo on all American exports of steel, scrap iron, and oil. At the same time, the State Department entered into sensitive diplomatic negotiations in Washington with the Japanese ambassador, Kichisaburō Nomura, and special envoy to the United States, Saburō Kurusu. It was a last-ditch effort to avert a war.[5]

The Japanese government, though, was merely stalling and had little intention of reaching a political settlement or of curbing its military ambitions. In November 1941 as negotiations in D.C. continued, the Japanese military leadership dispatched a powerful naval armada under the command of Admiral Isoruku Yamamoto towards the American territory of Hawaii.[6] Consisting of six aircraft carriers, two battleships, and two heavy cruisers, the fleet launched a surprise and devastating air attack against American military installations on the island of Oahu on December 7, 1941.[7]

That Sunday morning, much of the United States' Pacific fleet was at anchor at Pearl Harbor, oblivious to the impending attack. Within minutes, Japanese planes sank eighteen ships, including five of the Navy's most formidable battleships. The USS *Arizona* (BB-39) was sunk when a Nakajima B5N2 "Kate" bomber dropped an 1,800-pound, armored-piercing bomb which struck the ship near its #2-gun turret. The shell exploded below deck, detonating 1.7 million pounds of gunpowder stored in the ship's magazine.[8] In an instant, 1,177 sailors and Marines perished. Most of their bodies (1,102) would never be recovered, forever entombed on the skeletal remains of the submerged ship.

Nearby, the USS *Oklahoma* (BB-37) was struck by several air-launched torpedoes. The crippled ship capsized at its mooring dock; 429 members of its crew were killed. Subsequent salvage efforts recovered 388 remains, but the bodies were so badly mutilated and commingled that they were considered to be individually unidentifiable and were buried as unknowns.[9] On the very first day of America's de facto entry into World War II, the United States had sustained 3,752 combat casualties—2,273 killed and 1,479 wounded.[10] The dead, including hundreds of unknowns, were quickly buried, mostly in existing cemeteries in Nuuamu and at the Schofield Barracks, and the Kaneohe Naval Air Station.

The day after the attack, President Roosevelt delivered an impassioned speech before an emergency session of Congress. The President declared that December 7, 1941, would forever be remembered as "a date which will live in infamy."[11] After chronicling and documenting Japanese deceit and aggression, the President urged Congress to issue a declaration of war, pledging that: "No matter

(National Archives)

The USS Oklahoma *capsized at Pearl Harbor, December 7, 1941. After salvage operations, 388 bodies from the ship were deemed to be unidentifiable and were buried as unknowns.*

how long it may take us to overcome this premeditated invasion, the American people in their righteous might will win through to absolute victory...With confidence in our armed forces -- with the unbounding determination of our people -- we will gain the inevitable triumph -- so help us God."[12]

The Senate responded by unanimously voting in favor of the war resolution. In the House of Representatives, the vote count was 388 yeas to one nay. The stalwart pacifist, Jeanette Rankin of Montana, was the only member of Congress to dissent. She justified her principled opposition to the war on the grounds that: "As a woman, I can't go to war and I refuse to send anyone else."[13] Rankin was the only legislator to have voted against American involvement in both of the world wars.

On December 11, honoring its Tripartite Pact (1940) alliance with the Japanese, Germany declared war on the United States. For the first time in American history, the United States faced the daunting prospect of waging a two-ocean, global war. Over the next four years, the nation would mobilize 16 million men to serve in the nation's armed forces. These servicemen were destined to see combat in distant and diverse locations. They would fight in the hot deserts of northern Africa in 1942 as well as at the Bulge during the brutally cold winter of 1944/45. Marines and GI's would assault entrenched Japanese forces on little known tropical islands (Tarawa, Eniwetok, Saipan, Kwajalein, Iwo Jima, et al.) while U.S. naval forces would engage rival enemy surface fleets in mortal combat. Japanese Kamikazes would inflict massive naval casualties in 1945 while submarines covertly prowled the seas preying on vulnerable allied shipping. In the four years of actual combat, over 416,000 American would die; of these, 79,000 servicemen were classified as either missing-in-action or unknown.[14] Only the American Civil War had exacted a greater toll on the nation's citizenry.

AFTER PRESIDENT ROOSVELT'S call to arms, the nation began to mobilize its massive industrial resources in support the war effort. Simultaneously thousands of patriotic young men and women flocked to military recruiting centers to volunteer to serve in the American armed services while the nation's military leadership began to develop a strategy to fight and defeat the Axis powers.

In early 1942, despite the loss of the Philippines Islands and other setbacks, the Navy began convoying the first American troops to England. In the Pacific, LTC Jimmy Doolittle successfully launched a squadron of 16 land-based B-25 bombers from the carrier, USS *Hornet*, and was able to attack the Japanese cities of Nagoya, Yokohama, and Tokyo. Although mostly symbolic and strategically insignificant, the daring raid boosted American morale and was seen as inflicting some revenge for the attack on Pearl Harbor. Two months later, Fleet Admiral Chester Nimitz and the Navy's Pacific Fleet were able to defend the American military garrison on Midway Island while carrier-based planes sank four Japanese aircraft carriers and one heavy cruiser.[15] It was the nation's first decisive victory against the Imperial Japanese Navy.

On August 6, 1942, all of the American newspapers were filled with stories about the global war. In Washington, D.C., the *Evening Star's* main headline read: "Red Reserves Strive to Check Nazi Gains." The battle for the Russian city of Stalingrad was just beginning and its outcome would likely determine the fate of the Soviet Union. In Northern Africa, the *Star* informed its readers that British bombers had launched an aerial assault against entrenched German positions at El Alamein in preparation for a combined allied offensive against General Erwin Rommel's famed Afrika Korps. The news also covered the visit of Queen Wilhelmina of the Netherlands to Washington, D.C. The 61-year old exiled monarch delivered an address to a special joint session of Congress. The Queen valiantly proclaimed that her occupied homeland would never submit to Nazi occupation and defiantly declared that the Dutch maxim was: "No surrender."[16] Of lesser note, in an obscure section of the newspaper was a small obituary notice. SGT Edward F. Younger, a 44-year old postal service employee, had suffered a heart attack and died at the Hines Memorial Hospital in Chicago. He was to be buried the following week at Arlington National Cemetery.

SGT Younger had received considerable publicity after having been given the honor of selecting the American Unknown Soldier in 1921. With the return to peace, though, the United States quickly consigned World War I to its historical memory and Younger left the army to return to civilian life. He lived in relative obscurity working as a civil service employee while living in Chicago with his wife, Agnes, and the couple's two children. Younger remained active in the Veterans of Foreign Wars (VFW) and was frequently invited to speak to veterans and patriotic groups about his role in the drama surrounding the burial of the Unknown Soldier. He visited Arlington Cemetery on occasion, most notably on May 30, 1930, when he proudly placed a wreath at the Tomb while wearing his old military uniform as well as his VFW hat.

Younger's flagged-draped casket arrived by train at Washington's Union Station on Wednesday, August 12. A small honor guard contingent from the American Legion, the VFW, and the Military Order of Cooties had assembled there to escort SGT Younger's coffin to Arlington where Younger was scheduled to lay-in-state in the small chapel at the Amphitheater for a few hours before the committal services.[17]

Younger was buried that afternoon in Section 18, just a short distance from the Memorial Amphitheater and the Tomb of the Unknown Soldier. His grave was marked by a plain, white tablet government headstone, virtually indistinguishable from those of his compatriots who had died during the Great War. There was no acknowledgment, inscription, or indication of the pivotal role that SGT Younger had played in the selection of America's Unknown Soldier some 21 years earlier.

AS A MATTER of government policy, the military's Graves Registration units had been decommissioned at the end of World War I. Their services were deemed to be unnecessary during times of peace since the armed services could rely upon local, civilian morticians and private funeral homes to deal with any isolated in-service deaths or training accidents. With the onset of World War II, however, the GRS was resurrected, albeit slowly. Considered to be primarily administrative units, the training and deploying of forensic morticians was initially assigned a low priority, subordinate to the more pressing need to mobilize and supply desperately needed combat forces. As Alvin Stauffer notes in his official history of Quartermaster Corps operations during World War II: "In the haste of arranging for the feeding, quartering, the training of troops...little attention had been given to care of the dead."[18] As such, during the initial stages of the war, GRS units were woefully understaffed despite the growing need to bring order and discipline to the recovery and identification of the dead.

Still, the military had learned important lessons from its experiences during the first world war. A typical GRS unit consisted of 260 enlisted men and five officers. As support troops, once combat operations had subsided in an area, GRS soldiers would sur-

(National Archives)

Two sailors pay tribute to the American dead. Graves Registration Units were deployed to bury combat casualites in newly created, temporary cemeteries.

vey a battlefield and conduct "sweeping operations" in an effort to locate all American casualties.[19] The unit's primary responsibility was to collect, evacuate, and identify bodies and then transfer these remains to centralized collection stations for additional process-ing. The bodies had first to be searched for any unused ammunition, hand grenades, military ordnance, or other weapons.[20] Since it was logistically impossible to transport the dead across thousands of miles of ocean during wartime, all casualties were interred in newly established, temporary cemeteries.[21] The individual graves had to be dug by hand and this arduous physical labor was detailed to specially assembled, ad hoc burial details. Ideally, graves would measure 5 feet deep, 2 feet wide, and 6.5 feet long and would be laid out in a symmetrical grid pattern.[22]

All American soldiers and sailors wore two identical stainless-steel dog tags into battle during World War II. These identification disks served as proof of identity for any serviceman killed-in-action. After a body was recovered and buried, one of the deceased's dog tags was nailed to the grave marker while the other was placed in the corpse's mouth to re-verify a soldier's identity in any subsequent reinternment.[23] Letters and personal effects were also effectively used to prove the identify of a soldier while technological advances in fingerprint analysis and dental record identification greatly reduced the number of unknowns.[24]

THE WAR IN the Pacific was generally one of maneuver rather than that of fixed position. The island-hopping strategy devised and developed by the Navy's leadership required American troops to make regular amphibious landings on remote tropical islands and atolls. Once captured islands were secured, they were frequently abandoned or held by a small contingent of garrison troops while the main American force moved on to the next Japanese stronghold. The temporary cemeteries established on these remote outposts were left to be consolidated and improved at a later date.

The Imperial forces proved to be a determined and formable enemy. Japanese soldiers preferred dying in battle, often in suicidal banzai charges, to the dishonor of surrender.[25] On the island of Tarawa, of the 4,200 Japanese defenders, only 17 soldiers lived to surrender to American forces. On Iwo Jima, just 200 enemy soldiers surrendered from an initial force of over 22,000 men.

(National Archives)

A Graves Registration soldier sprays sodium arsenite on the bodies of dead American marines on Iwo Jima. Battlefield sanitation became a major priority due to the tropical heat and torrential rains in the Pacific Theater.

Casualties were enormous in the Pacific Theater and it often took days or weeks before GRS troops were able to safely enter an area to tend to the dead. Even then, Japanese snipers posed a hazard to recovery teams. The tropical heat and constant rain made battlefield sanitation the most important priority for GRS troops. Rapidly decaying bodies on the battlefield had to be liberally sprayed with sodium arsenite to reduce odor and deter destructive insects.

The horrors of the Pacific war were typified on the island of Saipan. GRS troops had been assigned to survey a small, one-mile square area of the battlefield. During the intense, hand-to-hand fighting, 406 marines were killed, their bodies intermingled with those of hundreds of Japanese dead. It was reported that: "the difficulties of locating bodies among thousands of Japanese dead, of recovering bodies from shell holes which had filled with water, and the collection of bodies which had been badly shattered by mortar fire...the delay in evacuating our dead...had a depressing effect on the morale of troops in the area."[26]

Out of necessity, Grave Registration units had to bury the enemy's dead as well. Every effort was made to separate these soldiers from allied casualties and to inter them in separate cemeteries.[27] But the sheer number of enemy corpses precluded the digging of individual graves, so bulldozers were often deployed to escavate massive trenches. These large burial pits were filled in and marked only with a sign estimating the number of men interred there.[28]

The intensity of fighting on remote islands and heavily jungled areas meant that American combat units regularly had to deal with their own dead. In 1944, GRS troops were delayed in reaching Los Negros in the Admiralty Islands. The fighting for the island's crucial airfield had been fierce and unrelenting.[29] When GRS troops were finally able to arrive, they discovered a chaotic situation: "Many grave markers bore no information whatever; identification tags were attached to markers by strings rather than by screws; and Japanese bodies were not separated from American remains. Frequently, no effort was made to identify the unknown dead. As recording clerks were generally unavailable, facts needed to verify an identification were seldom indicated...some burial reports contained no information about the cause of death and neither listed nor noted the disposition of personal effects though they might have given valuable clues to identity."[30] This situation was in stark contrast to the battle on the Japanese island of Okinawa late in the war. There, experienced and battle-hardened GRS units were able to establish and organize eight military cemeteries on the island, including two that were for the exclusive use of the United States Marine Corps. The remains of 9,227 GI's and Marines had all been properly buried with only 328 remains classified as unidentifiable.[31] Each grave was marked by a white, wooden cross or star of David and a small 48-star American flag.

(National Archives)

A makeshift grave for an American soldier killed during the Palawan Massacre in 1944. All of the temporary military cemeteries would be consolodated and centralized after the war in both theaters of operations.

THE FIGHTING IN north Africa and in Europe during World War II was similarly fierce but more conventional. There were usually clearly delineated lines of battle and this enabled GRS troops to establish traditional cemeteries safely behind the steadily advancing armies. Still, it was a difficult mission since during the peak of the fighting (1944/45), GRS troops were having to process and bury over 500 American casualties each and every day.[32]

In March of 1945, General George Patton's 5th Division crossed the Rhine River and marched into Nazi Germany. Orders were issued that no U.S. soldiers should be buried on German soil. Instead, all remains were to be transported to predetermined collection points and then transported to GRS cemeteries in either Belgium or the Netherlands.[33] This policy proved to be impractical due to the high number of casualties incurred during the final offensives of the war, but eventually, the remains of all American soldiers were removed to allied concentration cemeteries after the end of the war.[34]

The massive saturation bombing campaigns launched against German cities had resulted in hundreds of allied aircraft being shot down over enemy territory. The ultimate fate of many of these air crews often was uncertain and contributed to a high number of missing-in-action (MIA). Since no bodies were recovered, government telegrams were sent out by the score informing stateside family members of the underdetermined status of their loved one. This vague classification caused uncertainty and consternation, but at least provided some solace in faint hope that a missing airman may have somehow survived his crash and been captured by the enemy. In-theater military commanders were deluged with letters from frantic family members desperate for any news concerning their missing loved one's fate. A typically poignant letter requested information concerning the fate of Captain John R. Walker:

> On July 14, 1943, he was shot down near Evereux, France. He was in a Spitfire. He was listing as 'missing in action.' I heard no other word from the government...I have tried to be patient all the past year, while waiting for definite news...I can't bear up un-

der the strain of not knowing for sure—or—this horrible uncertainty and indefiniteness...Is it possible that both the dog tags and plane identification can be destroyed so that I would never get any message except 'missing in action?'...I don't know how to plan my life when I don't know for sure about my husband. I've asked myself a thousand times a day for a whole year: Is he dead or is he alive? The worst part of it is we have a young son to be considered. If he is definitely known to be dead, please tell me the truth. I wish to be informed. I don't know whether to keep hoping and planning he is alive.[35]

As the allied armies advanced through France, Belgium, and the Netherlands, liberating cities, towns, and villages, local civilians assisted GRS search teams in helping locate the isolated graves of missing airmen and paratroopers who had been shot down or killed behind enemy lines. Major Joseph Shomon, who served with the 611th Quartermaster Graves Registration Company in France, recounts: "they showed us where Americans were buried, gave us access to burial records of Allied fliers, and even helped us disinter the bodies from their own cemeteries."[36]

Another major problem for GRS troops was the increasing number of soldiers, sailors, and airmen who died in common, catastrophic disasters that left their known remains commingled but impossible to identify individually. For the first time, the military authorized group burials. Oversized grave markers were used to indicate a mass burial, with the stone listing the names of all service members or crew, along with their individual ranks and the nature of the tragedy (plane crash, ship explosion, etc.).[37]

German forces finally surrendered to the allies on May 8, 1945. Later that summer, after the atomic bombings of Hiroshima and Nagasaki, the Japanese also agreed to surrender terms, finally bringing an end to the second World War. After four years of bitter and fierce combat, over 78,000 American soldiers, fully 20% of all casualties, remained classified as missing. This number included over 20,000 remains that had been recovered but were "Known but to God."[38]

BY THE FALL of 1945, the American people were exhausted and weary of war. The civilian-led "Bring Our Boys Home" campaign demanded that the government immediately return all of the country's soldiers and sailors to the United States and forced a rapid demobilizing of the nation's armed services. It also had the adverse effect of severely limiting the number of active duty troops available for post war clean-up and recovery operations.[39] There were literally hundreds of American cemeteries scattered throughout Africa, Europe and the Pacific. Many were in poor condition and located in remote and inaccessible areas.[40] It was imperative that these cemeteries be centralized and consolidated, but it was an Herculean task that would take years to accomplish.

Fully aware of the difficulties ahead, the military postponed all repatriations of the known dead for six months but promised Gold Star families: "that every desire of the next of kin [will] be fulfilled" and that they would eventually have the right to return their loved ones to the United States wholly at government expense.[41] The financial expense would be enormous. It was conservatively estimated that it would cost $700 to return each body from abroad. With 300,000 remains expected to be returned, over $210,000,000 would have to be budgeted to fund the effort.[42] Additionally, hundreds of surplus Liberty ships would have to be commandeered and repurposed for transport of the dead.[43]

Following the precedents established after World War I, the consolidation of the cemeteries in the Atlantic theater of operations proceeded relatively smoothly. Eventually 12 centralized burial grounds were established in Europe as well as one in Tunisia. All were placed under the administration of the American Battle Monuments Commission.[44] The Pacific, though, posed unique obstacles due to the remoteness of many of the temporary island cemeteries. The recovery of remains for reburial was difficult since: "Many individual grave markers were missing, knocked down, or disarranged. Some of the burial places were so badly over grown that they were scarcely recognizable as cemeteries."[45] Other graves had been disturbed and desecrated by vandals searching for war relics and valuables. There was also the problem of the disproportionate number of missing-in-action and unknowns since: "many deaths occurred at sea or on beaches where bodies were swept out into the ocean, thus becoming unrecoverable. Plane crashes over oceanic expanses added to the number of non-recoverable dead."[46]

It was ultimately decided to create just two concentration cemeteries for the Pacific dead. One was established in Manila and would be under the direction of the American Battle Monuments Commission.[47] The other cemetery was to be constructed on the island of Oahu. Since Hawaii was still an American territory, it would fall under the jurisdiction of the Veterans Administration.[48]

In February 1948, Congress appropriated the necessary funds for the establishment of the National Memorial Cemetery of the Pacific (the Punchbowl) in Honolulu.[49] The picturesque site was located above the city in a dormant volcanic caldera. The cemetery made its first interment in January 1949 when the remains of an American unknown soldier who had died during the Japanese attack on the island on December 7, 1941 were buried.[50] Over the ensuing three months, Phase 1 (January 4 through March 25, 1949), 9,940 soldiers, sailors, and Marines were buried at the Punchbowl cemetery, with an average of 200 interments per day. Most of these American servicemen had died during fighting in China, Burma, Saipan, Guam, Okinawa, and Iwo Jima. The new cemetery remained closed to public visitation during this time while infrastructure construction on walkways, approaches, and memorials continued.[51] Phase 2 (June 13 through June 23, 1949) saw an additional 1,778 interments, casualties mostly from the battles for Wake Island and Formosa.[52] Eventually, over 13,000 World War II dead would be buried at the National Memorial Cemetery of the Pacific. Each of the graves was initially marked by the traditional white, Christian cross or six-pointed Star of David. Unbeknownst to the general public, though,

(National Archives)
The National Memorial Cemetery of the Pacific (the Punchbowl) in Honolulu, Hawaii. The cemetery was one of two created to bury the American dead from the Pacific Theater after the end of the war.

the military had always deemed these grave markers as temporary and in 1951, all were removed and replaced by flat, granite stones. This led to a major controversy and a public outcry, but the Quartermaster General justified the action, claiming: "Crosses do not mark the graves of our dead in other national cemeteries. No cross marks the burial of our revered Unknown Soldier. From Arlington to Golden Gate, from Puerto Rico to Hawaii, the Government's markers in national cemeteries for all our hero-dead are of the traditional designs…[s]ome are upright and some are flat. None is in the form of a religious emblem."[53]

IT WAS TACITLY assumed that once the war was over, an Unknown Serviceman from World War II would be buried at the Tomb. On September 6, 1945, just four days after the Japanese Instrument of Surrender had been signed on board the USS *Missouri*, Congressmen Melvin Price of Illinois introduced the sanctioning legislation for just such a burial at Arlington.[54] The resolution was passed into law (Public Law 429) the following year on June 24, 1946. It mandated that the military bury a World War II Unknown: "near or beside the remains of the Unknown American Soldier of the First World War."[55] The legislation further ordered that this be completed by no later than May 30, 1951. "By that time," it was believed that "the American Graves Registration Service would have searched for, recovered, identified, declared unidentifiable, or declared non-recoverable most of the dead of World War II."[56]

The popular legislation, however, had failed to consider the stark realities and logistical challenges that were being faced by the military after four years of brutal, global combat. The Quartermaster Corps predicted that battlefield cleanup operations would take years to complete. Moreover, the GRS had established a staggering 454 cemeteries in 86 different countries during the war. These burial grounds contained the remains of hundreds of thousands of American soldiers, sailors, airmen, and Marines. Most of these remains would eventually have to be disinterred and returned to the United States. Included in these stark statistics were thousands of remains that were still classified as "unknown." Brigadier General G. W. Horkan maintained that the GRS's main post-war priority was to re-examine and identify as many of these as possible by: "using every scientific means to identify these bodies."[57] He also warned that: "we cannot bring a body back to Washington to be buried as an unknown soldier until we have exhausted every means known to identify those that are now unknown. The time element is very problematic."[58]

Regardless of these realities or potential consequences, the military was forced to comply with the provisions of the new legislation even though no one knew how to accommodate a second crypt at the existing Tomb. This prospect had never been considered during the development of the original design. Any subsequent memorial would have to be of equal stature to that of the World War I Unknown and the military knew that this was going to cause a huge "public relations problem" as well as serious "architectural problems and some engineering problems".[59]

The structural details for the construction of a new crypt or a new tomb remained unresolved by 1948, but contingency plans still had to be developed for the selection and burial of a World War II Unknown. The initial proposal called for disinterring five sets of unidentifiable remains. These bodies would come from all of the geographic regions where American forces had been engaged during the war: Europe, the Far East, the Mediterranean, the Pacific, and the Africa-Middle Eastern sector. The unknown candidates would be brought to Philadelphia and the formal selection of the World War II Unknown Serviceman would take place at Independence Hall on May 26, 1951. Interment at Arlington would take place the following day, Memorial Day.[60]

GENERAL OF THE ARMIES, John J. Pershing, died on July 15, 1948 at Walter Reed Hospital in Washington, D.C. The former commander of the American Expeditionary Forces had been in declining health for several years, suffering from complications from congestive heart failure as well as the effects of a serious stroke. Pershing had been a full-time resident at the hospital since 1944 and was confined to a special wing that had been set up to accommodate his needs. The General was 87 years old.[61]

The official plans for General Pershing's state funeral had long been established by the Military District of Washington, but the public announcement of his demise had to be delayed since President Truman was en route back to Washington by train and unavailable. The President had been in Philadelphia attending the Democratic National Convention which had just nominated him for re-election. Immediately upon arrival at Union Station that morning at 5:15 AM, staff informed Truman of Pershing's passing. The White House soon thereafter issued an official statement noting the General's: "tireless energy, unswerving loyalty and constant devotion to duty."[62] The

President ordered all of the nation's flags lowered to half-staff during the official mourning period. Truman stated that: "In World War I, [Pershing] led the greatest army this country had, up to that time, been called to assemble...the nation will ever hold him in grateful remembrance."[63]

Pershing was the highest-ranking military officer in American history. Although throughout his later career, he only wore four silver stars on his uniform, he was senior to all of the nine five-star generals that had been appointed during World War II.[64] Only George Washington would ever achieve a comparable rank, albeit posthumously. The first President was awarded his six-star grade by act of Congress during the nation's bicentennial celebrations in 1976.[65]

General Pershing's casket was first taken to the Walter Reed chapel where a private viewing was held for close friends and family members. An honor guard from the 3D Infantry was assigned to stand vigil. The next day, at 1 PM, the coffin was removed from the chapel and taken by hearse to the U.S. Capitol for the official laying-in-state in the Rotunda. It was placed upon the Lincoln catafalque, the same bier that had held the remains the Unknown Soldier from World War I some 27 years earlier. After brief, official ceremonies, the Capitol was open to visitation to allow the general public to view the opened casket.[66]

The state funeral for General Pershing was held on Monday, July 19. The casket was carried down the steps of the Capitol building and placed upon a gun caisson drawn by six white horses. A black, caparison horse followed directly behind, its riderless saddle carrying a sheathed sword with boots reversed in stirrups to signify the death of a fallen leader. Generals Eisenhower and Bradley marched on foot in the mile-long procession as it slowly made its way down Constitution Avenue, over the Memorial Bridge and into Arlington National Cemetery. Over 300,000 people gathered along the parade route despite a brief, soaking summer rain storm.[67]

(National Park Service)
The arrival of the casket of General John J. Pershing, 19 July 1948, at his gravesite at Arlington National Cemetery. Pershing commanded American forces during World War I and was the highest ranking military officer in the nation's history.

When the caisson reached the east plaza of the Memorial Amphitheater, it stopped directly in front of the Tomb of the Unknown Soldier. It was meant to be a deeply symbolic moment—the commander of all of the American forces in World War I paying final tribute in death to one of his own common soldiers who made the supreme sacrifice during the war. Pershing had been instrumental in his selection and burial in 1921 and even dedicated his wartime memoirs, *My Experiences in the First World War*, "To The Unknown Soldier."[68]

Pershing's flag-draped casket was then carried by joint service body bearers into the Memorial Amphitheater through the south entrance to the apse area for a brief Episcopal ceremony. Among the mourners on stage was President Harry Truman, who, as a young man, had served with Battery B, 129th Field Artillery and had been one of Pershing's junior officers.

At the conclusion of the Amphitheater service, the casket was returned to the awaiting caisson on the plaza. The funeral procession then proceeded to the gravesite located in Section 34. Pershing had expressed a desire to be buried among his men and his grave would be marked only with a standard government headstone. A short Anglican committal ceremony was conducted by chaplain Major General Luther D. Miller and the Very Reverend John Suter at the gravesite before Pershing's mortal remains were committed to the soil.[69]

In 1968, Pershing's grandson, 1LT Richard W. Pershing, was killed in Vietnam during the Tet Offensive while serving with the 101st Airborne. He was buried next to the General.[70]

AS THE DEADLINE was rapidly approaching for selecting and interring a World War II Unknown, the Commission of Fine Arts was seriously debating proposals for the construction of an appropriate crypt on the plaza. All of the members were well aware that the existing Tomb was the nation's most cherished shrine to American servicemen and had become a nationally revered landmark. Indeed, the Commission acknowledged that: "The massiveness of the Tomb of the Unknown Soldier and the approach providing for it makes the Tomb outstandingly distinctive among the monuments of the world."[71] So any substantive architectural changes to the plaza or the Memorial Amphitheater building would prove contentious and could potentially disrupt the Tomb's delicate aesthetics.

It was decided to keep the deliberations secret to avoid any unnecessary controversy while allowing members to discuss alternatives openly, without public censure. Several serious alternatives were proposed, presented, discussed, and debated, including the possibility of constructing two identical crypts in front of the existing Tomb. This would require disinterring the World War I Unknown and re-burying the remains on the plaza in a new crypt adjacent to the World War II Unknown Serviceman. The Lorimer Rich-designed Tomb would remain in place as a common monument to both Unknowns, since it had never inscribed with any identifying date. This design, though, was quickly vetoed on the grounds that the American people would see disturbing the existing grave of the World War I Unknown as an act of defilement.[72] Indeed, the military made a forceful argument that: "...the actual moving of the body would be resented by all peoples in the country, as disturbing the grave of a man who has been buried there as long as he has."[73] An Army colonel further explained that: "...veterans would object to touching this tomb at all, they would consider it a desecration."[74]

Another idea that initially seemed promising was to construct a duplicate tomb on the plaza that would be: "similar in size, design and material to that of World War I."[75] This approach was favored by Lorimer Rich, who prepared preliminary architectural drawings for presentation to the Commission.[76] His first plans required radical structural revisions to both the existing plaza and to the Memorial Amphitheater building. The underused Trophy Room would be completely demolished, as would its east steps. This would open up the Amphitheater's circular colonnade and create a magnificent vista that would serve to frame and accentuate the two identical Tombs located on the plaza. Quartermaster General, Major General K.L Hastings, objected to these radical alterations, noting that: "... we have wondered about the reaction of Congress to the destruction of the monument which received many thousands of dollars in appropriated funds several years ago and was dedicated to all the dead of all our wars."[77] Chairman of the Fine Arts Commission and civil engineer, Gilmore David Clarke, likewise questioned the appropriateness of destroying or fundamentally altering an existing structure: "When the suggestion came for opening up the view from the back of the amphitheatre straight through to look out over Washington as one scheme which would involve the destruction of the Carrère and Hastings Building, we raised the question in our own minds as to the propriety of it, because, after all, our predecessors on this Commission approved of it at one time or another...it has always been a question in our minds as to whether, with a change in the Commission, we feel justified in destroying something that our predecessors have once approved...just because tastes change is no

(Commission of Fine Arts)

An aerial view of the Memorial Amphitheater and the Tomb of the Unknown Soldier. A proposal was made to tear down the Trophy Room and open up the colonade area to frame a new tomb for a World War II Unknown.

(Commission of Fine Arts)

A modified model by architect, Lorimer Rich. This rejected proposal called for the construction of an identical Tomb on the plaza for the World War II Unknown and tearing down the steps to the Trophy Room.

reason why we should express our views by destroying what was in perfectly good taste thirty years ago."[78] Rich's first proposal was eventually rejected by the Commission of Fine Arts, after members: "expressed disapproval of that scheme, since it would mean virtual destruction of a memorial building that had been erected and dedicated to honor the Grand Army of the Republic."[79] Rich modified his plans to retain the Trophy Room but proposed removing the east steps to create a larger plaza area to accommodate another tomb. This idea was rejected as well.

After two years of contentious deliberations and impasse, it was agreed in June 1950 that the current Tomb would have to suffice as a monument for both Unknowns and that the World War II Unknown would be buried in a newly constructed vault. The Quartermaster General described the plan as follows: "...a shaft be built, a permanent shaft, in front of the present monument or sarcophagus, and the body lowered to a prepared vault beneath the present World War I vault on the day of the interment. That mean[s] that the present World War I vault would not be disturbed in any way, that both would be buried under the present sarcophagus erected there."[80] The *New York Times* explained further: "Rather than construct a second monument and perhaps disturb the simplicity of the war memorial's setting...an opening...at the west side of the monument [will] provide access to the burial vault. The opening will be lined with black marble and through this space at the interment ceremonies will pass the casket of the World War II hero."[81]

But even after finally reaching an agreement on how to actually inter a World War II Unknown, serious concerns were raised about what would happen in the event of future conflicts. Army General Renfrow hypothetically asked: "Of course, the question of building one new sarcophagus for World War II brings up the question: Where would you put World War III, if you had it?"[82] He acknowledged that: "...the veterans of World War I...want to hold this tomb as the center tomb for all the honors to be conferred and not permit the World War I man to be shoved aside, as the new ones come along."[83]

The other issue the was faced by planners concerned the inscription on the existing Tomb's west-facing façade. Secretary of State, General George C. Marshall, ardently felt that the engraving needed to be altered to accurately reflect the new burial of the World War II Unknown. This would be a relatively simple process and require altering only two words. The new inscription would read: "Here Rest in Honored Glory American Heroes Known but to God." President Truman authorized the change.[84]

With all of the contentious issues finally resolved, it was now possible to proceed with the actual selection process for a World War II Unknown. Potential candidates were to be chosen by the military prior to March 15, 1951, with the selection process taking place at Independence Hall in Philadelphia that May. The final burial at Arlington was scheduled for Memorial Day. The *Evening Star* reported: "The selection of the body of the 'Unknown Serviceman' of World War II will take place immediately following the burial or reburial of all known dead of the late war...this will probably occur sometime during 1951.[85]

On June 25, 1950, Communist North Korea (DPRK) launched a full-scale military invasion of South Korea (ROK). This foreign policy crisis forced President Truman to order a cessation of all ceremonial planning for the burial of the World War II Unknown, as the United States began to formulate its response to this overt act of North Korean aggression.

———————

THE KOREAN WAR was never constitutionally declared by Congress. It was, instead, a conflict of presidential prerogative rather than of Congressional decree and the first American war to be fought with limited military objectives. This often led to frustrations and uncertainty.

The DPRK invasion of the South was initially spectacularly successful. In just a matter of days, the South Korean capital of Seoul had fallen; ROK forces had been routed and were in full retreat. The demoralized remnants of the army, aided by an injection of American forces, were finally rallied near Pusan in the southeastern corner of the Korean peninsula. President Harry S Truman authorized the General of the Army, Douglas MacArthur, to resupply and reinforce the beleaguered armies from his headquarters in occupied Japan. Truman denounced the "breach of the peace" and called upon the United Nations Security Council to act by authorizing military intervention.

The Soviet representative to the UN, Jacob Malik, was boycotting meetings of the Security Council in protest over the continuing presence of Chiang Kai-shek's Republic of China as one of the five permanent members of the body. The Soviets insisted that the Nationalists be expelled, and that official recognition be granted to the "legitimate" government of Mao Tse Tung's People's Republic of China (PRC).[86] Thus, no Soviet delegate was present at the Security Council meeting on July 7 to cast a veto of UN Resolution 84. It passed with a vote of seven for, none against, with three abstentions, and authorized the use of military force in the defense of South Korea as part of an international police action to deter open aggression.[87] Ultimately, 21 nations would contribute combat forces to Korea, although the bulk of the fighting was again left to the United States armed services.

General MacArthur was able to deploy enough troops to hold onto the Pusan perimeter. In September, in a bold and daring effort to outflank the over-extended DPRK's forces, MacArthur ordered a perilous, amphibious landing at Inchon. The attack was a complete surprise and successfully cut off DPRK supply lines. In a desperate effort to preserve their army, the North Koreans retreated north across the old 38th parallel boundary. Rather than declare victory with the restoration of the pre-war borders, MacArthur received permission from the Joint Chiefs of Staff to pursue the enemy and "to conduct military operations north of the 38th parallel in Korea," but was restricted from bombing bridges spanning the Yalu River or attacking communist sanctuaries and supply centers in Manchuria.[88]

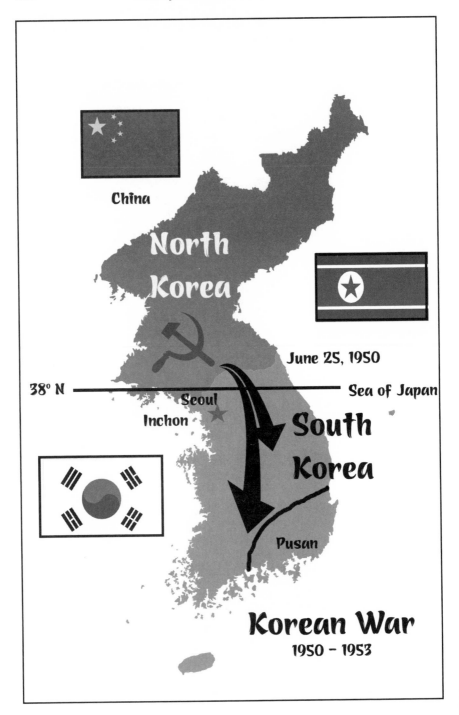

By late November, total victory seemed imminent. But, as UN troops approached the Chinese border, Mao Tse Tung intervened with over 300,000 fresh troops from the Chinese People's Liberation Army (PLA). It was a decisive move and a major escalation of the war. General MacArthur noted: "Red China...[had] entered into open war against the United States forces and those allied with us."[89] Moreover: "the limitless capabilities of the entire Chinese nation, with Soviet logistical support," posed a mortal threat to the UN war effort.[90]

The ensuing brutal winter fighting forced American and UN forces to withdraw after sustaining staggering losses. At the Battle of the Chosin Reservoir (27 November-13 December 1950), the United States alone incurred 17,843 casualties, killed and wounded, including 4,894 who were listed as missing-in-action. The bodies of recovered Marines and GI's were so badly frozen that they had to be thawed in special heating rooms before they could be processed and prepared for burial.[91]

THE GRAVES REGISTRATION SERVICE was again reactivated at the onset of hostilities in Korea. By September 1950, though, there were only 30 GRS soldiers in-country and this small contingent of men was responsible for dealing with all of the American battlefield deaths. Despite being woefully understaffed, the GRS successfully tagged and buried hundreds of soldiers in newly created, utilitarian in-country cemeteries.[92]

As the war progressed and intensified, though, the battle lines became fluid and unpredictable. Out of necessity, many isolated military units were once again forced to bury their own dead in crude graves that were: "often no more than a hasty drop in a foxhole or a shallow indention scratched at the bottom of a shell crater covered with a scattering of earth."[93] The muddled military situation also resulted in several previously established GRS cemeteries being overrun by enemy forces and virtually destroyed, thereby increasing the overall number of Americans classified as missing.

(National Archives)
A military chaplain prays over the bodies of American servicemen killed during the Korean War. In three years of bitter combat, the United States lost 36,914 men.

In February 1951, the United States military stopped all in-country burials and, for the first time, initiated a policy of concurrent return for soldiers killed-in-action. From this point forward, the dead would be transported by ship from the port of Inchon to the Central Identification Unit at Camp Kokura, Japan. There, the bodies would be examined, identified, embalmed, and prepared for return to Fort Lee, Texas for additional processing.[94] A few months later, the removal of KIA's from Korea was conducted exclusively by air evacuation.[95]

THE KOREAN WAR deteriorated into a bloody stalemate with neither side gaining any significant advantage. For two years, the battle lines were relatively stagnant, with the armies entrenched near the original 38th parallel boundary. In November 1952, General Dwight

Eisenhower was elected as the nation's 34th President of the United States. Shortly before taking office, he fulfilled a campaign promise by personally visiting South Korea to assess the military situation. Several weeks later, Josef Stalin, the Premier of the USSR, died, and the ensuing internal political turmoil over succession cast doubt over the continuation of Soviet military and economic support for the communist North Korean regime.[96] These events served as a catalyst for armistice negotiations. A cease fire was finally agreed to and signed at Panmunjom on July 27, 1953. It called for: "a complete cessation of all hostilities" and essentially a return to the status quo antebellum.[97]

During the three years of sustained fighting in Korea, over 1,789,000 men had served in the American armed services. The United States lost a staggering 36,914 men killed during the war, of which 8,126, some 25% of the total number of casualties, remained classified as missing. This number included 848 remains which had been recovered but were deemed to be unidentifiable. All of these unknowns were eventually re-interred at the National Memorial Cemetery of the Pacific, the "Punchbowl," in the territory of Hawaii.[98]

THE CEASE FIRE IN Korea led to a renewed interest in completing the long-postponed interment of an Unknown from World War II. But because of the nation's most recent war, Congress promptly amended its initial legislation to mandate the additional burial of an Unknown Serviceman from the Korean War. This decision effectively negated the previously approved new vault plan and further complicated the complex architectural issues on how to appropriately modify the existing Tomb to accommodate further interments.[99]

There was already a public debate about making any major changes at the Memorial Amphitheater. Indeed, for many Americans, the Tomb had transcended from being a gravesite to becoming a sacred national monument that symbolically honored all American servicemen who had died while in service to the country, regardless of the conflict. Charles M. Beverly echoed these sentiments, writing to a newspaper in 1956: "I think that a single tomb is enough," while A.W. Edwards went even further suggesting: "In the broadest sense, the present tomb can signify all of our war dead...it can be envisioned as representing other service dead, as well...Our soldier is quite sufficiently the truest and most meaningful translation of all our war dead into a proud and impressive memorial. Its beautiful simplicity and its stern young guard leave nothing to be desired. Let the tradition stand!"[100] An army private, P.J. Powers, concurred, claiming that: "In my opinion, additional entombments would only lessen the pride and reduce the symbolism of the monument."[101] Even a World War II Gold Star mother felt that the existing Tomb of the Unknown Soldier was adequate, poignantly noting that: "My son gave his life on Iwo Jima, yet I think of the Tomb as a memorial to him and all of the boys of all wars who made the supreme sacrifice."[102] A more sardonic critic dismissed plans for additional burials by flippantly asserting: "OK! So, let's dig up an unknown from our Civil War—one from the North and one to represent the South. And say, what about the Alamo? If we let them change the Tomb, we might as well move the Capitol to someplace else."[103]

There was, though, a large percentage of Americans who favored burying Unknowns from World War II and Korea at Arlington. Mary E. Brown argued in a persuasive letter to the Washington *Daily News*: "I am in favor of burying a World War II unknown servicemen and also a Korean War unknown serviceman at Arlington. I think it is only fitting and respectful to the families of the other war dead." Z. H. O'Neal put it succinctly: "Didn't the dead of World War II give as much as the dead of World War I?"[104]

The ongoing public debate aside, the military was proceeding with its planning for the Congressionally mandated interments. Architect Lorimer Rich was again commissioned to work out designs for the new memorial vaults. After considering various options and inspecting scale models erected on site in April 1956, he settled upon the construction of two identical crypts flanking the existing Tomb marked with only a plain white marble crypt cov-

(Commission of Fine Arts)
Scale models of possible crypt covers on display at the Tomb, April 1956. Ultimately, it was decided to use flush, white marble stones for the World War II and Korean Unknowns and to inscribe them only with the dates of the conflicts--1941-1945 and 1950-1953.

ers.[105] Measuring 8'2" x 3' x 6," these gravestones would be set flush with the ground and inscribed only with the dates of their respective conflicts—1941-1945 for the World War II Unknown and 1950-1951 for the Korean Unknown. The inscription on the main Tomb's façade was now considered to be generic enough to remain unchanged, although the dates 1917-1918 would be added to the base of the monument for continuity and to acknowledge the presence of the World War I Unknown. A $139,100 government contract was awarded to John McShane, Inc. for the construction and preparation of the new crypts. During the construction phase beginning in November 1957, a six-foot privacy fence was erected on the plaza to hide the work from public view. The sentinels were temporarily relocated to the lower steps on the east side of the Tomb, as were all wreath ceremonies.[106]

WHILE CONSTRUCTION WAS proceeding on the new crypts at Arlington, the selection process for the two new Unknowns began. Choosing a representative Unknown from World War II, however, posed unique problems since American forces had been engaged in combat operations over a wide geographical area. In order to be truly representative of all of the nation's combat forces, it was determined that two candidates would have to be selected, one from the European/North Africa theater of operations and the other from the Pacific theater. Once the two preliminary candidates had been officially designated, the bodies would then be brought together for a final selection ceremony. Their two caskets had to be identical and indistinguishable in order to forever conceal the actual geographic origin of the candidate that was ultimately selected as the Unknown Serviceman from World War II.

The draft plan for selecting the Unknowns from World War II and Korea was finally approved by all branches of the armed services on November 7, 1957.[107] For the Transatlantic selection, a list of 290 potential candidates was compiled from the 13 American cemeteries in France, Belgium, Luxembourg, the Netherlands, Italy, and Tunisia. It was further ordered that: "Upon disinterment of the remains of a selected candidate-unknown, the officer in charge of the recovery team will conduct a thorough investigation for any identification media not heretofore annotated on the records for the particular candidate-unknown. If any identification media are discovered, the candidate-unknown will be immediately re-interred, and an alternative candidate-unknown will be disinterred and similarly investigated."[108] By late April 1958, the bodies of 13 unknowns had been successfully disinterred with each remain verified for nationality and certified by the officer in charge of the recovery team as unidentifiable. These bodies were then placed: "into a transfer case" and all "records, papers, files or transcripts that pertain to the particular remains" were burned, leaving no trace.[109]

Each of the 13 caskets were sent to the Army Mortuary in Frankfurt, Germany. There all of the bodies were: "identically en-

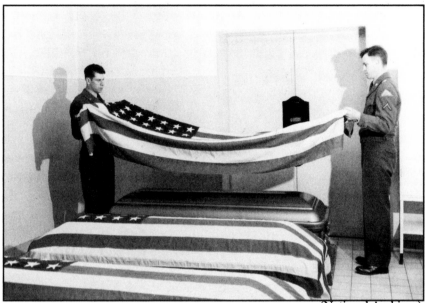

(National Archives)

The caskets of the 13 candidates-unknown from the Transatlantic theater are covered with American flags prior to the selection ceremonies. The bodies were all placed in identical caskets to disguise their point of orgin.

(National Archives)

Major General Edward G. O'Neill selects the Transatlantic candidate, World War II Unknown. The ceremony was held at the Epinal American Cemetery.

shrouded…to preclude any possibility of identity as individual un-knowns."[110] The bodies were then carefully re-casketed, covered with an American flag, and rearranged to prevent any possible link to a specific region in accordance with orders that: "the remains will be prepared and interchanged between caskets by separate mortuary teams to insure that there is no way of identifying any candidate with a specific cemetery."[111]

The caskets were finally convoyed to the Epinal American Cemetery in France, where the final selection ceremony for the Transatlantic Unknown was scheduled for Monday, May 12. The identical, flagged-draped caskets were assembled on the terrace of the cemetery's central memorial building located at the north end of the Court of Honor. A large, 48-star American flag flew at half-staff. The honor of selecting the Unknown was given to Major General Edward G. O'Neill, commanding general of the U.S. Army Com-munication zone.[112] General O'Neill made his selection by placing a round floral wreath consisting of red and white carnations before one of the caskets. "Taps" was then played, followed by the National Anthem. After the conclusion of the brief ceremonies, the casket of the Candidate-Unknown from the Transatlantic Theater was carried by a joint service casket team to an awaiting hearse. The unselected candidates were reburied without any further acknowledgment or recognition.[113]

The Transatlantic Unknown was transported to the Ameri-can NATO Air Base at Toul-Rosières and flown to Naples, Italy on board a Lockheed C-130 Hercules transport. From there, the casket was conveyed to the port and loaded onto the destroyer, USS *Blandy* (DD-943). The ship left Naples heading for a scheduled rendezvous with the guided missile heavy cruiser, USS *Canberra* (CAG-2), off of the Virginia Capes. _____

THE SELECTION OF the Korean Unknown Serviceman proved to be a relatively simple affair in contrast to the complexities sur-rounded the World War II Unknown. As of 1958, there were 9,037

CERTIFICATE

15 May 1958

We, the undersigned, certify that all records and identifying materials
known to exist in this command, concerning the four unknown remains from the
Korean Conflict, which were disinterred at the National Memorial Cemetery of
the Pacific on 7 May 1958, have been destroyed.

JAMES J. HUMES
Lt Cmdr, MC
U. S. Navy

IRA P. NORFOLK
Major, USMC

JACOB E. RUBENSTEIN
Major, QMC
U. S. Army

I. C. MCLEAN
Lt Cmdr, USCG

HUGH V. MCBRIDE
Major, USAF

(National Archives)

Signed affidavit attesting to the destruction of all records concerning the disinterments of the unknowns. This was done to ensure perpetual anonymity.

(National Archives)

Sergeant Ned Lyle selects the Unknown Serviceman from the Korean War at the National Memorial Cemetery of the Pacific. There were 848 unknowns from the war, all reinterred at the Punchbowl in Hawaii.

men still classified as missing-in-action from the war.[114] The 848 recovered bodies that were certified as unidentifiable had all been interred at a single location, the National Memorial Cemetery of the Pacific (the Punchbowl) in Honolulu, Hawaii.[115] A classified inventory of the most likely candidates for the Korean Unknown was compiled and from this list, four bodies were disinterred on May 7. Their remains were taken to the U.S. Mortuary at Kapalama Basin in Honolulu and then carefully examined. It was verified that no identification was possible and the bodies were then: "wrapped in new burial sheets and blankets and placed in four new identical caskets."[116] They were finally removed to a special holding area and placed under a strict military guard with no one allowed admittance.[117] All records and files concerning the selection process and disinterments were ordered destroyed to ensure perpetual anonymity.

On May 14, Colonel Austin Miller entered the holding area containing the caskets. He secretly rearranged the four coffins to further obscure any possible clues as to their place of origin. The next morning, four hearses returned the unknowns to the Punchbowl cemetery for the scheduled 11:00 AM selection ceremonies. Master Sergeant Ned Lyle, a Korean War veteran and Distinguished Service Cross recipient, was given the honor of making the final selection of the Unknown. MSG Lyle placed a wreath before one of the assembled caskets and that coffin was moved a short distance away to a covered canopy area near the cemetery's flag pole to allow visitors to pay their respects to the Unknown Serviceman from the Korean War. The three unselected candidates were reburied at the cemetery. At 5:00 PM, the Korean Unknown was taken back to the Kapalama Basin mortuary to await the selection of the Pacific Theater Candidate Unknown, scheduled for the following day.[118]

AFTER THE END of World War II, all of the American unknowns from the Pacific theater had been reinterred during post-war cleanup operations to either the Fort McKinley Cemetery in the Philip-

(National Archives)
Four of the Transpacific candidates arrive at Hickam Air Force Base from Fort McKinley Cemetery in Manila.

pines or to the National Memorial Cemetery of the Pacific in Hawaii.[119] There were 32 unknowns from the American cemetery in the Philippines under consideration as candidates for the Transpacific Unknown. On April 29, four remains were disinterred, and flown on-board a Douglas C-54 transport to Hickam Air Force Base. Immediately after arrival, the caskets were taken to the Army Mortuary where the bodies were re-examined and re-casketed.[120]

Likewise, American Army officials selected the grave locations of six unknowns at the Punchbowl. The individual plots were written down on cards, sealed in envelopes, and placed in a traditional Hawaiian koa wood bowl. Chaplain LTC Clarence Hobgood then drew two of the cards at random and these bodies were disinterred and taken to the Army mortuary for further preparation for the official selection ceremonies.

The identical caskets of the six unknown candidates were transported to Hickam on the morning of May 16. Each casket was carried by six airmen to the base's grassy mall area near its iconic water tower. It was an appropriate setting since the airbase was located adjacent to the Pearl Harbor Naval Station and both installations had been attacked on December 7, 1941, some 17 years earlier.

Each of the six identical caskets was draped by an American flag and lined up under a canopy. Colonel Glenn T. Eagleston

(USAF) was given the honor of making the final selection of the Transpacific Unknown.[121] Eagleston was a highly decorated pilot who had served with the 354th Fighter Group during World War II and flew 100 combat missions in support of American troops. He was credited with shooting down 18 German aircraft during the war. In Korea, Eagleston had advanced to jet-fighters and successfully flew an impressive 84 combat missions. His decorations included the Distinguished Service Cross, the Silver Star, the Distinguished Flying Cross, and the Legion of Merit.[122]

After a short pause, Colonel Eagleston made his selection by placing a white lei on one of the assembled caskets. Staff Chaplain Colonel Howell G. Gum rendered a prayer followed by the playing of the National Anthem. After the conclusion of the ceremonies, the

(National Archives)

The Transpacific Candidate Unknown is carried to an awaiting hearse. The body was flown with the Korean Unknown to Cuba.

Transpacific Candidate Unknown was taken to the Kapalama Basin mortuary. His casket and that of the Korean Unknown were placed inside protective shipping containers. The bodies were then transported to NAS Barber's Point where at 3:45 PM, they were loaded onto an awaiting aircraft to be flown to the American base at Guantanamo Bay, Cuba.[123]

THE CASKETS ARRIVED in Cuba and were transferred on May 23 to the guided missile cruiser, the USS *Boston* (CAG-1). The ship set sail for a prearranged rendezvous, scheduled for three days later, with the USS *Blandy*. The destroyer was completing its Atlantic crossing, returning the Transatlantic Candidate Unknown back to the United States.

On May 26, at 0747 hours, the *Boston* carefully maneuvered alongside the *Blandy* near the coast of Virginia. With the ships traveling parallel to one another and in tight formation, the captains matched speed while their respective crews established an open water, highline transfer. The Transatlantic Unknown's casket was conveyed across the open water from the *Blandy* to the deck of the much larger cruiser. This difficult and perilous ship-to-ship procedure was completed in just 30 minutes despite bad weather and a persistent rain. Now, with all three caskets of the Unknowns safely onboard the *Boston*, the two Navy vessels proceeded in tandem to the Virginia Capes where the USS *Canberra* (CAG-2) awaited.[124]

A few hours later, the *Canberra* came into sight off the Virginia coast. The two missile cruisers, now on identical headings and traveling at a constant speed of 10 knots, had just 100 feet separation as they established another mid-ship, highline transfer. With their crews manning-the-rails in dress whites, all three caskets of the Unknowns were individually conveyed to the *Canberra's* deck. Once onboard, the World War II Candidates Unknown were taken below decks. In a missile compartment, Navy morticians removed the steel caskets from their shipping containers. The bodies were then transferred to identical, ceremonial bronze coffins and the new caskets

(US Navy)

The first Unknown's casket is transferred by highline from the USS Boston *to the USS* Canberra *where the selection ceremony for the World War II Unknown would take place off of the Virginia Capes.*

were secretly repositioned in order "to preserve their anonymity and insure no clue to their identity or theater of origin."[125] At the same time but in a separate compartment, the Korean Unknown Serviceman's body was also being re-casketed for a final time.

Once all of the preliminary preparations had been completed, the three flagged-draped caskets were carried top-side to the *Canberra's* deck and placed on individual catafalques directly under the ship's Terrier missile launcher. The Korean Unknown was situated in the center position, flanked by the World War II candidates, their caskets now indistinguishable in terms of point of origin. A Navy/ Marine honor guard stood watch as the ship's band played Chopin's "Funeral March."[126]

(US Navy)

Hospital Corpsman First Class, William R. Charette, selects the World War II Unknown Serviceman. The unselected World War II candidate was buried at sea with full military honors.

Hospital Corpsman First Class, William R. Charette was given the honor of selecting the World War II Unknown.[127] Charette was the Navy's only active duty Medal of Honor recipient. He had received his decoration for "conspicuous gallantry and intrepidity at the risk of his life above and beyond the call of duty" during the Korean War while serving as a medic with a Marine Corps rifle company.[128]

Charette made his choice shortly after noon by placing a wreath in front of one of the caskets, thereby officially designating the remains as America's Unknown Serviceman from World War II. With the conclusion of the formal ceremonies, the nearby *Blandy* carefully pulled alongside of the *Canberra*. The huge missile cruiser was unable to transverse the Potomac River's shallow waters, so the bodies of the Unknown Servicemen from World War II and the Korean War had to be again transferred by highline to the shallow draught *Blandy*. The destroyer would then transport both Unknowns on their final journey to Washington, D.C. for the scheduled Memorial Day funeral rites at Arlington National Cemetery.

On the *Canberra*, the unselected World War II candidate's body had been taken below deck and was prepared for burial at sea. According to the Navy's after-action report: "the body of the unselected Unknown, removed from the ceremonial casket, [was] wrapped in the traditional white sailcloth, and draped with the flag."[129] At 2:00 PM, "the order, 'Bury the dead,' was passed over the loudspeaker...the ship stopped in her course... the national ensign was...lowered to half-mast, [as] the band played a dirge, [and] the ship's company massed in formation."[130]

The shrouded body was carried by six Navy sailors, each wearing a black mourning armband, to the starboard side of the ship where the crew had assembled and rendered the appropriate military honors. Christian chaplains and a Jewish rabbi delivered final prayers for the Unknown while the casket team bowed their heads in respect. Then the command was given to "commit" the body to the sea. The sailors deftly tilted the mahogany sliding board over the ship's railing and the body "loaded with 200 pounds of lead and sand" silently slipped into the ocean below "and settled in 113 feet of water" some 33 miles off of Cape Henry Lighthouse. The official coordinates of the burial were recorded as 36°57' N latitude and 75°19 W longitude. Having completed its final duty, the *Canberra* returned to its home port of Norfolk, while the *Blandy*, now escorted by the USCGC *Ingham* (WPG-35), turned course up the Chesapeake Bay. The ships made their way to the mouth of the Potomac River and then anchored overnight near Piney Point, Maryland.[131]

———————

THE NEXT DAY, the *Blandy* reprised the journey of the USS *Olympia* to the Washington Navy Yard. The ship arrived on May 27 at 12:35 PM, a day prior to the scheduled arrival ceremonies for the

Unknowns. With the ship tightly moored at Pier #1, the caskets of the World War II and Korean Unknown Servicemen remained under guard overnight on the ship. Early the next morning, the two flagged-draped caskets were relocated to the rear fantail area of the ship. A welcoming delegation, comprised of members of the clergy and military honor guard units, assembled onshore, led by the Secretary of Defense, Neil McElroy, and Secretary of the Treasury, Robert Anderson. The U.S. Navy Band initiated the start of the ceremonies by playing a selection of hymns and then, at 9:25 AM, the body of the World War II Unknown was carried off of the *Blandy* by a joint service casket team. It was followed shortly thereafter by the coffin of the Unknown Serviceman from the Korean War. The two caskets were then placed into separate hearses as a 21-gun salute was rendered in their honor.[132]

The flags at the Navy Yard were, like all flags throughout the nation, at half-staff in honor of the Unknown Servicemen. President Eisenhower had issued a proclamation declaring a three-day period of mourning:

> *Whereas* on this Memorial Day, in the National Cemetery at Arlington, the remains of two unknown Americans who gave their lives in service overseas during the Second World War and during the Korean conflict, will be interred; and

> *Whereas* these two Unknown Americans represent almost eighty thousand Americans killed in the Second World War and more than eight thousand Americans killed in the Korean conflict whose bodies lie unidentified in resting places abroad; and

> *Whereas* their two caskets will arrive in the City of Washington on May 28, 1958, to lie in state in the rotunda of the United States Capitol until final interment: *Now, Therefore, I, Dwight D. Eisenhower*, President of the United States of America, do hereby

direct that the flag of the United States be flown at half-staff on all buildings, grounds, and naval vessels of the Federal Government in the District of Columbia and throughout the United States and its Territories and possessions, and at all United States embassies, legations, consular offices, and other facilities abroad, including all military facilities and naval vessels and stations, when customarily flown, on May 28, May 29, and May 30, 1958.

As a sign of our national gratitude and concern, I also urge my fellow citizens to display our country's flag at half-staff at their homes and other appropriate places during this period.[133]

The motorcade to the Capitol was led by a motorized police escort and mirrored the original parade route for the World War I Unknown some 27 years earlier. Upon arrival at the East Front, 12 military body-bearers removed the two caskets from their respective hearses and slowly carried the coffins up the steps, passing through the traditional armed services cordon and into the Capitol Rotunda. The casket of the World War II Unknown was gently placed upon the Lincoln catafalque, occupying the senior position. The Korean Unknown's coffin was placed upon a specially built, duplicate black-shrouded bier immediately adjacent to the World War II Unknown. During the two-day mourning period at the Capitol, the two coffins would be regularly rotated so that each of the Unknowns would have the honor of resting on the famous Civil War-era Lincoln catafalque.[134] Over the next two days, a five-member, joint service honor guard stood the death watch at the Capitol. Tomb Guard SSG James Cardamon, who was assigned to this duty since his relief was not on duty at Arlington, remembers that the honor guard was rotated every hour. The impressive silent guard change was carefully choreographed and conducted without verbal commands but signaled through heel clicks and precise counting.[135]

(National Archives)
The Unknowns lying in state at the U.S. Capitol. The caskets were rotated regularly so that each Unknown had the honor of resting upon the Lincoln catafalque.

Vice President Richard M. Nixon and Speaker of the House Sam Rayburn led the Congressional delegations.[136] Both men placed their individual wreaths in front of the two caskets. Also present for the Rotunda formalities were distinguished members of the diplomatic corps as well as officials from various government departments and agencies. Shortly after the conclusion of the brief ceremonies, the Capitol building was open to public visitation. Over 28,000 people paid their respects during the ensuing two days while the bodies lay-in-state.[137]

THE BURIALS OF the World War II and Korean Unknowns occurred during the peak of Cold War tensions between the United States and the Soviet Union. It was a time when a nuclear holocaust seemed possible and it was hoped that the Unknowns would serve as a universal reminder of the human consequences of war. In that spirit, Congress and the President dedicated Memorial Day 1958 to the goal of maintaining a lasting peace. The resolution called upon all citizens to observe the "day for Nation-wide prayer for [a] permanent peace."[138]

As protocol dictated, former President Harry S Truman was invited to participate in the Arlington services for the Unknown. Truman, though, was unable to attend, responding to President Eisenhower's formal invitation, writing: "Your letter and invitation to attend the Memorial Day Ceremonies at Arlington National Cemetery were highly appreciated and I regret very much that Mrs. Truman and I cannot be there. Unfortunately, we will be out of the country."[139] Also invited to the Memorial Day services were all of the nation's living Medal of Honor recipients.[140] On Friday morning, the day of the burials, a special White House briefing was held for those Medal of Honor recipients who could attend. Among the distinguished MOH veterans who were present at the Rose Garden event were MSG Prull B. Huff and SGT Gerry Crump. These two men had been pre-selected to assist President Eisenhower during the Amphitheater ceremonies later that afternoon with the presentation of the Medal of Honor to the two Unknowns.[141] Also there was HM 1C William Charette, who had selected the World War II Unknown onboard the *Canberra* just four days earlier.[142]

President Eisenhower made brief remarks to the distinguished group, using the opportunity to reinforce the Memorial Day theme of a lasting peace. He told the assembly that: "Because you have been such great fighters, I am quite certain that all of you feel a great compulsion to be a fighter for peace. The cornerstone for fighting for peace and winning the peace is the strength of America-first of all, its spiritual strength, its determination to stand before the world as an exemplar of those ideals and principles of human dignity and freedom and liberty in which we so deeply believe."[143] After his remarks, the President and Vice President Richard Nixon remained behind to greet personally each soldier and serviceman and to thank them for their distinguished service.

The weather that day in Washington for the funeral of the Unknowns was seasonably hot and humid with the high temperature hovering around 87 degrees. As a precaution, the military set up several medical aid stations at strategic intervals along the parade route, as well as at Arlington, to treat any of the thousands of spectators who might succumb to heat stroke or other weather-related ailments.[144] In fact, throughout the day, over 400 people sought medical aid, including Associate Justice of the Supreme Court, Charles E. Whittaker.[145]

At 1 PM, the caskets of the two Unknowns were carried out of the Rotunda and down the East Steps to the Capitol plaza. There, the flagged-draped coffins were placed upon two identical gun caissons, each cloaked in black mourning cloth and pulled by six grey-white horses. In the distance, a saluting battery stationed at the Washington Monument could be heard as the large mourning procession, led by honor guard contingents representing all branches of the military services, left the Capitol grounds and turned westward down Constitution Avenue towards Arlington National Cemetery.[146]

It took over an hour and half to make the 3-mile journey through Washington, D.C. and across the Memorial Bridge and into Arlington. As the two Unknowns passed through the cemetery's main gate, twenty jet fights and bombers flew directly over the pro-

(National Archives)
The funeral procession for the Unknowns crosses the Memorial Bridge and into Arlington National Cemetery. Over 300,000 mourners lined the parade route.

cession in the missing man formation. The caissons arrived at the Amphitheater's West Entrance at precisely 2:40 PM.[147]

A capacity crowd of three thousand had been invited to attend the memorial services at the Amphitheater. Some 24 different types of tickets were issued to various dignitaries and government officials, including Medal of Honor recipients, members of Congress, diplomats, high ranking military brass, and veteran organizations. Controversially, though, no tickets had been allotted to Gold Star mothers and widows.[148] Overflow crowds gathered on the plaza below the Tomb and in surrounding sections to listen to the services broadcast on loudspeakers.

The formal ceremonies began after the President and Vice President took their respective positions on the dais under the apse. At 3:02 PM, the two caskets were conveyed to the stage area, followed by the playing of the National Anthem. A two-minute period of silence was then observed in honor of all of the nation's military dead.[149]

The printed program listed an official commemorative address by President Eisenhower, but the White House had decided that the President would forgo delivering formal remarks. Instead, after being given the two Medals of Honor by SGT Crump and MSG Huff, Eisenhower read only an abbreviated 26-word, version of the MOH citations for the Unknowns in order to: "do away with a period of time when the President is at the podium without any apparent action."[150] In the absence of any formal presidential remarks, it was left to others to define the meaning of the day's events. In its follow-up coverage of the events, *National Geographic* author, Beverley

(National Archives)
President Dwight Eisenhower presents the Medal of Honor to the World War II Unknown Serviceman during services held at the Memorial Amphitheater, May 30, 1958.

(National Archives)
The interment services for the World War II and Korean Unknown Servicemen. President Eisenhower and Vice President Nixon led the mourners.

Bowie, provided a context for the symbolism of the day's events. In the November issue, Bowie wrote: "A hero's death? Perhaps. No one will ever know. But we do know he gave that life for his country, and we take this sacrifice to stand for all the unseen, unrecorded deeds of courage and compassion performed in these conflicts by the obscure many."[151]

After scripture readings and prayers, the President and Vice President were escorted inside to the south portion of the Trophy Room as the Unknowns' caskets were carried to the plaza for the final committal ceremonies. At 4:06 PM, President Eisenhower took his position directly in front of the World War II Unknown, while Vice President Richard Nixon stood before the casket of the Korean Unknown. Committal prayers were rendered by Army, Navy, and Air Force chaplains representing all of the major religious faiths.

(Library of Congress)

The Memorial to 2,111 unknown soldiers who died during the American Civil War. The monument is located a short distance from the Arlington House Mansion and is adjacent to the Old Amphitheater.

(Library of Congress)

The dedication ceremonies for the Confederate Memorial, 4 June 1914. President Woodrow Wilson declared: "this chapter in the history of the United States is closed and ended."

(Library of Congress)

The ground breaking for the new Memorial Amphitheater, 1 March 1915. The Secretary of the Navy, Josephus Daniels, and Judge Ivory Kimball used a ceremonial shovel to symbolically begin construction on the new building.

(Philip Bigler)

The grave of Judge Ivory Kimball in Section 3 at Arlington National Cemetery. Kimball was the leading force behind building the Memorial Amphitheater, but he died before it was completed.

(National Archives)

Pacifists at the nation's Capitol protesting Woodrow Wilson's impending request for a Declaration of War against Germany. Many Americans opposed sending soldiers to fight in the European war.

(National Archives)

The first AEF troops arrive in Paris during World War I. Over 4.7 million American troops were mobilized during the war.

(American Battle Monuments Commission)
President and Mrs. Wilson at the Suresnes American Cemetery near Paris. The President and First Lady paid tribute to American war dead on Memorial Day, 1919.

(National Archives)
The dedication ceremonies of the Memorial Amphitheater, 15 May 1920. The new, open-air structure could hold 5,000 guests for services.

(Library of Congress)
An aerial photograph of the newly completed Amphitheater, 1920. Both the Confederate Memorial and the Mast of the USS Maine Memorial are visable. The Tomb of the Unknown Soldier would not be added until the following year.

(National Archives)
The graves of American war dead at the Aisne-Marne Cemetery, France. It was estimated that over 116,000 Americans lost their lives during the war in just seven months of actual combat.

(National Archives)

A disinterment team removes the casket of an American soldier for return to the United States. Families of identified soldiers killed during the war were given the option to return their loved one's remains to the United States for burial. Over 70% of Gold Star families chose to do so.

(National Archives)

The repatriation of the remains of 23 American sailors to Arlington National Cemetery, 2 November 1923. These sailors were among the 58,119 American soldiers and sailors who died from influenza during the war. They were serving onboard the USS *Pittsburgh when they died and were initially interred in Rio de Janerio.*

(Library of Congress)

President Warren G. Harding and General John J. Pershing walk down Pennsylvania Avenue behind the caisson of the Unknown Soldier, 11 November 1921.

(Library of Congress)

The committal service for the Unknown Soldier on the plaza of the Memorial Amphitheater.

(Library of Congress)

The Tomb of the Unknown Soldier at Arlington, circa 1922. The original sarcophagus was intended to be temporary and was often disparaged by critics as an "unfinished block." It was routinely disrespected by ill-informed tourists to the cemetery.

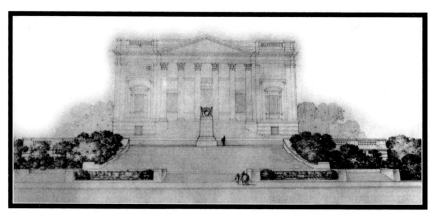

(Commission of Fine Arts)

Thomas Hasting's architectural design concept for completing the Tomb of the Unknown Soldier. As the chief architect of the Memorial Amphitheater, Hastings felt that he was the person most qualified to finish the Tomb.

(Library of Congress)

An early effort to prevent tourists from disrepecting the Tomb. As early as 1922, veterans groups and Gold Star Mothers were urging the military to place an armed, military guard at the Tomb.

(Library of Congress)

President Calvin Coolidge places a wreath at the Tomb, 1924. Note the early roadways directly below the original Tomb.

(Library of Congress)

Secretary of War, Patrick Hurley, breaks ground on 19 December 1930 for the new approaches to the Tomb. Army Chief of Staff, Douglas MacArthur, looks on.

(Library of Congress)

Construction at Tomb of the Unknown Soldier, circa 1931. Much of the original plaza area had to be demolished for the construction of a new stairway approach.

(Library of Congress)

President Franklin Roosevelt places a wreath at the newly completed Tomb of the Unknown Soldier circa 1935.

(National Archives)

A Japanese aerial photograph showing the attack on Pearl Harbor. As early as 1943, there was a movement to bury an Unknown from World War II at Arlington.

(National Archives)

Soldiers removed a dead American GI killed during the Malmedy massacre in Belgium. The Graves Registration Service was charged with recovery and identification of all remains.

(National Archives)

A Korean girl places a wreath at the grave of an American Soldier at the United Nations cemetery in Pusan, 1951. The United States lost 54,246 soldiers killed in action during three years of combat operations.

(US Navy Photograph)

The two unknown World War II candidates flank the casket of the Korean Unknown (center) on the USS Canberra. *The selection ceremony was conducted at sea on 26 May 1958.*

(National Archives)

The funeral procession for the World War II and Korean Unknowns crossing over the Memorial Bridge into Arlington.

(National Archives)

Members of the Tomb Guard stand vigil over the casket of the Vietnam Unknown Serviceman, Memorial Day, 1984.

```
0 019

MSC RANDOLPH AFB TEXAS GOVT PD CASUALTY MESSAGE,  11 MAY          19 72  C- PERSONAL


MR AND MRS GEORGE C. BLASSIE            WU:  DELIVER - DO NOT PHONE
405 PADDLEWHEEL DRIVE
FLORISSANT, MISSOURI  63033             REPORT DELIVERY

IT IS WITH DEEP REGRET THAT I OFFICIALLY INFORM YOU OF              (THE DEATH
OF YOUR) FIRST LIEUTENANT MICHAEL J. BLASSIE.                      .
         (HE WAS KILLED IN ACTION IN)  SOUTH VIETNAM
ON  11 MAY 1972.  HE WAS THE PILOT OF AN A-37 AIRCRAFT ON A COMBAT MISSION.
WHILE ON A PASS OVER THE TARGET HIS AIRCRAFT RECEIVED INTENSE GROUND FIRE AND
CRASHED.
```

(National Archives)

Telegram dated 11 May 1972 informing the Blassie family of their son's death after his plane was shot down by "enemy gunfire." Colonel Charles Gunn, in a subsequent condolence letter, wrote that LT Blassie's wingman observed an "explosion and instense fire resulting from the crash" and that there was "no possibility of survival...Recovery efforts by ground forces are impossible at the present time do to instense combat operations and large concentrations of enemy troops in the area."

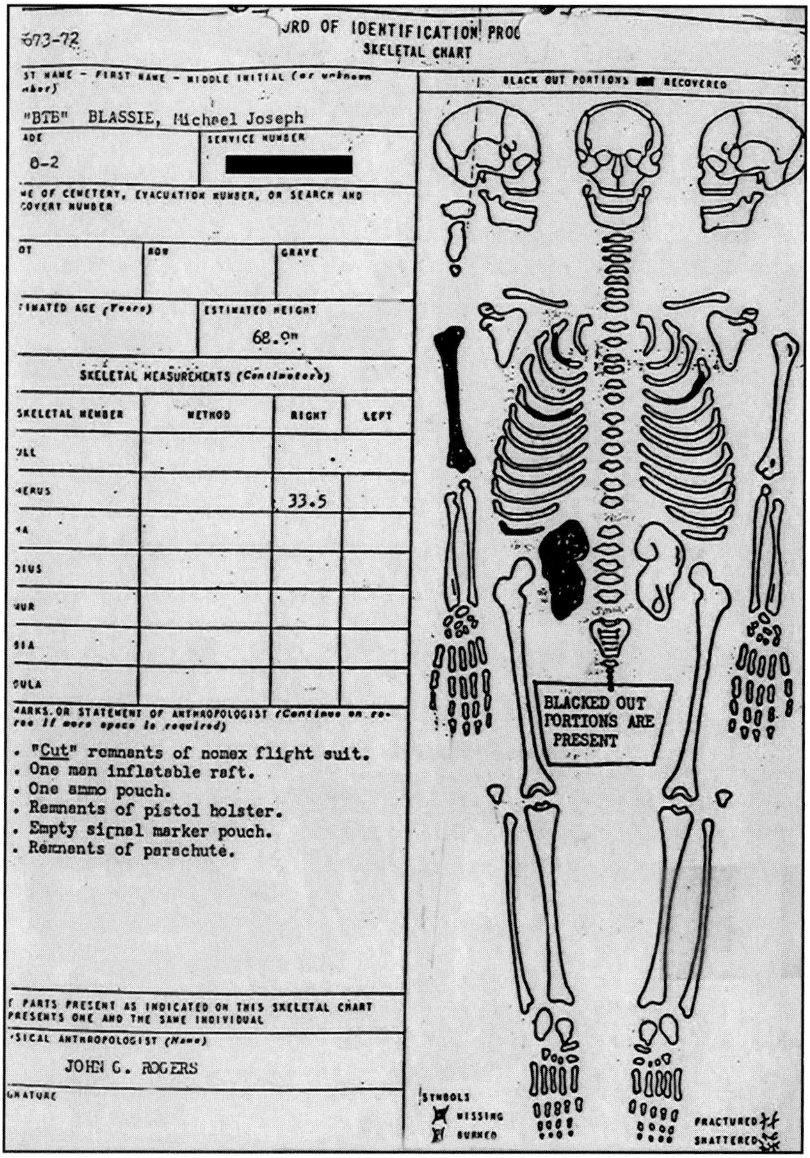

673-72

...RD OF IDENTIFICATION PROC
SKELETAL CHART

ST NAME - FIRST NAME - MIDDLE INITIAL (or unknown ...ber) "BTB" BLASSIE, Michael Joseph	
...ADE 0-2	SERVICE NUMBER [redacted]
...E OF CEMETERY, EVACUATION NUMBER, OR SEARCH AND ...COVERY NUMBER	

OT	ROW	GRAVE

...IMATED AGE (Years)	ESTIMATED HEIGHT 68.9"

SKELETAL MEASUREMENTS (Centimeters)

SKELETAL MEMBER	METHOD	RIGHT	LEFT
...ULL			
...MERUS		33.5	
...NA			
...DIUS			
...MUR			
...BIA			
...BULA			

...MARKS OR STATEMENT OF ANTHROPOLOGIST (Continue on reverse if more space is required)

- "Cut" remnants of nomex flight suit.
- One man inflatable raft.
- One ammo pouch.
- Remnants of pistol holster.
- Empty signal marker pouch.
- Remnants of parachute.

...T PARTS PRESENT AS INDICATED ON THIS SKELETAL CHART ...PRESENTS ONE AND THE SAME INDIVIDUAL

...SICAL ANTHROPOLOGIST (Name)
JOHN G. ROGERS

...GNATURE

BLACK OUT PORTIONS RECOVERED
BLACKED OUT PORTIONS ARE PRESENT
SYMBOLS
MISSING
BURNED
FRACTURED
SHATTERED

(National Archives)

A working skeletal chart from the Army Central Identification Laboratory in Honolulu, Hawaii for the remains classiefied as "believed to be" those of LT Michael Blassie. Six bones along with a few artifacts were recovered from the crash site in October 1972 but these items were still deemed insufficient to make a positive identification.

C - E - R - T - I - F - I - C - A - T - I - O - N

21 March 1984

REMAINS OF TSN 0673-72 (X-26)

Anthropological processing of the remains designated as TSN 0673-72 (X-26) has failed to support a positive identification with any known casualty of Southeast Asia. All efforts since 4 November 1972 to establish a positive identification have proven negative. The portions of the recovered remains do not include the identification criteria that can be matched exclusively to an individual and it is highly improbable that continued identification processing would be successful. These remains are determined to be unidentifiable.

JOHNIE E. WEBB, JR.
MAJ, GS
Commanding

(National Archives)

The official certification from MAJ Johnie Webb that the remains of X-26 were unidentifiable and eligible for burial as the Vietnam Unknown Serviceman.

(National Archives)

The funeral for Air Force 1LT Michael Blassie. Advances in DNA technology lead to his identification as the Vietnam Unknown Serviceman in 1998.

The brief 9-minute ceremony was concluded after the President and Vice President placed wreaths before the caskets and the customary firing of a 21-gun salute and a playing of "Taps." The 3rd Relief of the Tomb guard immediately took up an honor guard position on the plaza while the general public was allowed to solemnly pass by the biers holding the two bronze caskets.[152]

IMMEDIATELY AFTER THE ceremonies, President Eisenhower motorcaded to the nearby North Parade Ground at Fort Myer. There he boarded a military helicopter and flew to his farm in Gettysburg, Pennsylvania. The President made his way to the Gettysburg Country Club to play nine holes of golf. The remainder of his weekend was devoted to more golf, barbecues with his family and grandchildren, and conducting farm business.[153] Vice President Richard Nixon and his wife, Pat, left Arlington and flew to St. Catherine's Island, Georgia for a short vacation.[154]

After the cemetery closed for the night, the caskets were lowered into their vaults and a temporary covering was placed over the open graves. The crypts could not be sealed with the white memorial stones until that Monday when a construction crane was brought onto the plaza to lift the heavy marble.

As America returned to work after the Memorial Day holiday, few were aware that some seven months earlier, Captain Harry Griffith Cramer had been killed while serving as a military advisor to a Special Forces contingent of the Army of the Republic of Vietnam (ARVN) near Nha Trang during a live-fire exercise.[155] According to the official report, Captain Cramer died: "while engaged in [an] exercise demonstrating principles of vehicle ambush, [the] deceased was in vicinity of man throwing TNT block which exploded while in throwing position."[156] The premature detonation of the explosive had killed Cramer along with several South Vietnamese trainees. Few Americans had ever heard of a place called Vietnam nor were they aware of the growing presence of United States military forces in that region of Southeast Asia.

Endnotes

1 Franklin D. Roosevelt. "Message to Congress—State of the Union: 3 January 1940." Franklin: Master Speech File, 1898-1945 available at: http://www.fdrlibrary.marist.edu.

2 *Ibid.*

3 *Ibid.*

4 Iris Chang. *The Rape of Nanking: The Forgotten Holocaust of World War II.* New York: Basic Books, 1997, pp. 101, 315.

5 Homer N. Wallen. *Pearl Harbor: Why, How, Fleet Salvage and Final Appraisal.* Washington, D.C.: Government Printing Office, 1968, pp. 18-19.

6 The six Japanese carriers were the *Akagi, Kaga, Soryū, Zuikaku, Kiryū,* and *Shaleaku. Ibid.,* p. 88.

7 Although the naval base at Pearl Harbor was the primary target, the Japanese also targeted the Schofield Barracks, Bellous Field, Wheeler Field, Hickam Field, and the Kaneohe Naval Air Station.

8 Thurston Clark. *Pearl Harbor Ghosts: A Journey to Hawaii Then and Now.* New York: William Morrow and Company, Inc., 1991, p. 188.

9 Wallen, p. 108.

10 The final death toll was 2,036 killed from the Navy, 215 killed from the Army along with 22 MIA's. Wallen, p. 108.

11 Franklin Roosevelt's Declaration of War Speech, 8 December 1941, available at: http://www.presidency.ucsb.edu/ws/?pid=16053.

12 *Ibid.*

13 "Jeanette Rankin casts sole vote against WWII." History Channel: available at: https://www.history.com/this-day-in-history/jeanette-rankin-casts-sole-vote-against-wwii.

14 World War II Accounting, Defense POW/MIA Accounting Agency, available at: http://www.dpaa.mil/Our-Missing/World-War-II/.

15 The *Akagi, Kaga, Hiryu,* and *Soryū* were all sunk by American airplanes. All four carriers had participated in the attack on Pearl Harbor the previous year.

16 *The Evening Star* edition, August 6, 1942, p. A-1.

17 "Rights for Sargt. Younger at Arlington Tomorrow," The *Evening Star*, p. A-10.

18 Alvin P. Stauffer. *The Quartermaster Corps Operations in the War Against Japan*. Washington, D.C.: Center of Military History, 2004, p. 249.

19 Steven E. Anders. "With All Due Honors: A History of the Quartermaster Graves Registration Mission" available at: http://old.qmfound.com/grave.htm, p. 4.

20 Shomon, p. 109.

21 Stauffer, p. 249.

22 It took roughly 90 minutes to dig a standard grave. See Stauffer, p. 249; Shomon, p. 109.

23 Joseph Shomon. *Crosses in the Wind: Graves Registration Service in the Second World War*. New York: Stratford House, Inc., 1947, p. 98.

24 Stauffer, p. 249.

25 The Japanese *bushido* code, the way of the warrior, meant that surrender would bring dishonor to a soldier. The term "banzai charge" came from Japanese troops yelling "*Tenno Heika Banzai!*" (Long live the emperor, ten thousand ages!) during an attack. See: http://world-war-2.wikia.com/wiki/Banzai_Charge.

26 Stauffer, p. 255.

27 Shomon, p. 106.

28 *Ibid.*, pp. 252, 254.

29 "Los Negros, Admiralty Island Campaign 1944: War Department; Combat Bulletin #3, available at https://www.youtube.com/watch?v=s1z9RO1K2Bg.

30 Stauffer, p. 251.

31 The fighting in the Pacific accounted for one quarter of all American casualties in World War II, but due to the nature of combat, there was a higher number of missing-in-action and unknowns. Indeed, over water losses were common, which meant that bodies were unrecoverable. Furthermore, the Navy lost numerous ships in combat to submarines, surface warfare, and Kamikaze suicide planes. *Ibid.*, p. 257.

32 Shomon, p. 91.

33 *Ibid.*, pp. 103, 104.

34 *Ibid.*, p. 109.

35 Letter from Mrs. John Walker to Brigadier General E.R. Quesada, 14 August 1944. Letters to Brigadier General Elwood Richard Quesada. Dwight D. Eisenhower Library: Papers 1920-1967, Box 1. Captain Walker's remains were never recovered; he is still listed as MIA by the Defense POW/MIA Accounting Agency. http://www.dpaa.mil.

36 *Ibid.*, p. 49.

37 The largest group burial at Arlington National Cemetery took place after the Coast Guard ammunition ship, the USS *Serpens*, exploded at Guadacanal on 29 January 1945. The remains of 250 men were consigned to 50 caskets and buried as a crew in Section 34. Dean W Holt. *American Military Cemeteries: A Comprehensive Illustrated Guide to the Hallowed Grounds of the United States, Including Cemeteries Overseas.* Jefferson, N.C.: McFarland & Company, 1992, p. 4.

38 Brigadier General G.W. Horkan testimony before the Commission of Fine Arts, 24 March 1948; Michael J. Allen. *Until the Last Man Comes Home: POWs, MIAs, and the Unending Vietnam War.* Chapel Hill: University of North Carolina Press, 2009, p. 2.

39 Edward Steere and Thayer M. Boardman. *Final Disposition of World War II Dead:1945-1951.* Washington, D.C.: Office of the Quartermaster General, 1951, p. 59.

40 Shomon, p. 149.

41 Steere, pp. 31, 36.

42 *Ibid.*, p. 51.

43 *Ibid.*, p. 344.

44 Two in Belgium; one in Luxembourg; five in France; one in the Netherlands; two in Italy; one in the United Kingdom and one in Tunisia.

45 *Ibid.*, p. 417.

46 *Ibid.*, p. 477.

47 The Manila American Cemetery consists of 152 acres and is the final resting place for 17,184 American soldiers, mostly from campaigns in New Guinea and the Philippine Islands. See the American Battle Monuments Commission at https://www.abmc.gov/.

48 The Philippine Islands had also been an American territory prior to World War II, but the country was granted its independence on 4 July 1946.

49 The Punchbowl National Cemetery consists of 112 acres and is the burial place for such notables as Senator Daniel Inouye, astronaut Ellison Onizuka, and journalist Ernie Pyle.

50 Holt, p. 225.

51 Steere, p. 504.

52 The cemetery averaged 144 burials per day during this period. *Ibid.*, p. 504.

53 Quartermaster General letter to Senator Paul Douglas, December 1952 available at: http://cem.va.gov.

54 *The Unknowns of World War II and Korea.* Washington, D.C.: U.S. Department of Defense, p. 1.

55 Public Law 429 available at: http://www.loc.gov.

56 *The Unknowns of World War II and Korea*, p. 1.

57 Brigadier General G.W. Horkan's testimony before the Commission of Fine Arts, 24 March 1948, pp. 5, 6.

58 *Ibid.*, p. 6.

59 *Ibid.* p. 6.

60 B.C. Mossman and M.W. Stark. *The Last Salute: Civil and Military Funerals 1921-1969.* Washington, D.C.: Department of the Army, 1971, p. 93.

61 *Ibid.*, p. 28.

62 Harry S Truman. "Proclamation on the Death of General John J. Pershing" available at: http://www.trumanlibrary.org.

63 *Ibid.*

64 The nine five star generals and admirals were: General of the Army: George C. Marshall, Douglas MacArthur, Dwight D. Eisenhower, Omar Bradley; General of the Air Force: Henry "Hap" Arnold; Fleet Admiral: William D. Leahy, Ernest King, Chester Nimitz, and William "Bull" Halsey. Marshall (Sect. 7, #8198), Bradley (Sect. 30, #428-1-2), Arnold (Sect. 34, #44A), Leahy (Sect. 2, #932), and Halsey (Sect. 2, #1184) all are buried at Arlington National Cemetery.

65 Andrew Glass. "General John J. Pershing dies at 87, July 15, 1948," available at: http://politico.com.

66 Mossman, p. 33.

67 *Ibid.*, p. 41.

68 John J. Pershing. *My Experiences in the First World War.* New York: De Capo Press, 1995.

69 Pershing is buried in Sect. 34, #S-19-LH; Mossman, p. 43.

70 Richard W. Pershing (25 October 1942—17 February 1968), Sect. 34, #S-19-RH.

71 Minutes of the Meeting of the Commission of Fine Arts, 26 April 1932.

72 Minutes of the Meeting of the Commission of Fine Arts, 11 February 1949.

73 General Renfrow quoted in Meeting of the Commission of Fines Arts, 20 February 1950, p. 27.

74 Colonel Freeman quoted in Meeting of the Commission of Fine Arts, 20 February 1950, pp. 30, 31.

75 Minutes of the Meeting of the Commission of Fine Arts, 6 May 1949.

76 "Tomb of the Unknown Soldiers," *The Quartermaster Review*, January-February 1964: available at http://old.qmfound.com/tomb_of_the_unknown_soldiers_1964.html.

77 Major General K.L. Hastings quoted in the Proceedings of the Commission of Fine Arts, 10 January 1950, p. 2.

78 Chairman Gilmore David Clarke quoted in the Proceedings of the Commission of Fine Arts, 10 January 1950, pp. 3,4.

79 Minutes of the Meeting of the Commission of Fine Arts, 21 June 1949.

80 General Renfrow quoted in the Proceedings of the Commission of Fine Arts, 20 February 1950, p. 20.

81 "Tomb of 'Unknown' to Enshrine Two," *New York Times*, 18 June 1950.

82 Proceedings of the Commission, 20 February 1950, p. 26.

83 *Ibid.*, p. 31.

84 "Tomb of the Unknown Soldier," *Quartermaster Review*.

85 "The Monthly Print Clinic," *The Evening Star*: 19 December 1948, B-6.

86 Mao's forces had defeated the Nationalist Chinese in 1949 and forced them into exile on the island of Formosa (Taiwan).

87 The three abstentions in the Security Council voting were India, Egypt, and Yugoslavia. The USSR was absent and thus could not exercise its right of veto.

88 Douglas MacArthur. *Reminiscences*. McGraw-Hill Book Company, 1964.

89 *Ibid.*, p. 374.

90 *Ibid.*, p. 375.

91 Charles W. Honaker. *The Dead Were Mine*. Charles W. Honaker, 2014, p. 2.

92 Judith Keene. "Bodily Matters Above and Below Ground: The Treatment of American Remains from the Korean War." *The Public Historian*, vol. 32, no. 1, 2010, pp. 59–78. *JSTOR*, JSTOR, www.jstor.org/stable/10.1525/tph.2010.32.1.59, p. 65.

93 *Ibid.*, p. 65.

94 Allen, p. 129; Keene, p. 66.

95 Keene, p. 67.

96 Josef Stalin died on 5 March 1953 at the age of 73.

97 No peace settlement has ever been negotiated in Korea. The cease fire remains in effect. See the Korean Armistice Agreement available at: https://en.wikipedia.org/wiki/Korean_Armistice_Agreement.

98 Allen, p. 2.

99 Public Law 975. Government Publishing Office available at: https://www.gpo.gov/fdsys/pkg/STATUTE-70/pdf/STATUTE-70-Pg1027-2.pdf. This legislation was passed into law on 3 August 1956.

100 A.W. Edwards. "Unknown's Tomb," The *Evening Star*, 16 November 1956.

101 "Pro and Con on a Second Unknown Soldier," Washington *Daily News*, 26 March 1956.

102 Mrs. Arthur Allen quoted in "Pro and Con."

103 Mrs. Jesus F. Blas quoted in "More Views About 2d Unknown Soldier," *Washington Daily News*, 29 March 1956.

104 Mary E. Brown and Z. H. O'Neal quoted in "Pro and Con."

105 Models of the crypt covers were temporarily placed at the Tomb on 5 April 1956 for inspection.

106 "Work to Start on Crypts for 2 Unknown Soldiers," *Interment of the Unknowns of World War II and Korea*. Chief of Information, Military District of Washington, National Archives, RG 92.

107 Mossman, p. 97.

108 "Work to Start."

109 "Memorandum: Selection and Interment of the Unknown Soldier of World War II and Korea, 5 November 1957. National Archives, RG 92.

110 *Ibid.*

111 *Ibid.*

112 Major General Edward O'Neill (24 March 1902 – 9 January 1979), Sect. 30, #1081.

113 Mossman, p. 98.

114 "Great Care Taken to Keep Unknown Heroes Secret," *Washington Post*, 20 May 1958.

115 Keene, p. 70.

116 "Tomb of the Unknown Soldiers," *The Quartermaster Review.*

117 National Archives, RG92.

118 *Ibid.*

119 The Fort McKinley Cemetery is now called the Manila American Cemetery.

120 "Tomb of the Unknown Soldiers," *The Quartermaster Review.*

121 "Acceptance and Delivery of the Trans-Pacific World War II and Korean Unknown," National Archives, RG 92.

122 Colonel Glenn Eagleston (12 March 1921 – 7 May 1991). He is inurned at the Columbarium at Arlington National Cemetery, Court 3: Sec. G, Col. 5, Niche 5.

123 "Acceptance and Delivery of the Trans-Pacific World War II and Korean Unknowns," National Archives, RG 92.

124 After Action Report: "US Atlantic Fleet Phase of the World War II and Korean Unknown Project," Record Group 92, Entry (A1 1898D), Records of the Office of the Quartermaster General Box 1-3, [Location: 390/8/3/1-2], National Archives.

125 *Ibid*.

126 Mossman, p. 99.

127 William R. Charette (29 March 1932–18 March 2012).

128 Charette bravely saved several Marines during combat on 27 March 1953. Despite being wounded himself, he "continued to administer medical aid to the wounded in his own unit and to those in adjacent platoon areas." *The Congressional Medal of Honor: The Names, the Deeds*. Forest Ranch, CA.: Sharp & Dunnigan, 1984, pp. 181-182.

129 Record Group 92, National Archives.

130 "Tomb of the Unknown Soldiers," *The Quartermaster Review*.

131 *Ibid*.

132 Mossman, p. 100.

133 Proclamation 3243-Display of the Flag at Half-Staff Upon the Occasion of the Return and Final Interment of Two Unknown Americans Killed in the Second World War and Korean Conflict, 17 May 1958, available at the American Presidency Project: https://www.presidency.ucsb.edu.

134 *Ibid*., pp. 107, 110.

135 SSG James Cardamon. Telephone Interview. 25 October 2018.

136 Vice President Richard Nixon had just returned from a goodwill trip to South America where he visited eight countries. During his last stop in Caracas, Venezuela, his motorcade was assaulted by Communist protestors. The Secret Service drew their weapons to protect the Vice President's limousine from being overturned. Nixon returned to Washington's Military Air Transport Service (MATS) terminal at National Airport on May 15 and was greeted by President Eisenhower

and the First Lady. Richard Nixon. *Six Crises*. Garden City, NY: Doubleday & Co., Inc. 1962, p. 228.

137 President Dwight Eisenhower did not visit the Capitol during this period.

138 "Prayer for Peace," White House Central Files: Official File, 1953-1961, Box 458. Dwight D. Eisenhower Library.

139 Letter from Harry S Truman to Dwight D. Eisenhower, 23 May 1958, White House Central Files: Official File, 1953-1961, Box 458, Dwight D. Eisenhower Library.

140 According to White House files, letters were sent to 128 Army, 34 MarineCorps, 47 Navy, and 9 Air Force Medal of Honor recipients. White House Central Files.

141 MSG Prull B. Huff (23 June 1918-21 Sept. 1994) & SGT Gerry Crump (18 Feb. 1933-10 Jan. 1977). SGT Huff received his MOH for actions in Carano, Italy in 1944, while SGT Crump received his medal for heroic actions during the fighting on Hill 284 in Korea, 1951.

142 Presidential Schedule for 30 May 1958.

143 President Dwight D. Eisenhower. Remarks to Congressional Medal of Honor Winners, 30 May 1958 available at: http://www.presidency.ucsb.edu/ws/index. php?pid=11077.

144 Mossman, p. 111.

145 Jack Raymond. "Unknowns of World War II and Korea Enshrined," *New York Times*, p. 1.

146 White House Central Files.

147 Mossman, p. 118.

148 The public was allowed to take any vacant seats once the Presidential party had arrived and the ceremonies had begun. *Ibid.*, p. 118.

149 Presidential Schedule for 30 May 1958.

150 Colonel Schulz memorandum to Tom Stephens, 26 May 1958, White House Central Files. Also see McElya, p. 230.

151 Beverley M. Bowie. "Known But to God," *National Geographic Magazine*, November 1958, p. 601.

152 James Cardamon. Written Interview. 21 October 2018.

153 Presidential Schedule for 30 May 1958.

154 The Nixon's were at St. Catherine's Island from 30 May **through 7 June.**

155 Cramer was killed on October 21, 1957. He is considered **to be the first Amer**ican to be killed in the Vietnam War.

156 See the West Point website at: http://www.west-point.org/.

(National Archives)
The casket of the Unknown Serviceman from the Vietnam War en route to Washington, D.C. for his state funeral.

Chapter VI

The Vietnam Unknown

The veterans of the Vietnam generation served with high professional compe-
tence, with courage, and with honor. America has a deep moral obligation to
these fine men and fine women. – Gerald R. Ford

The Geneva Conference of 1954 effectively marked the end to the French effort to reassert control over its pre-World War II colonies in Southeast Asia. After having suffered a disastrous and humiliating military defeat at Dien Bien Phu, French forces surrendered to the Viet Minh. The agreement called for the French to withdraw all of its remaining military forces from Vietnam and approved a temporary partition of the country along the 17th parallel until unifying elections could be held. The Democratic Republic of Vietnam (North Vietnam) was placed under the control of Ho Chi Minh, the communist leader, while the Republic of Vietnam (South Vietnam) was to be ruled by Emperor Bao Dai and later by President Ngo Dinh Diem.

Since the Truman administration and the advent of the Cold War, the United States was committed to containing communism and preventing its spread to vulnerable countries around the world. The People's Republic of China was believed to be the greatest threat to the vulnerable, infant democracies in Asia. In April 1954, at a press conference, President Dwight Eisenhower first enunciated the "Domino Theory." The President stated: "Finally, you have broader considerations that might follow what you would call the 'falling domino' principle. You have a row of dominoes set up, you knock over the first one, and what will happen to the last one is the certainty that it will go over very quickly. So you could have a beginning of a disintegration that would have the most profound influences." [1] The Eisenhower administration soon began a massive financial and military aid program designed to assist South Vietnam. From 1955 until 1961, the United States contributed over $7 billion dollars in economic development grants and money to expand the South's military defenses.[2] At the same time, China and the Soviet Union were funding the North Vietnamese in a war of national liberation against the Diem regime. Large numbers of guerrilla fighters were infiltrating from the North through Laos and Cambodia. This led Eisenhower to commit the first contingent of American military advisors to assist the Army of the Republic of South Vietnam (ARVN) in combating the growing threat.

By the end of his second term of office, President Eisenhower was becoming increasingly disenchanted with the corruption of the South Vietnamese government and the lack of progress in the ever-widening war. With now over 900 military advisors deployed, the President was convinced that the American people would not tolerate another limited war, one with vague military objectives and of undetermined length.[3] Still, when Eisenhower left office in January 1961, the situation in Southeast Asia was confused at best.

The new president, John F. Kennedy, began his administration by boldly promising: "that we shall pay any price, bear any burden, meet any hardship, support any friend, oppose any foe to assure the survival and the success of liberty."[4] Determined to stop communist expansion, he filled his administration with young, ambitious, and well-educated men whom journalist David Halberstam described, somewhat sardonically, as the "best and the brightest." These close advisors included General Maxwell Taylor and Robert S. McNamara.[5] Both men were fully confident in their own abilities and believed that they could manipulate world events through the

Map of Vietnam and Southeast Asia.

development of new doctrines, theories, and formulas, all verified through scientific, statistical analysis. Taylor, who would later serve as Chairman of the Joint Chiefs of Staff, became the key architect of Kennedy's Vietnam strategy. He proposed that the military adopt a doctrine of flexible response, which called for gradual escalation of the nation's military reaction predicated upon new circumstances. It required developing, innovating, and deploying different types of limited warfare. In Vietnam, this meant the extensive use of special forces, soldiers specifically trained and skilled in fighting a guerrilla insurgency which was being waged by an unconventional enemy.[6]

The Secretary of Defense, Robert McNamara, brought to the Pentagon a strong skepticism and distrust of the nation's traditional military leadership. He demanded "Weekly Headway Reports" to gauge the progress being made in Vietnam. This would evolve into using body counts as statistical proof that the South was winning the war. Both McNamara and Taylor grossly underestimated the human element in the war and failed to adequately consider the North Vietnamese army's determination and tenacity.[7] By the end of 1963, the Kennedy administration had dramatically increased American troop strength in Vietnam by committing 16,300 American advisors to the region to help instruct the Army of the Republic of Vietnam on military tactics. Kennedy's assassination that November further muddled the foreign policy morass although his successor, Lyndon Johnson, pledged to continue Kennedy's policies in regard to Southeast Asia and retained his most trusted advisors.

The following year, two American destroyers, the USS *Maddox* and USS *Turner Joy*, were allegedly attacked by North Vietnamese torpedo boats while on patrol in international waters in the Gulf of Tonkin. President Johnson asked for authorization to expand American involvement in the war and Congress passed the fateful Gulf of Tonkin Resolution on August 10. It authorized the President: "to take all necessary measures to repel any armed attack against the forces of the United States and to prevent further aggression."[8] By granting the President unilateral, broad war-making powers, the Congress had once again ceded its constitutionally prescribed power

(National Archives)
President Lyndon B. Johnson signing the Gulf of Tonkin Resolution. The Congressional act gave the President broad war-making powers in Vietnam.

and responsibility to declare war. In the first retaliatory air strikes unleashed against North Vietnam, Navy LTJG Everett Alvarez's A4 Skyhawk was shot down over enemy territory. He would remain a prisoner-of-war for the next eight and a half years.[9]

The escalation of the war by the Johnson administration continued throughout 1964. By December, there were 23,000 American advisors stationed in Vietnam and the United States had already lost 149 servicemen killed-in-action, including 19 men who were officially listed as missing-in-action.[10] In February 1965, the United States Air Force began a massive bombing campaign, euphemistically named Operation Rolling Thunder, against military targets in North Vietnam.[11] The first Marine combat divisions were sent ashore at DaNang on March 8 and began American ground combat operations the following month.[12] Troop strength swelled to 184,300 by the end of 1965, finally peaking in 1968 with 536,100 American soldiers deployed to Vietnam. Casualties correspondingly soared. In 1968, alone, 16,592 American servicemen and women were killed in Vietnam, an average of 319 per week.[13] Following past precedents, the recovery and return of the dead became a national priority.

———

THE UNITED STATES armed services established several large military compounds along the coastal areas of South Vietnam during the war. These vast complexes were used for supply, R&R, and the rapid deployment of troops. Since there were no defined battle lines in Vietnam, much of the war was fought using counter-insurgency tactics, search and destroy missions, and massive air power. American helicopters enabled the rapid injection of combat troops into remote and inaccessible hostile areas. They were also used effectively to quickly evacuate the wounded and the dead from the battlefield. Enemy forces, though, soon began to target the helicopters, and as the war progressed and intensified, these aircraft were increasingly susceptible to Soviet and Chinese supplied rocket-propelled grenades (RPG's) and anti-aircraft missiles.

The unique nature of the fighting in Vietnam posed significant challenges for the military's Graves Registration troops (abbreviated GRREG during the Vietnam War) who were stationed in-country. Since there were no real safe areas, GRREG troops often had to be flown into heavily jungled areas and remote landing zones to recover the dead who had been left behind during intense fighting. NVA and VC forces knew well of the American commitment to retrieve the remains of all of its soldiers who had been killed-in-action, so GRREG troops were frequently targeted and ambushed while on recovery missions. Moreover, the enemy surreptitiously booby-trapped allied corpses with trip wires, hidden hand grenades, and planted explosive devices which were designed to detonate whenever a dead body was moved or disturbed.[14]

The worst recovery missions for GRREG troops were aircraft crash sites. The force of impact and the inevitable fires from aviation fuel caused catastrophic damage to the wreckage and ravaged the remains of pilots and air crews. SGT Bill Honaker, who served with the Graves Registration Platoon, Company A, 9th Supply and Transportation Battalion, 9th Infantry Division, explained the difficulties faced by his troops when they were surveying a crash site: "Our job was to somehow recognize, separate, and keep each remains intact along with personal effects and ID tags associated with each one. All of the remains were charred and unrecognizable, devoid of anything that would give a clue to their ID."[15] Since many air operations during the war were conducted over densely jungled areas and near third party countries, such as Cambodia and Laos, these crash sites were inaccessible, the remains of those unfortunate air crews were deemed unrecoverable and classified as missing-in-action. This also was true for those pilots shot down over North Vietnamese territory by surface-to-air (SAM) missile sites.

(National Archives)
A helicopter staging area for combat operations in Vietnam. Helicopters were used extensively for deploying troops and evacuating casualties. As the war progressed, the aircraft became increasingly vulnerable to enemy rockets and small arms fire.

The majority of American casualties, though, were recovered by their own platoons and quickly evacuated from the battlefield by helicopter. All of the dead were transported to centralized collection points (CP) located on the larger American bases. The military post mortuaries, though, were intentionally constructed in out-of-the-way locations and built to be inconspicuous so: "that other soldiers were not demoralized by the thought of someone dying."[16]

Once on base, GRREG personnel would examine, process, and attempt to identify the remains. Often, a member of a deceased soldier's platoon would be asked to verify an identity and to sign a "Statement of Recognition." Once the deceased's identity had been preliminarily confirmed, a formal death certificate would be issued by a medical doctor.[17] Any personal effects (PE) recovered from the bodies were carefully collected, inventoried, and bagged for shipment to the deceased's next of kin.[18]

After the initial processing, bodies were sealed in an olive-colored, rubberized "Human Remains Pouch" (HRP or body bag) and then flown onboard large C-130 transports to one of the two in-country military mortuaries, located at DaNang and Ton Son Nhut Air Force Base, Saigon. There, the remains were once again examined and verified before being embalmed by military morticians. At the height of the Vietnam War, the Saigon mortuary had 22 embalming tables in continual use.[19]

As part of the military's policy of concurrent return, once final processing was completed, the dead were transferred to special shipping areas where the bodies were placed in aluminum transport caskets for return to the United States. The major entry points for American casualties from Vietnam were Travis Air Force Base in California and Dover Air Force Base in Delaware. Once state-side, the bodies were dressed and re-casketed before being returned home to their next of kin.[20] All casualties were assigned a military escort to accompany the remains on their final journey and to ensure proper dignity and decorum. These attendants would also provide comfort and support to grieving families.[21] The entire process from battlefield casualty to state-side burial usually took less than two weeks.[22]

The Graves Registration units were among the unsung heroes of the Vietnam War. These men were committed to providing an accurate accounting of all American losses, frequently risking their own lives in dangerous search and recovery operations. As a result of their efforts, there were virtually no American unknowns from the Vietnam War, and only 5% of the nation's total casualties were classified as missing.[23]

THE VIETNAM WAR was controversial from the onset and became increasingly divisive as the Johnson administration gradually increased American troop strength and casualties correspondingly mounted. Television news coverage of the war nightly beamed graphic, raw footage of the fighting in Southeast Asia into the nation's living rooms. The networks documented the brutality of the conflict, but often failed to provide appropriate context. The overall impression was that the military was waging a war but was making little progress against a resolute enemy that was proving to be both elusive and cunning. On January 17, 1968, with over a half a million troops deployed to Southeast Asia, President Lyndon Johnson delivered his annual State of the Union address to a joint session of Congress. The President used the nationally televised occasion to boast about the significant progress that was being made in Vietnam, boldly proclaiming that: "The enemy has been defeated in battle after battle."[24] Less than two weeks later, the NVA and VC launched the Tet Offensive, a massive, all-out assault against 36 provincial capitals as well as on the major South Vietnamese cities of Hue and Saigon.[25] The most shocking televised images were those of the U.S. Embassy under siege. The compound's walls had been successfully breached by 19 Viet Cong sappers and the grounds became an urban battleground. Harry G. Summers writes: "Although all [of the enemy] were killed before they could enter the chancery building, itself, pictures of that skirmish gave the false impression that Saigon had been overrun."[26] Indeed, the Tet Offensive became a major turning point in the war. Although it was ultimately a military defeat for the North Vietnamese, it further polarized the nation and encouraged the anti-war movement. It also effectively ruined the Johnson presidency. On March 31, the President shocked the nation by announcing that he would not seek re-election.

THE FIRST MAJOR anti-war protests began in early 1965. Before long, college campuses throughout the country became hotbeds of dissent as students organized and participated in draft card burnings, teach-ins, sit-ins, and moratoriums. American soldiers were denounced and demonized while hundreds of thousands of protestors regularly converged on Washington, D.C. in an all-out effort to end the war. In January 1968, the resolute pacifist and former Congresswoman, Jeanette Rankin, now 87-years old, led a large women's peace protest in the nation's capital.[27]

All political demonstrations and protests were strictly forbidden by regulation at Arlington National Cemetery. Superinten-

(Library of Congress)

Anti-war protestors marching across the Memorial Bridge towards Arlington National Cemetery. The Vietnam War divided the nation and war protests were common on college campuses and in major cities across the nation.

dent Jack Metzler rigorously enforced this proscription and was often forced to lock the main gates to deny protestors access to the cemetery's grounds. The stoic presence of the Tomb sentinels generally discouraged anti-war demonstrators from disrupting the hallowed ambiance at the Tomb of the Unknown Soldier. The exception, though, was a week-long protest conducted by Rebecca Shelley, an 82-year old pacifist.[28] For years, Shelley daily dressed in mourning garb to protest America's involvement in the Vietnam War. In 1969, she suddenly appeared at the Tomb, standing barefoot and silent on the plaza for eight straight days. When she finally began shouting, Shelley was immediately challenged by the Tomb sentinel on duty and local law enforcement escorted her from the cemetery.[29]

(Philip Bigler)

The grave of SSG William Spates. Spates was one of two Tomb Guards who was killed-in-action during the Vietnam War. He is buried near the Tomb of the Unknown Soldier.

There was additional controversy at Arlington when one of the Tomb Guards, SGT Michael C. Sanders (TGIB #64), made headlines by expressing his opposition to the war in a newspaper interview. The sensational story became national news and was featured in stories on NBC News as well as in the *Washington Post*.[30] Sanders political views, though, were not typical and were in stark contrast to the views of most of the other sentinels. Indeed, SSG William Spates (TGIB #33), volunteered for duty in Vietnam and was killed in an enemy mortar attack in Pleiku in 1965. He was buried in Section 48, directly adjacent to the Tomb of the Unknown Soldier.[31] Likewise, Tomb Guard Marvin Franklin (TGIB #50) was killed while serving with the 1st Cavalry Division in Binh Dinh, RSV in 1967.[32]

RICHARD NIXON WON the presidency in 1968, partially by campaigning on the pledge to bring "peace with honor" to Vietnam. His plan called for a gradual turnover of combat operations to the South Vietnamese military forces while simultaneously withdrawing American combat troops. Nixon explained: "we [w]ould train, equip, and inspire the South Vietnamese to fill the gaps left by departing American forces."[33] The policy, known as Vietnamization, was announced in early 1969 and it allowed the United States to begin the slow process of disengagement from the war. By 1972, American military presence had been slashed to just 24,200 troops.

Although the war was still ongoing, President Nixon first raised the possibility of burying an Unknown from the Vietnam War during a Veterans Day visit to Arlington National Cemetery in 1971. It was, appropriately, the fiftieth anniversary of the burial of the World War I Unknown, which President Nixon noted in his prepared remarks: "Fifty years ago a soldier known to God alone was returned to America from the foreign land where he fell in defense of freedom. He was buried in Arlington National Cemetery on Armistice Day, November 11, 1921, and his memory consecrated for all time to those who have died that this nation might live."[34] The President recalled that he and President Eisenhower had been at Arlington 13 years earlier to participate in the ceremonies surrounding the burials of the Unknowns from World War II and Korea and that: "Soon, another Unknown may come to rest on this hallowed hill. We pray he will be the last."[35]

Despite the ongoing political disagreements over the war, there was bipartisan support in Congress for the burial of a Vietnam Unknown. On June 18, 1973, Public Law 93-43, Sec. 9 of the National Cemeteries Act passed, authorizing the interment of an Unknown from Vietnam, despite the lack of qualified remains. It read:

(Library of Congress)
President Richard M. Nixon and First Lady Pat Nixon during the Inauguaral Parade in Washington, D.C., 20 January 1969. Nixon was elected on a pledge to bring "peace with honor" in Vietnam.

(a) The Secretary of Defense is authorized and directed to cause to be brought to the United States the remains of an American, who was a member of the Armed Forces of the United States, who served in Southeast Asia who lost his life during the Vietnam era, and whose identity has not been established, for burial in the Memorial Amphitheater of the National Cemetery at Arlington, Virginia.

(b) The implementation of this section shall take place after the United States has concluded its participation in hostilities in South-east Asia, as determined by the President or the Congress of the United States.[36]

But unlike previous resolutions concerning the Unknowns, the legislation contained no specific deadline, nor did it establish any time frame for a selection and burial of a Vietnam Unknown.

It was hoped that a future burial of an Unknown would unify the country and elevate the Vietnam War to a position of equality with the nation's other twentieth century conflicts. It could also provide some degree of repentance for the callous treatment that the nation's 3.4 million Vietnam veterans had received from the general public. As historian Micki McElya notes: "the failure to inter an unknown (from the Vietnam War) was tantamount to dishonor."[37]

IN JANUARY 1973, the United States signed the Paris Peace Accords, fulfilling Nixon's promise to end America's involvement in Vietnam during his first term of office. The agreement required the withdrawal of the last American combat troops and provided for the prompt return of the nation's 591 POW's still being held by the North. President Nixon had secretly reassured South Vietnamese President, Nguyen Van Thieu, that: "the United States will react very strongly and rapidly to any violation of the agreement" and that any breach of the truce by the North Vietnamese would lead to an American response with "full force."[38] The Watergate scandal, though, soon shattered the Nixon presidency, forcing his resignation from office in August 1974. He was succeeded by his recently appointed and Congressionally approved Vice President, Gerald R. Ford.[39]

Nixon's promises to President Thieu were rendered moot after the Congress drastically slashed military aid to South Vietnam, essentially crippling the nation's combat capabilities. On March 5, 1975, North Vietnam launched a Korean-style invasion of the South with over 20 divisions of hardened combat troops. The communist leadership was supremely confident that the United States would not intervene or provide air support to the besieged ARVN forces.[40] Despite this foreign policy crisis, Congress obstinately refused to authorize any emergency military appropriations, and it wasn't long before the Army of the Republic of Vietnam collapsed from the onslaught. The Ford administration was left with few alternatives and ordered the evacuation by helicopter of last 300 American personnel from the U.S. embassy in Saigon. Code named Operation "Frequent Wind," carrier-based Marine rescue helicopters were sent to the rescue. The pilots were forced to evade enemy sniper fire and navigate in poor weather conditions, but successfully saved all of the embassy staff as well as hundreds of loyal, South Vietnamese civilians who were considered to be "at risk" in the impending communist takeover.[41]

South Vietnam surrendered to the North on April 29 and the NVA occupied Saigon the following day. President Thieu was forced to resign and went into exile in Taiwan where he bitterly complained that the United States had betrayed his country and committed: "an injustice, lack of responsibility and inhumanity toward an ally…the shirking of a responsibility."[42]

(National Archives)
President Gerald R. Ford consults with his advisors, Vice President Nelson Rockefeller and Secretary of State Henry Kissinger in the Oval Office in April 1975. The White House ordered the evacuation of the United States embassy in Saigon during the final North Vietnamese offensive against the South.

In a speech at Tulane University, President Ford attempted to consign the humiliating and embarrassing defeat to the past. The President told students: "Today, America can regain the sense of pride that existed before Vietnam. But it cannot be achieved by re-fighting a war that is finished as far as America is concerned. As I see it, the time has come to look forward to an agenda for the future, to unify, to bind up the Nation's wounds, and to restore its health and its optimistic self-confidence...We, of course, are saddened indeed by the events in Indochina. But these events, tragic as they are, portend neither the end of the world nor of America's leadership in the world."[43] There was no mention or acknowledgement of the 58,209 Americans who had died defending South Vietnam from communism, or of the 2,646 servicemen who were still classified as missing-in-action.[44]

THE NATION'S BICENTENNIAL celebrations in 1976 marked the 200th anniversary of American independence and were a welcome respite from the recent events in Vietnam. Vast crowds of tourists were expected to converge on Washington, D.C. during the year-long commemorations and over 35 million people were predicted to visit Arlington National Cemetery.[45] This enormous increase in visitation would be unprecedented, making it obvious that major renovations to the Memorial Amphitheater were gravely needed in order to accommodate the expected large crowds. In a stark assessment of the current situation, it was reported that: "The area of the Tomb of the Unknowns is not presently equipped to handle the large number of visitors that come to view the ceremony of the changing of the guard."[46] Hundreds of tourists literally surrounded the Tomb each hour to watch the Changing of the Guard ceremony and were restrained by only a few temporary stanchions linked together by chains. The report continued: "Their presence, at peak times, overwhelms the [Changing of the Guard] ceremony, allowing only a limited number of people to have an unobstructed view. As critical as the situation is now, it can only continue to become more confused, as the number of tourists will increase in the near future."[47]

Tourists at the Tomb of the Unknown Soldier. For the nation's Bicentennial celebrations, it was decided during renovations to the Memorial Amphitheater, to restrict access to the plaza area to keep visitors away from the Tomb and prevent them from interfering with the guard change.

A two million dollar renovation project for the Amphitheater was approved by the Commission of Fine Arts. Beginning in 1973, new terraces and balustrades were added to the east front of the Amphitheater to help improve the viewing experience for tourists at the Tomb. These additions were to be constructed from Danbury marble in order to closely match the Amphitheater's existing stone. To ensure order and dignity at the Tomb: "Massive stanchions and chains [are to] be installed to separate public areas from the ceremonial areas. The monumental stairs and plaza area to the East of the Tomb will be closed off to the public and will only be used for ceremonial occasions."[48] Unfortunately, this meant that few tourists would ever see the east façade of the Tomb with its three allegorical figures of "Peace, Victory, and Valor." The new restrictions, though, would provide an: "undisturbed panorama…from the viewing area west of the Tomb."[49]

During the 18 months of construction, it was decided to renovate the Trophy Room and to construct a new barracks for the Tomb Guard. The new Tomb Quarters were built under the south terrace area and included an office for the Sergeant of the Guard, a kitchen and dining area, a ready room, a sleeping area, and a day room.[50]

It was also an opportune time to construct a new crypt for an Unknown on the plaza: "even though no unknown American military dead have yet been found in Vietnam."[51] The Vietnam crypt would be located in the center of the plaza, directly in front of the Lorimer Rich monument and positioned in-between the two existing crypts of the Korean and World War II Unknowns. The empty grave, though, was to be carefully camouflaged with gray, stone pavers in order to make it practically invisible to the general public. The cost for the new crypt was placed at $15,000. During the construction work on the Amphitheater and the plaza, the entire area was closed to public visitation and a privacy fence was erected to conceal the ongoing work. The Tomb Guard was temporarily relocated to the memorial steps and all ceremonies were conducted on the east side of the Tomb during this period.

THE CRYPT AND the Amphitheater renovations were all finished well in advance of the nation's Bicentennial. But 1976 was not only a time of celebration and patriotism; it was a presidential election year as well. Gerald Ford was attempting to win the presidency in his own right since he had inherited the office through his appointment under provisions of the XXV Amendment after the resignations of Vice President Spiro Agnew (1973) and President Richard M. Nixon (1974). Ford, however, had little advantage from incumbency since he was still widely perceived by much of the electorate to be an accidental president. His approval ratings had also declined

(National Archives)
President Gerald R. Ford places a wreath at the Tomb of the Unknown Soldier on Veterans Day. During the renovation of the Amphitheater and the construction of the new crypt for a Vietnam Unknown Soldier, all ceremonies were held on the east steps. A plywood privacy fence was erected to hide the work from the public.

dramatically after he issued a pardon to President Nixon and by the summer of 1976, his popularity was at a anemic 45%.[52] By contrast, his Democratic opponent was a relatively unknown ex-governor from Georgia named Jimmy Carter. A devout Christian and a man of impeccable honesty, Carter seemed to many to be a refreshing counterpoint to the unpleasantness of the Watergate scandal.

During the campaign, in an effort to put aside the divisions caused by the Vietnam War, Governor Carter favored a full and un-conditional amnesty for the over 50,000 draft-dodgers, military deserters, civilian protestors, and dishonorably discharged veterans.[53] President Ford had proposed an alternative amnesty plan, one that required a period of alternative service, a path by which these individuals could work their way back to a restoration of full citizenship rights.[54] In a speech to the VFW, Ford told his audience that: "All, in a sense, are casualties, still abroad and absent without leave from the real America."[55] Ford's alternative service approach, though, was never politically popular and was seen by many to be just another government program and bureaucratic nightmare. As a result, Congress refused to fund the program.[56]

The Vietnam War remained an issue during the 1976 election campaign. It had only been a year since the South had collapsed and the country reunified under communist rule. The dramatic scenes of the humiliating evacuation of the American embassy in Saigon were still vivid in the nation's memory, as were the horrific scenes of thousands of loyal, forsaken Vietnamese citizens being abandoned by the United States to an uncertain fate. There was also the issue about how the millions of American veterans who had served during the Vietnam War were being treated by their fellow citizens. For many, this was a national disgrace and something that needed to be rectified.

Congressman Paul Findley of Illinois was a strong advocate for honoring the service of all Vietnam veterans. In a letter dated August 2, 1976 to President Ford, he wrote: "While our combat participation in the Vietnam War may have been a grievous error, the men who served and died in this conflict nevertheless deserve every recognition and honor. The courage and conviction, determination and devotion that they displayed in a strange, distant war must place them in the very front ranks of all heroes in our history. It is my fervent hope that Vietnam combatants will receive the same tributes as the soldiers from our other wars."[57]

Findley was convinced that by promptly burying a Vietnam Unknown at Arlington National Cemetery, it would elevate the war to co-equal status with the nation's other twentieth century conflicts and finally recognize the honorable service of the nation's veterans in Southeast Asia. His letter to President Ford continued: "I have been informed that there are now ten unidentified remains in the Army Central Identification Laboratory in Hawaii. If these bodies cannot be identified, I think it appropriate that one of these men be interred at the Tomb of the Unknown Soldier in Arlington. Additional delay can serve no purpose and deprives tens of thousands of Vietnam veterans of the recognition they deserve...it has now been over three years since hostilities were officially terminated for Americans...if identification has not been possible to date, the chances for success in the future must be remote at best."[58]

Findley's well-intentioned letter was forwarded to the White House Military Office and to the Secretary of Defense for further consideration and response. On August 26, Charles Leppart, the Deputy Assistant to the President, replied at length in an effort to address the Congressman's concerns. Leppart noted that the United States was still engaged in a vigorous effort to locate and identify all of the nation's soldiers who were listed as missing-in-action. Moreover, the ten remains in Hawaii were not considered suitable for an Unknown soldier; seven were name-associated and were expected to be identified soon, after further corroborating evidence. Two of the remains could not be positively confirmed to be Americans and were thus eliminated from any consideration. Leppart wrote: "In summary, none of these nine remains is within the criteria utilized for the selection of the Unknowns for World War I, World War II, and the Korean War."[59] He continued: "The three years which have elapsed since Vietnam hostilities were officially terminated...are not considered to be excessive when compared to the approximately twelve years which elapsed between the cessation of hostilities for World War II and the selection of an Unknown to commemorate the service of millions of veterans who served in that war."[60]

Despite Charles Leppart's thoughtful and reasoned response, Congressman Findley still introduced a resolution in Congress calling for the immediate burial of an Unknown Serviceman from Vietnam and enlisted the support of 40 co-sponsors. The legislation noted that the crypt at the Tomb was complete and had been "prepared for the remains of a Vietnam Unknown Soldier."[61] Findley completely disregarded the dubious status of the remains in Hawaii, implying that: "the remains of several unknown soldiers from Vietnam are at the Army Identification Laboratory in Hawaii" and could thus be used for the selection of the Unknown Serviceman.[62]

The same day that he introduced the resolution on the Unknown, Findley sent a "personal and private" letter to Jack Marsh, the Counselor to the President. In it, he highlighted the enormous political benefits that President Ford could receive from interring an Unknown just prior to the election. He wrote: "Jack, this is a natural for the President. He could do it this year on Veterans Day, October 25, and gain more votes than he could with any other initiative he might make between now and election day…since the crypt for a Vietnam Unknown is already authorized by Congress and in place, it is as certain as death and taxes that someday a President of the United States is going to bury a Vietnam Unknown there. I just think it should be President Ford, and that he should do it before the election."[63]

In the letter, Findley discounted the careful response from Charlie Leppart that he had received a few days earlier and which had rejected the idea of a quick burial of a Vietnam Unknown. Findley wrote:

> If you talk to the people who wrote the attached letter
> for Charlie Leppart, they will give you basically two
> reasons why this should not be done:

(1) That someday they hope to be able to identify the bodies they have, even though one has been there for nine years. So what! Would it make the symbolism of the Tomb of the Unknown for the American people any less important if someday they decide that the body they buried might be identified? In the meantime, how about all the Vietnam Vets, the Missing, and the 55,000 dead, and all their families who are not being properly recognized because someone is worried that someday they may be able to put a name on the Unknown. If that mentality had prevailed two decades ago, we would never have buried any Unknowns at Arlington from any of our wars.

(2) Some believe that you need a whole body, or a substantial portion of one, to bury. The fact is, if you have 85% of a body—the accepted standard for the World War II Unknown—you can identify the soldier today through advanced techniques. Frankly I don't see what difference it makes if we bury only a small portion of an Unknown Soldier—a limb if that is all there is. We would be doing it to honor the memory of the thousands who died in Vietnam, and that honor will be in no way diminished just because there isn't a whole body to bury. That honor comes from the emotion and gratitude of those who live on, not from the contents of the casket placed at the Tomb of the Unknown Soldier. If we fail to honor our Vietnam dead at the Tomb of the Unknowns, we surely diminish our country's own honor in the eyes of those brave men who answered their country's call when the time came.[64]

Congressman Findley's correspondence caused a flurry of internal, confidential White House staff memos. Jack Marsh did not want to politicize the burial of an unknown, and asked that Bill Hyland, the White House National Security Adviser, to meet with Findley to explain the administration's objections.[65] This task was eventually delegated to Frank Sieverts, who was actively involved with POW/MIA matters at the State Department. In a handwritten note on White House stationary, Mitt Mitler explained that Sieverts: "understands the problem—no unidentified body available and we shouldn't move in Findley's direction until MIA matter is settled."[66]

To its credit, the Ford administration refused to succumb to political opportunism and refused to proceed with the burial. Superintendent of Arlington National Cemetery, Raymond Costanzo, acknowledged that the crypt may forever remain empty. In an interview with the *New York Times*, Costnazo stated: "We were so enormously efficient over there. We've had the Vietnam crypt ready for two years now, but I don't know, it may never be used."[67] In the general election, Jimmy Carter defeated President Ford. His narrow margin of victory in the Electoral College was 297 to 240.

THE NEW PRESIDENT, Jimmy Carter, visited Arlington National Cemetery on Veterans Day, 1977. In his speech, Carter acknowledged the absence of the Vietnam Unknown Soldier: "We are here to commemorate the dead. The Tomb of the Unknown Soldier was dedicated in 1921, and the body of an Unknown Soldier from the First World War was buried here. Later, we had the bodies of unknown soldiers from the Korean war and the Second World War. We don't have the body of a Vietnam veteran, because every body so far discovered has been identified."[68] He also took the time to recognize the honorable service of the nation's Vietnam-era veterans: "And I think there's a special debt of gratitude on the part of American people to those young men and women who served in Vietnam, because they've not been appreciated enough."

The following year, in lieu of burying an Unknown, President Carter authorized the installation of a large bronze memorial plaque in the Trophy Room at Arlington to recognize the service of the nation's Vietnam veterans. The plaque read: "The People of the United States of America Pay Tribute to Those Members of Its Armed Forces Who Served Honorably In Southeast Asia During the Vietnam Conflict." In his remarks during a bill signing, the President said: "We've never had an unidentified or unknown soldier from the Vietnam war. All those who died and whose bodies were recovered have been identified...there should be a means to honor those who died in Vietnam, and a special plaque will be installed [at Arlington]."[69]

(Philip Bigler)

A plaque honoring Vietnam veterans in the Trophy Room at the Memorial Amphitheater.

LORIMER RICH, THE architect who had designed the main Tomb of the Unknown Soldier as well as the crypts for the World War II and Korean Unknowns, died on June 2, 1978 at his home in Camden, New York. He was 86 years old.[70] In addition to his work at Arlington, Rich had a distinguished career and was credited with having designed 21 federal buildings and post offices for the United States government. In his later years, he was an instructor at Columbia University before retiring in 1971.

Rich had served in the military during World War I, working primarily on developing gas masks for use by American troops in Europe. He never saw combat and left the military shortly after

the armistice. With Arlington
National Cemetery's rigorous
restrictions on burial, Rich was
ineligible for in-ground interment based upon his military
service record.[71]

Immediately after his
death, Rich's wife, Martha,
contacted their Congressman,
Donald J. Mitchell, to see if
anything could be done to allow for the architect's cremated remains to be buried at
Arlington, given his instrumental role in the development
and evolution of the Tomb of
the Unknown Soldier. Mitchell promptly contacted Frank
Moore, a White House assistant
on Congressional Relations,
who forwarded Mrs. Rich's request to President Jimmy Carter. Moore wrote: [Rich] does

(Philip Bigler)

The grave of Lorimer Rich, the designer of the Tomb of the Unknown Soldier. His burial was authorized by President Jimmy Carter.

not qualify for burial in Arlington under the present regulations, unless you make an exception. I believe that Mr. Rich's contribution
to the beauty of Arlington warrants his burial there."[72] The President initialed the request, approving it without any comment. On
June 21, Lorimer Rich was buried in close proximity to the Tomb he
had designed, in Section 48. His grave was marked with a standard,
government-issued stone and bore the inscription: "Designer, Tomb
of the Unknown Soldier." His wife was interred upon her death in
the same grave 9 years later.[73]

FOR THE NEXT several years, there was little progress on the possibility of designating an Unknown Serviceman from the Vietnam

War. There were still over 2,500 Americans classified as missing-in-action. Included in this number were 450 casualties who were categorized as "over water losses."[74] This meant that these airmen and crews were presumed to be dead (PTD) but that their bodies were deemed to be unrecoverable.[75] Thus, their names could be eliminated from any recovered remains and were precluded from being considered for the Unknown.[76]

The rapid helicopter insertion and evacuation tactics which typified military operations during the Vietnam War had virtually eliminated casualties from being classified as unknown. Moreover, very few American combat fatalities were caused by enemy artillery fire. Indeed, the vast majority of U.S. deaths were the result of "small arms fire, mines, rockets, mortars and grenades...There were fewer instances of the sort of mutilation that made identification impossible."[77] Coupled with the policy of concurrent return of remains along with major advances in forensics (blood typing, dental records, fingerprints analysis, physical characteristics, et al.), this meant that there were virtually no unknowns from the Vietnam War. As the *New York Times* reported: "advances in forensic science, and the fact that an unusually large number of engagements in Vietnam involved only small arms, limited the number of unknowns from the nation's most recent war. There were relatively few cases of mutilation so severe that identification was impossible."[78]

By 1981, only four partial remains were still classified as unidentifiable at the Army Central Identification Laboratory in Hawaii. The most likely candidate for the Vietnam Unknown was designated as X-26. These ossa-remains consisted of just six small bones and fragments (four ribs, part of a pelvis and a humerus) and represented less than "nine percent" of the human body.[79] The paucity of bones made positive identification extremely difficult, but it was not considered to be impossible.[80]

The National League of Families membership was comprised of the families of servicemen who were classified as missing-in-action or previously held as prisoners-of-war. The group was politically active and extremely influential. The organization demanded: "the fullest accounting for those still missing, and the reparation of all recoverable remains."[81] Members opposed any effort to select or designate an Unknown Soldier because they feared that it would lead to the United States issuing a blanket "presumed to be dead" (PTD) classification for all MIA's and thus end all efforts to recover remains still missing in Southeast Asia.[82] Indeed, Ann Mills Griffiths, whose brother, LCDR James B. Mills, was shot down in 1966 and classified as MIA, claimed that to select an Unknown as this time would be a political act that was not justified based upon the current circumstances.[83] In a classified memo to the Secretary of Defense, now Secretary of the Army, John O. Marsh, reported that: "the Central Identification Laboratory in Hawaii (CILHI) continues to indicate further concerns about the eligibility of any of the four candidates."[84] According to Colonel Chet J. Bobiski: "It's better than the alternative. Soldiers deserve names, dead or alive."[85] These arguments initially prevailed and any potential planning for a burial was placed on a temporary hold.

JAN SCRUGGS SERVED as an Army corporal in Vietnam. In 1979, he founded the Vietnam Veterans Memorial Fund, and began to seek financial support for a new memorial on the Mall in Washington, D.C. to honor all of those who had served during the Vietnam War. An architectural design competition was held under the stipulation that all submitted proposals would advance and foster the desired "national unity and reconciliation" while remaining political neutral by avoiding "any statement about the correctness of the war."[86] Eventually 1,421 entries were submitted for final review and evaluation. These designs varied drastically in concept, design, and scale. To ensure impartiality, all of the submissions were judged without attribution to the artist/architect. Eventually, the proposals were culled down to 39 finalists. After further review, entry #1,026 was selected. It was a powerful, minimalist design that was the work of a young, 21-year old Yale undergraduate student by the name of Maya Lin.

(National Archives)
President Ronald Reagan visiting the new Vietnam Memorial. The monument was designed by Maya Lin and listed the names of all of the American servicemen and women who died while serving in Vietnam.

The new monument was to be prominently located on re-cently cleared land in close proximity to the Lincoln Memorial. Lin's memorial would be constructed in the shape of a "V."[87] On its black, mirrored marble walls, the names of the over 58,000 American sol-diers, servicemen, and nurses who had died during the Vietnam War would be etched into the stone chronologically, beginning in 1959 and continuing through 1975. Each name would be indicated with either a diamond "♦" for killed-in-action, or a plus sign "+" to indi-cate a serviceman was still missing-in-action.

Maya Lin's proposed monument was widely criticized by the political press and by some members of Congress. It was variously denigrated as: "a black gash of shame," a "degrading ditch," and "a monument to defeat."[88] These criticisms were moderated somewhat with the addition of an American flag pole and later by a three-figure statue of combat soldiers designed by Frederick Hart, as well as a monument to military nurses sculpted by Glenna Goodacre.[89]

The Vietnam Veterans Memorial was dedicated over the Veterans Day holiday in 1982. One of the featured speakers at the event was, appropriately, Navy pilot and POW, Everett Alvarez, who had been shot down over North Vietnam in 1964.[90] The detractors and critics of Maya Lin's design were proven to be spectacularly wrong. "The Wall," as it would become popularly known, was, in fact, a work of genius and immediately became one of the most visited memorials in the nation's capital. It was cherished by the Vietnam veterans, who said it represented the "welcome home" parade they never received. The memorial was part of a growing national catharsis to give the proper recognition to the Vietnam veterans who had served the nation during the war. According to one veteran, Stephen Sossaman: "The Vietnam Veterans Memorial has proven to be far more powerful and important than anyone could have ever imagined. One source of its power is the inclusion of names, an insistence on the humanity of every individual counted among the dead. Each of those names represents a unique individual with a unique set of life experiences."[91] It also served to restore the lost identity of hundreds of American soldiers and servicemen who remained missing-in-action.

———

PRESIDENT RONALD REAGAN did much to help redefine the Vietnam War for the American people and to finally bring honor to those American veterans who had served in Southeast Asia. In a heartfelt speech delivered to the VFW in August 1980, then candidate Reagan declared: "It is time we recognized that ours was, in truth, a noble cause...We dishonor the memory of 50,000 young Americans who died in that cause when we give way to feelings of guilt as if we were doing something shameful, and we have been shabby in our treatment of those who returned. They fought as well and as bravely as any Americans have ever fought in any war. They deserve our gratitude, our respect, and our continuing concern."[92] It was the start of an ongoing effort to seperate and exonerate American servicemen from the decisions made during the war by inept politicians and clueless Washington bureaucrats.

By 1984, some members of the Reagan administration decided that it was time to revisit the idea of burying an Unknown from the Vietnam War. It had been over a decade since the last American combat troops had left Vietnam and many patriotic and veteran groups, such as the VFW, were lobbying for an interment at Arlington as a way to appropriately recognize and honor the service of Vietnam-era veterans. The powerful and politically connected National League of Families, though, was still an obstacle. Members opposed any burial, fearing that the designation of a Vietnam Unknown would effectively end the search for MIA's. Senior members of the Reagan administration attempted to assuage these concerns by pledging that the government would continue its efforts to achieve the fullest accounting possible for all American missing servicemen. In March, finally yielding to the intense political pressure, the League's Executive Director, Ann Mills-Griffiths, cautiously withdrew the group's objections but with the caveat that: "under no circumstances must [burial] be allowed to signal any lessening of effort to account for POW/MIAs or to 'finally put the Vietnam War behind.'"[93]

The next month, Caspar Weinberger, the Secretary of Defense, issued a Pentagon press release that officially announced the planned burial of a Vietnam Unknown at Arlington National Cemetery on Memorial Day 1984. He claimed that: "after more than ten years of intensive effort, we have a remain which cannot be identified and is qualified for the Vietnam Unknown."[94] The Secretary went on to explain that: "The Tomb of the Unknowns is considered by many to be the greatest national monument to those who served, fought, and died during our wars. Those fine Americans who placed duty to their country above all else, deserved the highest recognition we can offer. We are now able to honor our Vietnam veterans...by placing one of their fallen comrades-in-arms alongside the national heroes of previous wars at the Tomb of the Unknowns."[95] Weinberger was careful to use the announcement to publicly reassure the League and the families of the missing that: "We must remember, there are almost 2,500 Americans still missing in Southeast Asia. For their families, the uncertainty and the pain continues. Our duty to them should be strengthened by this ceremony. The resolution of the fate of those gallant men still missing is, as the President has stated, a matter of highest national priority."[96]

There had been persistent rumors at Arlington for several months that an Unknown from Vietnam would soon be designated. Once the Pentagon confirmed that this would, indeed, take place, there was a sense of anticipation and excitement at the cemetery. Everyone knew the historical significance of such a burial and that it would be the most important occasion at Arlington since the burial of President John F. Kennedy some 21 years earlier.

The Tomb sentinels would have a central role during the interment ceremonies. [97] Acting Relief Commander (First Relief), Sergeant David Nicholson, remembers feeling honored and privileged to be at the Tomb at this important moment. His fellow Tomb Guard, SP4 Kevin Donovan, felt that the interment of an Unknown would be an opportunity to finally say "thank you to the Vietnam veterans."[98] Indeed, thousands of Vietnam-era veterans, many proudly wearing their military medals, made the pilgrimage to the Tomb over the next few weeks in anticipation of the forthcoming burial of one of their compatriots.

There was also widespread speculation at Arlington that the previous regulations which had rigorously governed the selection of the previous Unknowns had to have been either seriously modified or simply abandoned. Even without being privy to the classified information about the failed identification, it was presumed that any unknown had to be either an aviator or a member of a downed air crew. Only a cataclysmic crash and powerful explosion could have obliterated human remains to the degree as to make them unidentifiable. As Professor Michael Allen explains: "Unlike their predecessors who faced heavy artillery and aerial bombardment, few Americans killed in Vietnam were felled by weapons likely to destroy all identifying characteristics. Pilots and air-crews lost over enemy territory were the main exceptions."[99] Following the previous procedures governing the selection of earlier American unknowns, the military ordered all documents and related materials associated with

(National Archives)
Construction begins on preparing the crypt for the interment of the Vietnam Unknown Serviceman. The plaza was closed to the public for several weeks during the work.

the candidate-unknown's remains to be shredded and destroyed to ensure perpetual anonymity.

The preparations for the interment at the cemetery began in late April. Landscapers planted dozens of new shrubs and flowers in the immediate vicinity of the Amphitheater to beautify the area. A large, 20'x30' video viewing screen was contracted and erected at the cemetery's temporary Visitors' Center to accommodate the expected overflow crowds. Public access to the Amphitheater and plaza area was restricted and a large privacy fence was built around the immediate Tomb area. Construction crews began work on removing the granite pavers which had covered the unused center crypt for years in order to prepare it for the Memorial Day funeral. While this was being done, the adjacent crypt covers of the World War II and Korean Unknowns were cleaned and refurbished and the marble memorial stone for the Vietnam Unknown was retrieved from the Amphitheater's catacombs storage area. It was then inscribed by a stone carver with the dates of the Vietnam War: 1958-1975.[100] During this time period, the Tomb Guard was relocated to the east memorial steps and all scheduled wreath ceremonies were conducted in front of the Tomb's east façade.

SINCE THERE WAS only one remain at the Central Identification Laboratory deemed to be still unidentified, for the first time there could be no selection ceremony for an American Unknown. Instead, X-26 would be officially declared to be the Unknown Serviceman from the Vietnam War at a special "designation" ceremony held at the United States Naval base at Pearl Harbor, Hawaii on May 17. As 180 troops and sailors stood at attention, the flag-draped casket containing the remains of the Unknown was placed upon a bier covered in black mourning cloth at Bravo Pier 25. Admiral S. R. Foley delivered opening remarks, beginning the short services: "Our unknown hero...represents the finest of the generation who went to a far off land to fight for the ideals of freedom and human dignity."[101] Once the Admiral had concluded his speech and military chaplains recited prayers, U.S. Marine Sergeant Major Allan J. Kellogg, a Vietnam-era Medal of Honor recipient, placed a wreath of carnations at the foot of the casket. He stepped back and saluted, officially designating the Unknown Serviceman from the Vietnam War.[102] Admiral Foley then presented the Unknown with the Purple Heart medal and after the appropriate military honors were rendered, a squadron of F-4 Phantom jets from the Hawaiian Air National Guard flew over the dock in the missing-man formation. The formal ceremonies concluded with the Marine Corps band playing the traditional "Funeral March" by composer Frédéric Chopin.[103]

The casket of the Unknown Serviceman was then carried a short distance to the moored frigate, USS *Brewton* (FF-1086), where the entire crew in dress Navy whites stood at attention. The body was carried onboard by a joint service casket term and taken to the ship's stern flight deck, where it was placed under a four-man, Marine guard watch as the Unknown began his seven-day return journey to California.[104]

(National Archives)

Sergeant Major and Medal of Honor recipient, Allan Kellogg, designates the Vietnam Unknown Soldier. The ceremonies took place at Pearl Harbor, Hawaii.

(National Archives)

The Unknown Serviceman from the Vietnam War under guard on the flight deck of the USS Brewton *en route to California.*

THE *BREWTON* PASSED under the Golden Gate Bridge on Thursday morning, May 24, and sailed into the majestic San Francisco harbor. A short time later, the frigate docked at the Alameda Naval Air Station. There, an awaiting hearse transported the casket to Travis Air Force Base where the Unknown was scheduled to lay-in-state overnight in the base's chapel.

The next morning, the Unknown was taken to the flight line where it was loaded onboard an Air Force C-141B Starlifter transport. Air Force personnel also loaded dozens of wreaths and floral tributes onboard the aircraft to accompany the casket back to Washington, D.C. The plane arrived at Andrews Air Force Base at 2 PM where a small welcoming party awaited. Among the delegation were members of the cabinet and representatives of various veterans' or-

(National Archives)
The services for the Unknown at the U.S. Capitol Rotunda. President Ronald Reagan delivered brief remarks before the building was opened to the general public.

ganizations, as well as General William Westmoreland, the former commander of all American forces in Vietnam. The casket was carried to a nearby hearse and driven to the United States Capitol for the formal ceremonies.[105]

President Reagan and the First Lady arrived at the Capitol at 2:50 PM. Ten minutes later, an Army, Navy, and Marine color guard led the Unknown's casket into the Rotunda, where it was placed upon the Lincoln catafalque. After brief prayers, President Reagan delivered a short eulogy: "An American hero has returned home. God bless him." He continued: "We may not know of this man's life, but we know of his character. We may not know his name, but we know his courage. He is the heart, the spirit, and the soul of America…This young American understood that freedom is never more than one generation from extinction…On this day, as we honor our unknown serviceman, we pray to Almighty God for His mercy. And we pray for the wisdom that this hero be America's last unknown."[106] After concluding his remarks, the President placed a wreath in front of the bier. He and the First Lady returned to the White House, where they boarded a Marine helicopter for a short flight to the Camp David Presidential Retreat in Maryland.

Later that evening, the President confided in his diary: "He will lie in state in the rotunda til the Mon. funeral at Arlington. It's impossible to describe out thoughts when you stand before the casket. Who was he? A son, a husband & father? The answers known only to God."[107] The President and First Lady spent the rest of the holiday weekend enjoying horseback riding and relaxing with leisurely swims. Each evening, they screened a Hollywood movie before returning to Washington that Monday to participate in the official state funeral and interment ceremonies for the Unknown Serviceman from the Vietnam War.[108]

———

THE UNKNOWN SERVICEMAN lay-in-state for three days and nights in the Capitol Rotunda for a public viewing. During that time, thousands of American citizens solemnly passed by the bier to pay their respects. On Monday, May 28, the casket was carried out of the Capitol and down the East Steps where it was placed upon an Army gun caisson, drawn by six white horses. Marching units, military bands, and cadets and midshipmen from the nation's service academies made up the accompanying procession to Arlington National Cemetery. Despite overcast skies and a persistent threat of rain, thousands of people lined the entire three-mile funeral route. On the Memorial Bridge and the Memorial Drive approach to the cemetery, a cordon of 1,750 military men and women stood at attention to salute the national colors and the Unknown's casket as they passed by.[109] The scheduled flyover, however, had to be cancelled because of a low cloud ceiling.

The most poignant part of the funeral procession was unplanned and unexpected. Near the Vietnam Veterans Memorial, hundreds of veterans had gathered. These were once the boys that the nation called to war and who were now the men who had done their duty and served honorably during the Vietnam War. They were no longer young, but rather proud, seasoned veterans approaching middle age. Once the caisson and the accompanying military units had passed by, over 300 of these former GI's fell-in behind the main procession. They were dressed in their olive drab fatigues, jungle jackets, and boonie hats, providing a stark contrast to the official military units consisting of meticulously dressed young men and women in pressed uniforms and brightly shined brass. But in many ways, this disparate group of Vietnam veterans was iconic; they were finally marching in the parade that had been denied them upon returning home by an indifferent nation. Led by a lone bagpiper playing the evocative notes of "Amazing Grace," these vets were accompanying one of their comrades-in-arms on his final journey to the nation's most cherished burial ground.[110] There, he would be honorably laid to rest among the nation's other heroes.

The caisson arrived at the West Entrance of the Amphitheater promptly at 2 PM. The casket was still covered in translucent plastic to protect its interment flag in the case of rain. The joint service team of body-bearers carried the casket up the West Steps and into

The caisson arrives at the Memorial Amphitheater for the scheduled Memorial Day services.

the Amphitheater, around the North Colonnade and into the apse, where President Ronald Reagan and Secretary of Defense Caspar Weinberger awaited.

The official memorial services began with the Marine band playing the national anthem. Major General Patrick Hessian, Chief of Chaplains, then led the gathered mourners in prayer, which was followed directly by a one-minute period of observed silence. After further hymns and prayers, President Reagan presented the Unknown with the nation's highest military decoration for valor, the Medal of Honor. He then delivered his eulogy. "My fellow Americans," the President began. "Memorial Day is a day of ceremonies and speeches. Throughout America today, we honor the dead of our wars. We recall their valor and their sacrifices. We remember they gave their lives so that others might live. We're also gathered here for a special event -- the national funeral for an unknown soldier who will today join the heroes of three other wars."[111]

(National Archives)

President Ronald Reagan at the Amphitheater services for the Vietnam Unknown. The President presented the Unknown with the Congressional Medal of Honor and delivered an eloquent euolgy acknowledging the service of the nation's Vietnam veterans..

The President made sure to reaffirm the nation's commitment to the families of these servicemen who were still missing-in-action: "One way to honor those who served or may still be serving in Vietnam is to gather here and rededicate ourselves to securing the answers for the families of those missing in action… Vietnam is not over for them. They cannot rest until they know the fate of those they loved and watched march off to serve their country. Our dedication to their cause must be strengthened with these events today. We write no last chapters. We close no books. We put away no final memories. An end to America's involvement in Vietnam cannot come before we've achieved the fullest possible accounting of those missing in action."[112]

The moving address evoked the sentiments that President Reagan had earlier confided to his diary: "About him we may well wonder, as others have: As a child, did he play on some street in a great American city? Or did he work beside his father on a farm out in America's heartland? Did he marry? Did he have children? Did he look expectantly to return to a bride? We'll never know the answers to these questions about his life. We do know, though, why he died. He saw the horrors of war but bravely faced them, certain his own cause and his country's cause was a noble one; that he was fighting for human dignity, for free men everywhere. Today we pause to embrace him and all who served us so well in a war whose end offered no parades, no flags, and so little thanks."[113] The President concluded his speech with: "A grateful nation opens her heart today in gratitude for their sacrifice, for their courage, and for their noble service. Let us, if we must, debate the lessons learned at some other time. Today, we simply say with pride, 'Thank you, dear son. May God cradle you in His loving arms.'"[114]

After the President spoke, more prayers and psalms were read, then, following the benediction, the Unknown's casket was taken inside the Trophy Room followed by Reagan and the official

(National Archives)
President Ronald Reagan, Major General John L. Ballantyne, and Arlington Superintendent Raymond J. Costanzo salute the Unknown during interment ceremonies at the Tomb of the Unknown Soldier.

delegation. At the designated time, the casket was carried out of the east doors and down the steps, where it was placed upon a catafalque over the open crypt in front of the main Tomb. President Reagan, Major General John L. Ballantyne, and Arlington Superintendent Raymond J. Costanzo followed the casket onto the plaza. There, committal prayers were rendered by clergy from the Jewish, Orthodox, Catholic, and Protestant faiths. President Reagan, assisted by the Sergeant of the Guard, then placed a large, floral wreath in front of the casket. Traditional military honors followed with the firing of a twenty-one-gun salute and the playing of "Taps." The casket team then skillfully folded the Unknown's interment flag and presented it to the President of the United States. The Vietnam Unknown Serviceman had, at last, returned home.[115]

AFTER THE DIGNITARIES left the cemetery, four members of the Tomb Guard stood a rotating watch over the casket. The interment flag and the Medal of Honor were temporarily placed on display pedestals on the plaza for public viewing. Over the next several hours, thousands of people passed by the casket to pay their final respects.

Just after dusk, once the cemetery was closed to public visitation, Superintendent Raymond Costanzo and a few select staff returned to the plaza. The official ceremonies had long since concluded, but the casket still had to be lowered into its grave and the crypt closed and sealed. This is necessarily a logistical rather than a ceremonial exercise and is always conducted in private. But since it was a historic moment, Major General John Ballantyne and a few soldiers and marines were also there to render one final salute to the Unknown.

At 8:30 PM, Costanzo released the nylon straps on the metal frame that had been positioned over the crypt. The coffin slowly descended into the darkness of the burial vault. Afterwards, four members of a construction crew, each wearing a hardhat, carefully maneuvered a portable crane into place and lifted the heavy marble

(National Archives)
A construction crew positions the crypt cover over the grave of the Vietnam Unknown Serviceman as Arlington Superintendent Raymond Costanzo looks on.

crypt cover over the open grave. It was carefully lowered into place and the work crew sealed the grave. [116] By midnight, the task had been completed and everyone left the cemetery except for SGT David Nicholson and the sentinels of the First Relief who were on duty. There were no crowds, no newsmen, no pilgrims, no visitors—just the Tomb Guard silently maintaining their perpetual vigil.[117]

The crypt of the Vietnam Unknown Serviceman would remain sealed and undestrubed for the next 13 years, 11 months, and 14 days.[118]

Endnotes

1 Dwight Eisenhower, Press Conference, 7 April 1954, available at: https://www. nps.gov/features/eise/jrranger/quotes2.htm.

2 Robert McNamara. *In Retrospect: The Tragedy and Lessons of Vietnam.* New York: Times Books, 1995, p. 9.

3 H.R. McMaster. *Dereliction of Duty: Lyndon Johnson, Robert McNamara, the Joints Chiefs of Staff, and the Lies that Led to Vietnam.* New York: Harper Perennial, 1998, p. 10.

4 John F. Kennedy, Inaugural Address, 20 January 1961 available at the American Presidency Project: https://www.presidency.ucsb.edu/documents/inaugural-address-2.

5 Maxwell Taylor (26 August 1901-19 April 1987), Sec. 7A, #Lot 20; Robert S. McNamara (19 June 1906-6 July 2009), Sec. 2, #1233-A.

6 Taylor developed this policy to avoid the Eisenhower era doctrine of "massive retaliation" which required a nuclear response in the event of a major war with the Soviet Union. McMaster, p 10.

7 *Ibid.*, p. 58.

8 Gulf of Tonkin Resolution, 10 August 1964 available at: https://www.ourdocuments.gov/doc.php?flash=true&doc=98&page=transcript.

9 Alvarez was the first aviator to be captured during the war and second longest held American prisoner-of-war. Colonel Jim Thompson had been captured six months earlier by the Viet Cong. Everett Alvarez and Anthony S. Pitch. *Chained Eagle.* New York: Donald J. Fine, Inc., 1989.

10 McMaster, p. 202.

11 Harry G. Summers, Jr. *Historical Atlas of the Vietnam War.* Boston: Houghton Mifflin Company, 1995, p. 96.

12 *Ibid.*, p. 98.

13 Eight Army nurses died while serving in Vietnam—two in 1968: LT Pamela Donovan and LTC Annie Ruth Graham, Sec.21, #569. On 8 June 1969, 1LT Sharon A. Lane was killed in a rocket attack while serving with the 312th Evacuation

Hospital in Chu Lai. She was the only nurse to die by enemy action. See Philip Bigler. *Hostile Fire: The Life and Death of 1Lt. Sharon A. Lane.* St. Petersburg, FL.: Vandamere Press, 1996.

14 Charles W. Honaker. *The Dead Were Mine.* Charles W. Honaker, p. 88.

15 *Ibid.*, pp. 7, 103.

16 Charles W. Honaker quoted in *The Dead Were Mine*, p. 13.

17 Honaker, p. 25.

18 *Ibid.*, p. 13.

19 *Ibid.*, p. 18.

20 *Ibid.*, p. 3.

21 *Ibid.*, p. 53.

22 *Ibid.*, p. 3.

23 The percentage of missing-in-action was far greater in earlier wars than in Vietnam. In Korea, it was 25% while in World War II, the number was 20%. During the American Civil War, the number of missing is estimated to be around 50%. Michael Allen. *Until the Last Man Comes Home: POWs, MIAs, and the Unending Vietnam War.* Chapel Hill: University of North Carolina Press, 2009, p. 2.

24 Lyndon B. Johnson, State of the Union Address, 17 January 1968 available at: https://www.presidency.ucsb.edu.

25 Summers, p. 130.

26 *Ibid.*, p. 132.

27 McElya, p. 253.

28 Rebecca Shelley's papers are available at the University of Michigan. She died in 1984 at the age of 97.

29 McElya, pp. 257, 258.

30 *Ibid.*, pp. 256, 257.

31 See the Society of the Honor Guard at: https://tombguard.org/column/2015/10/we-remember-william-bill-spates-tgib-33/.

32 William Spates (8 September 1939-25 October 1965), Sec.48, #432; Marvin Franklin (15 July 1945-31 August 1967, burial at Chapel Hills Memorial Garden Cemetery in Oklahoma City, Oklahoma.

33 Richard M. Nixon. *The Memoirs of Richard Nixon.* New York: Grosset & Dunlap, 1978, p. 392.

34 Richard M. Nixon. "Statement Following the Laying of a Wreath on the Tomb of the Unknowns in Arlington National Cemetery," 11 November 1971 available at The American Presidency Project: http://www.presidency.ucsb.edu.

35 *Ibid.*

36 Public Law 93-43, National Cemeteries Act of 1973 available at: https://www. gpo.gov/fdsys/pkg/STATUTE-87/pdf/STATUTE-87-Pg75.pdf.

37 McElya, p. 262.

38 Letter from President Richard M. Nixon to President Nguyen Van Thieu quoted in *Historic Documents of 1975.* Washington, D.C.: Congressional Quarterly, Inc., 1976, p. 298.

39 Nixon's Vice President, Spiro Agnew, resigned from office on 10 October 1973. Under the provisions of the XXV Amendment, Nixon was allowed to appoint a new Vice President with the consent of both houses of Congress. Congressman Gerald Ford was confirmed and sworn in on 6 December 1973.

40 *Historic Documents of 1975.* Washington, D.C.: Congressional Quarterly, Inc., 1976, p. 280.

41 "Notes from Cabinet Meeting Regarding the Evacuation of Saigon, South Vietnam," 29 April 1975, available at: https://catalog.archives.gov/id/7367500/.

42 President Nguyen Van Thieu quoted in *Historic Documents*, p. 279.

43 President Gerald R. Ford, Speech at Tulane University, 23 April 1975 available at: https://www.presidency.ucsb.edu/documents/address-tulane-university-convocation.

44 Paul D. Mather. *M.I.A.: Accounting for the Missing in Southeast Asia.* Washington, D.C.: National Defense University Press, 1994, p. xx.

45 "Renovations to the Tomb of the Unknowns: Arlington National Cemetery," prepared by Mills, Petticord & Mills Architects, December 1971 available at the Commission of Fine Arts, p. A-2.

46 *Ibid.*, p. A-2.

47 *Ibid.*, p. A-2.

48 *Ibid.*, p. A-3.

49 *Ibid.*, p. A-3.

50 *Ibid.*, pp. A-3, B-2.

51 Jay Mathews. "3d 'Unknown's' Tomb Eyed," *Washington Post,* 1 July 1972, B2.

52 Roper Center at Cornell University. See: https://presidential.roper.center/.

53 Many of the political protestors had sought asylum in Canada during the war and were considered to be fugitives from justice. A report noted that for such individuals: "Full integration into the post-Vietnam world is difficult at best." "Vietnam: Veterans, Deserters, and Draft Evaders," available at the Gerald R. Ford Library.

54 *Ibid.*

55 Gerald R. Ford. *A Time to Heal: The Autobiography of Gerald R. Ford.* New York: Harpers and Row, 1979, p. 142.

56 *Ibid.*, p. 250.

57 Letter from Paul Findley to Gerald R. Ford, 2 August 1976. Gerald R. Ford Library.

58 *Ibid.*

59 Letter from Charles Leppart to Paul Findley, 26 August 1976. Gerald R. Ford Library.

60 *Ibid.*

61 Resolution Directing Interment of an Unknown Soldier from the Vietnam War in Arlington Cemetery, 1 September 1976. Gerald R. Ford Library.

62 *Ibid.*

63 Letter from Paul Findley to Jack Marsh, 1 September 1976. Gerald R. Ford Library. The Uniform Monday Holiday Act was designed to increase the number of three-day weekends for American citizens. It moved five federal holidays to Monday—Washington's Birthday, Memorial Day, Labor Day, Columbus Day, and Veterans Day. It was absurd to move established dates to a meaningless Monday since the holiday would no longer truly commemorate the intended event. George Washington's birthday, February 22, morphed into President's Day, a date

commemorating all chief executives. Veterans Day, however, was originally Armistice Day and November 11 had particular significance as a date since it marked the end of World War I. After seven October Veterans Days, the holiday was returned to its original November 11th date.

64 *Ibid.*

65 Memo from Jack Marsh to Bill Hyland, 13 September 1976. Gerald R. Ford Library.

66 Letter from Milt Mitler to Russ Rourke, 18 September 1976. Gerald R. Ford Library.

67 James T. Wooten. "Arlington Crypt Vacant, Awaiting Vietnam Unknown," *New York Times*, 1 May 1976.

68 Jimmy Carter, Speech at Arlington National Cemetery, 24 October 1977, available at: htts://www.presidency.ucsb.edu.

69 Jimmy Carter, Veterans Disability Compensation and Survivors Benefits and Housing Benefits Bills Remarks at the Bill Signing Ceremony, 18 October 1978, available at: https://www.presidency.ucsb.edu.

70 Lorimer Rich (24 December 1891-2 June 1978), Sec. 48, #288.

71 Memo from Frank Moore to President Jimmy Carter, 9 June 1978 available at: www.jimmycarterlibrary.gov.

72 *Ibid.*

73 Martha Ross Leigh (31 August 1894-6 January 1987), Sec. 48, #288.

74 As of 2018, the number of MIA from the Vietnam War has been reduced to 1,592.

75 Paul D. Mather. *MIA: Accounting for the Missing in Southeast Asia.* Washington, D.C.: National Defense University Press, 1994, p. 15; Evelyn Grubb and Carole Jose. *You Are Not Forgotten: A Family's Quest for Truth and the Founding of the National League of Families.* St. Petersburg, FL.: Vandamere Press, 2008, p. 318.

76 Grubb, p. 318.

77 Wooten.

78 David Shribman. "Vietnam Crypt Still Empty," *New York Times*, 25 October 1982, available at: https://www.nytimes.com/1982/10/25/us/vietnam-crypt-is-still-empty.html.

79 Michael J. Allen. "Sacrilege of a Strange, Contemporary Kind": The Unknown Soldier and the Imagined Community after the Vietnam War." *History and Memory,* vol. 23, no. 2, 2011, p. 109. JSTOR, JSTOR, www.jstor.org/stable/10.2979/histmemo.23.2.90.

80 *Ibid.,* p. 298.

81 Grubb, p. 318. Also see the National League of Families website at: http://www.pow-miafamilies.org.

82 *Ibid.,* p. 289.

83 LCDR Mill's remains were recovered from a shallow water crash site and identified in June 2018 by using DNA testing. See: https://www.bakersfield.com/news/remains-of-bakersfield-naval-aviator-identified-after-years-of-uncertainty/article_e6cc7c78-ab12-11e8-b49c-b7ce11ce7773.html. His remains were interred at Arlington National Cemetery on 24 June 2019, Sec. 60, #11803. Candice M English. "A Noble Cause: Government Manipulation of the Vietnam Unknown Soldier." Master's Thesis, Georgia College and State University, 2011, p. 48.

84 Memo from Secretary of the Army, John O. March, "Brussels for Secretary of Defense Weinberger, U.S. Mission of NATO," 3 December 1981.

85 Colonel Chet J. Bobinski, Army Casualty and Memorial Affairs Agency, quoted in Wooten.

86 Allen, p. 103.

87 The land was the site of the old Main Navy and Munitions complex that had been constructed in 1918. These wartime buildings disrupted the beauty of the National Mall and were ordered demolished by President Richard Nixon.

88 Elizabeth Wolfson. "The 'Black Gash of Shame'—Revisiting the Vietnam Veterans Memorial Controversy." *Arts21 Magazine,* 15 March 2017, available at: http://magazine.art21.org.

89 The Hart monument was added in 1984 and the Goodacre sculpture was dedicated in 1993.

90 The complete dedication ceremony of the Vietnam Memorial is available at: https://www.c-span.org/video/?88364-1/vietnam-veterans-memorial-dedication-ceremony-1982.

91 Stephen Sossaman. "Teach the Children Well," *Voices from the Wall.* Washington, D.C.: Vietnam Veterans Memorial Fund, 1998, p. 69.

92 Ronald Reagan, Address to the Veterans of Foreign Wars, Chicago, Il., 18 August 1980, available at: https://www.presidency.ucsb.edu.

93 Griffiths quoted in Allen, p. 111.

94 Press Release from the Joint Chiefs of Staff: Memorandum for Information # 17-84, Interment of an Unknown Serviceman from the Vietnam Era, 13 April 1984 available from the Library of Congress at http://www.loc.gov.

95 *Ibid.*

96 Caspar Weinberger quoted in William M. Hammond. *The Unknown Serviceman of the Vietnam Era.* Washington, D.C.: Center of Military History, 1985, p. 5.

97 Tomb Guard, SGT Lonny LeGrand remembered: "During my time there from 1981-1983 we had heard of the growing possibilities that there would someday soon be an Unknown from the Vietnam Era to be laid to rest there on the plaza. I would have loved to have been a part of something so great." SGT Lonny LeGrand. (TGIB #249). Written Interview. 7 November 2018.

98 SFC David Nicholson (TGIB #254). Written Interview. 12 October 2018; SP4 Kevin Donovan (TGIB #253). Written Interview. 22 October 2018.

99 Allen, p. 105. Professor Allen further notes: "…downed aviators were hardly ideal candidates for the Tomb. They were difficult to find (otherwise they would have been recovered when shot down)."

100 There was considerable debate at the Pentagon about how to date the Vietnam War. The 1958 date was designed to include the first American casualties caused by enemy action. In fact, the Vietnam Veterans Memorial initially began listing casualties beginning with 1959. MAJ Dale Richard Buis (Panel 1E/1) and MGT Chester M. Ovnand (Panel 7E/46) were the first names inscribed. They were killed in an enemy attack on their base at Bien Hoa on July 8 and the only American casualties for that year. The dates 1958-1975 were inscribed on the Unknown's marble crypt cover on May 23, 1984. Hammond, p. 7.

101 Admiral S.R. Foley, quoted in Hammond, p. 9.

102 Sergeant Major Kellogg received his Medal of Honor for his heroic actions at Quang Nam Province on 11 March 1970. Kellogg was helping a wounded Marine when an enemy soldier threw a hand grenade at them. Without concern for his own safety and well-being, Kellogg: "threw himself over the lethal weapon and absorbed the full effects of its detonation with his body, thereby preventing serious injury or possible death to several of his fellow marines." *The Congressional Medal of Honor: The Names, the Deeds.* Forest Ranch, CA.: Sharp & Dunnigan, 1984, pp. 90-91.

103 Hammond, p. 9.

104 "Interment of the Vietnam Unknown Serviceman," USS *Brewton* available at: http://ussbrewton.com/unknown.htm.

105 Hammond, pp. 9-10.

106 Ronald Reagan, Remarks at the U.S. Capitol, 25 May 1984, available at: www.presidency.ucsb.edu. Also available on Youtube at: https://www.youtube. com/watch?v=fQEVGZ3aZvw&t=992s.

107 Ronald Reagan, diary entry for 25 May 1984, available at the Ronald Reagan Library.

108 *Ibid.*

109 Hammond, p. 11.

110 McElya, pp. 279, 280.

111 Ronald Reagan, "Speech at the Memorial Amphitheater Honoring the Vietnam Unknown Serviceman," 28 May 1984, available at: http://www.presidency. ucsb.edu.

112 *Ibid.*

113 *Ibid.*

114 *Ibid.*

115 "Interment of the Unknown Serviceman of Vietnam, 28 May 1984, Official Program.

116 Hammond, p. 14.

117 Nicholson.

118 There were 5,097 days between the burial and the opening of the crypt on 14 May 1998.

(Department of Defense)

The empty crypt of the Unknown Serviceman from the Vietnam War.

Chapter VII

The Identification of X-26

We disturb this hallowed ground with profound reluctance. – William Cohen

During the spring of 1972, the NVA launched a major offensive against South Vietnamese positions in the III Corps region of Vietnam near An Lộc. With American troops having been reduced in-country to a token force of just 24,200 men, virtually all of the ground fighting was conducted by ARVN troops, although the United States did provide massive air support during the battle. High altitude B-52 bombers pounded communist sanctuaries near the Cambodian border while Air Force jets and Army helicopter gunships provided close-in ground support for the defending troops.[1]

Air Force pilot 1LT Michael Blassie was just 24 years old but was already a veteran of 130 combat missions in Vietnam.[2] On May 11, he was flying his Cessna A-37B Dragonfly near An Lộc. While on a low altitude napalm bombing run against attacking NVA and Viet Cong troops and tanks, Blassie's plane was struck by small arms fire. With aviation fuel streaming from his wing, 1LT Blassie reportedly took no evasive action and his aircraft crashed "at a nearly inverted altitude in the vicinity of coordinates XT732912."[3] A massive fireball was observed by accompanying planes, but no

(National Archives)
A Cessna A-37 B Dragonfly aircraft, the type of airplane flown by 1LT Michael Blassie when he was shot down by enemy fire in May 1972.

ejection chute was spotted.[4] The official military casualty report succinctly and conclusively stated: "1LT Blassie was pilot of an A37 aircraft on combat mission over An Lộc City, Vietnam, passed over target, aircraft took intense 20mm fire and crashed. Aircraft immediately exploded and burned. Crash was observed by 1LT Blassie's wingman. There was no possible chance for survival. Death was instantaneous. Decedent was performing official assigned operation duties..."[5]

Rescue helicopters were immediately dispatched to the crash site but were forced to abandon their mission after taking heavy enemy fire. No ground search was deemed to be possible due to NVA activity in the area. 1LT Michael Blassie was classified as "Killed-in-action—Body Not Recovered" (KIA-BNR).[6] He was one of just 759 Americans who were killed-in-action that year in Vietnam.[7]

Six months later on October 31, an ARVN patrol operating in the vicinity of An Lộc, stumbled upon a crash site in a heavily forested area. The platoon discovered a few bone fragments near a stream bed as well as remnants of an ejection seat from an American jet aircraft. They also located "a small portion of a NOMAX flight suit, a raft, ammo pouch, and part of a parachute."[8] Most important, the reconnaissance team found a military ID card and dog tags that had been issued to 1LT Michael J. Blassie, USAF, as well as $1000 in RVN currency, providing seemingly conclusive proof of identity.[9]

The news of the discovery reached the Joint Personnel Recovery Center that afternoon and Major Donald E. Lunday wrote a file memorandum entitled: "Subject: Body Recovery." It recorded that: "a recon patrol…discovered the remains of an American at coordinates XT716906. Also recovered were dog tags and an ID card identifying the individual as 1LT Joseph (sic) Michael Blassie, USAF…LT Blassie (JPRG #6518) was the pilot of an A-37 which crashed on 11 May 1972 in the vicinity of An Lộc. His status was KIA-BNR."[10]

Somehow, though, all of Blassie's personal items, critical in conclusively establishing his identity, were either "lost, misplaced, or stolen" while being transported to the U.S. Army mortuary at Ton Son Nhut.[11] In a follow up to his earlier memo, Major Lunday noted that the recovered remains had been received by the mortuary but that: "there are not sufficient remains for a positive ID. All that was recovered was four ribs, one pelvis, one humerus, a small portion of NOMEX flight suit, a raft, ammo pouch and part of a parachute."[12] The military did, however, classify the bones as TSN 0673-72 BTB (Believed to Be) Michael Blassie.

———

EVEN AFTER THE United States concluded its active military involvement in the war in Southeast Asia, the nation reaffirmed its strong commitment to locating and identifying all of the 2,646 servicemen still classified as missing-in-action from the Vietnam War. Under the provisions of the 1973 Paris Peace Accords, Article 8 stated that the North Vietnamese would assist American search and recovery teams in their efforts and help "to determine the location and take care of the graves of the dead so as to facilitate the exhumation and repatriation of the remains."[13] To facilitate these missions, the government created the Joint Casualty Resolution Center (JCRC), headquartered in Saigon. The agency was headed by Brigadier General Robert C. Kingston and maintained a dedicated and determined staff of 140 people. The primary purpose of the JCRC was to actively conduct "field search, excavation, recovery, and repatriation" of the remains of missing Americans from the war.[14] The agency worked closely with the newly created Army Central Identification Laboratory located at Camp Samae San, Thailand, in their ongoing efforts to identify all recovered remains.

The first investigations launched by the JCRC were conducted at previously known crash sites where American pilots had gone missing. In addition, the United States government offered monetary incentives of up to $150 to Vietnamese civilians who could help lead search teams to additional locations and graves where American remains could be found.[15] In the ten months immediately following the initiation of the recovery program, however, only 21 sets of remains were located, with just eleven of these proven to be of American origin.[16]

The work on recovery of MIA remains was hindered by the continuing deterioration of the military situation in South Vietnam. By the end of 1974, large portions of the country were under the control of the North Vietnamese and inaccessible. The following year: "all United States efforts at casualty resolution in South Vietnam had necessarily ceased."[17]

———————

THE REMAINS OF TSN 0673-72 BTB Blassie were moved on two separate occasions. The bones were first transferred from the Army Mortuary at Ton Son Nhut to Thailand in 1973. They were then returned to the United States as part of the relocation of the Central Identification Laboratory to their new facilities in Honolulu (CIL-HI).[18] Once in Hawaii, efforts continued to make a definitive, positive identification of the recovered bones but to no avail. Without corroborating physical evidence or the missing personal effects, TSN 0673-72 remained classified as unknown although the bones carried the BTB classification. Still, the circumstantial evidence surrounding the recovery of the remains was compelling. The bones had been discovered within six months of Michael Blassie's death and were found in the known vicinity of where his plane had crashed. There was only one other aircraft in the area that had been lost during that time frame and that was a Bell AH1G Cobra attack helicopter (Tail #69-1500). It was, ironically, shot down on the very same day as Blassie's plane. The helicopter, piloted by Captain Robert Williams and co-pilot, Captain Rodney Strobridge, was flying in support of ARVN ground forces. During the operation, the helicopter was struck by either by a SAM missile or small arms fire. It crashed in an undetermined location and the bodies of the two pilots were never recovered. Both officers were, like Michael Blassie, officially listed by the military as missing-in-action.[19] Army helicopters, though, were not equipped with either ejection seats or parachutes so the discovery of these items at the crash site where the TSN 0673-72 bones were recovered virtually precluded Williams or Strobridge from being considered as likely candidates for the remains.[20]

After years of frustrating failures and lack of progress, in an effort to end the impasse over identification, the CIL-HI hired a Japanese-American forensic anthropologist named Tadao Furue to re-examine the remains from the An Lộc crash site. Furue was widely believed to be a reputable and objective scientist capable of deriving critical physical and biological information from bone fragments through close clinical examination. After inspecting and studying the bones, the anthropologist concluded that the ossa-remains could not be those of Michael Blassie. He maintained that they were, instead, from an older individual who was shorter in physical stature than Blassie. Most important, Furue asserted that the bones came from a person with "O" blood type, effectively eliminating Blassie, since his known blood type was "A." These startling new revelations led the military to strip the BTB status from the TSN 0673-72 remains. On April 24, 1980, they were reclassified as unknown or, officially, X-26.[21] The official memo written that day stated: "after considering the circumstances of the incident involved, the completion of search and recovery operations, the circumstances of the recovery of remains, the identification findings presented by the U.S. Army Central Identification Laboratory...[it is] duly approved deletion of the 'Believed to Be' (BTB) name association from the following case [Michael Blassie]...[to] redesignat[e] to X-number [26]."[22]

In fact, Furue's scientific methods later proved to be seriously flawed and inaccurate. The small number of bones that he was able to study distorted his findings and certainly did not justify his conclusions, particularly in attempting to establish blood type.[23] Dr. Samuel Dunlap, a forensic anthropologist, who later worked at the Central Identification Laboratory, went further: "Furue's methods were 'completely worthless...He would take a bone fragment a couple of inches long and estimate the guy's height. That's impossible.'"[24]

———————

THE DECISION TO remove the BTB status of the remains served as a catalyst for declaring the remains as scientifically unidentifiable and qualified for interment at Arlington National Cemetery. A Pentagon spokesman announced in the spring 1984 that: "The information on the individual does not match anything we've got...we've used every trick, but we can't match him to any known missing soldier. We think, with a clear conscience, we can say this is a true unknown."[25]

Still, this case was unique from all of the previous selections of America's cherished Unknown Soldiers. In all of the other cases, there had been multiple unknown remains considered for a selection. These bodies had to be 80% intact in order to qualify for consideration. Moreover, the bodies of the candidates-unknown had been buried for extended periods of time and were disinterred from separate locations at different times. This ensured that all of the remains would be perpetually indistinguishable in terms of the place of death as well as the circumstances of recovery. By contrast, the minimal bones of X-26 had never been interred and were site specific. They had been subject to years of continual investigation and constant debate, all focused on reaching a definitive, positive identification.

Major Johnie Webb, who was in charge of the laboratory in Hawaii, was opposed to any efforts to certify X-26 as the Vietnam Unknown Serviceman. He argued persuasively that: "The selection must not be flawed. The high honor attributed to previously selected unknowns must not be compromised. A decision of non-selection may be more supportable than a decision of selection."[26] Webb's dire warnings, though, went unheeded, and without a conclusive identification, the X-26 remains were ordered to be officially designated as the Unknown Serviceman from the Vietnam War in the spring 1984. Webb remained privately conflicted by this decision but ultimately yielded to the intense pressures coming from the Pentagon and various veterans' organizations. Following earlier precedents, all of the documents relating to the new Unknown and the efforts at identification were to be shredded or destroyed. But Webb, on his own initiative, chose to preserve the important physical artifacts that related to the case. In fact, he sealed fragments of the recovered parachute and pieces of the life raft in the Unknown's casket prior to the designation ceremonies, later admitting: "I wanted to make sure everything stayed together. If the remains were going into the tomb, the artifacts needed to go to the tomb, so that at some point there was the historical perspective on what came in with those remains."[27]

The physical destruction of the written records surrounding the Unknown, however, did not erase the memories of the numerous individuals who had been involved over the years with the X-26 remains while they were at the CIL-HI. There were many people who knew all too well that the remains that were interred in the crypt at the Tomb of the Unknown Soldier had once been designated as BTB Lieutenant Michael Blassie, United States Air Force. It was a secret that would eventually be exposed to public scrutiny.

WITH THE BURIAL of the Vietnam Unknown, the era of political dissent and public division finally seemed to be over, replaced by the good times of peace, prosperity, and patriotism of the Reagan years. The National League of POW/MIA families continued their advocacy for soldiers who were still listed as missing-in-action. Every year, there were some notable successes as the remains of a few American veterans were repatriated to the United States from Southeast Asia and finally buried with full military honors. Part of these successes was due to the development of new DNA technology. It was a significant and exciting scientific breakthrough in the field of forensic medicine. As Sarah Wagner notes: "DNA became an arbiter of truth" and for the first time, science could eliminate all doubt about the identity of individual recovered remains.[28]

The search for the physical remains and additional evidence in the open case of the missing 1LT Michael Blassie continued as well. In September 1992, a recovery team was dispatched to the An Lộc region. At that time, Ly An, a former ARVN soldier, was interviewed by members of the American search party. An had been serving in the army in the area when Blassie was reported to have been shot down. He recalled hearing about the incident but could provide no substantive information or details. The team followed up their interview with a visit to one of the preported crash sites. Located at coordinates XT743904 in nearby Phu Binh hamlet: "The team found no material evidence. The site has been thoroughly excavated and was now being used as a reservoir."[29] Likewise, they were disappointed to discover that much of the surrounding area had changed dramatically since the end of the war. It had been converted into farmland and was under active cultivation. Furthermore, the vast majority of the residents of the hamlet had moved to the area well after 1972 and thus had no direct knowledge about any American casualties during the war.

A second search team returned to the region on September 7, 1994. This time, the group conducted a survey of three different locations looking for any wreckage or human remains. The first site investigated was XT732912. This was the transmitted coordinates of the actual crash site of Blassie's plane made on the day of the shoot down. It was now a rubber tree plantation and there was "no signs of a crash site or associated wreckage."[30] The second location that was visited was at XT716906 where the ARVN patrol in October 1972 reportedly discovered the human remains of X-26 some 22 years earlier. The investigative team found the region to be a "marshy area with scattered crops of various types...this area failed to yield any indications of aircraft wreckage or human remains."[31] The same was true for the third and final site, XT716904. The investigators concluded simply that there was: "no indication of wreckage, debris, remains or personal effects" to be found.[32] It seemed that whatever was known about Michael Blassie's fate had already been discovered and that there would never be any further evidence in his case. He seemed destined to remain forever missing-in-action.

TED SAMPLEY WAS the type of person that was easy to dismiss, a disgruntled Vietnam veteran determined to embarrass and make trouble for the U.S. government.[33] He certainly had an insatiable appetite for publicity as well as a history of preforming outrageous stunts and pranks. These included chaining himself to the White House fence, pouring oil on a Washington, D.C. highway, disrupting a presidential speech, and even assaulting a Senatorial aide.[34] Sampley also maintained a malicious personal vendetta against his fellow Vietnam veterans turned politicians: John Kerry, John McCain, and Colin Powell. Still, despite his personal flaws, Sampley was a fierce and relentless advocate for demanding a full accounting of all American POW's and MIA's.

Sampley self-published a modest newsletter entitled the *U.S. Veterans Dispatch.* In the July 14, 1994 edition, he authored a startling article entitled: "The Vietnam Unknown Soldier Can Be Identified."[35] Sampley alleged that the remains interred at Arlington National Cemetery could be identified and revealed publicly, for the first time, that the bones had once been classified as BTB Michael Blassie. Moreover, he asserted that the physical evidence that was recovered at the crash site included remnants of a parachute, pistol holster, inflatable raft, and flight suit which conclusively proved that

Blassie was, in fact, the Vietnam Unknown.[36] Sampley charged that: "The interment of that 'unidentifiable' U.S. servicemen in Arlington National Cemetery, beside the Unknown from World War I, World War II and Korea was supposed to be the ultimate symbolic gesture in healing the POW/MIA issue, the Vietnam War's 'sorest wound.' Instead, as it turns out, the entombment of the Vietnam Unknown was at the very best premature and at worst a politically expedient attempt to further close the books on the POW/MIA issue."[37]

Now, with the advent of DNA technology, Sampley claimed that it was possible to conclusively identify the remains in the Vietnam crypt, asserting that: "In 1984, as a result of the U.S. government's eagerness to lay to rest a Vietnam Unknown Soldier, it interred the remains of a missing American servicemen that today can be identified and accounted for through the U.S. government Central Identification Laboratory in Hawaii (CIL-HI)." He demanded that the remains at the Tomb be exhumed and that additional forensic testing be done: "If the experts at CIL-HI can identify American MIAs from minute tooth fragments, as they claim, then they should be able to right this wrong by determining through DNA if the remains of 1Lt. Blassie [are] in the tomb of the Vietnam Unknown Soldier."

These astonishing allegations led the family of Michael Blassie and those of other missing-in-action servicemen to demand additional information from the military concerning the status of their cases.[38] Jean Blassie, Michael's Gold Star mother, received a polite but unsatisfactory reply to her inquiry from the Deputy Assistant Secretary of Defense (POW/MIA Affairs), James Wold. In his correspondence, Wold provided a detailed chronological recap of the past events and the military's extensive efforts to locate and identify 1LT. Blassie's remains. He highlighted the two most recent trips to Vietnam made by MIA recovery teams and noted that their extensive and comprehensive searches had failed to uncover any additional evidence. Wold assured Mrs. Blassie that the partial remains that were interred at Arlington National Cemetery as the Vietnam Unknown: "in the mortuary's judgment…were not those of Lieutenant Blassie."[39] He concluded his letter: "We take our obligation to pursue cases of our brave service members and civilians very seriously. Above all, I want to assure you Lieutenant Blassie's sacrifice in service of his country will be honored forever by all Americans."[40]

THE SAMPLEY ALLEGATIONS led to a great deal of speculation and controversy surrounding the identity of the Unknown within the military and POW/MIA communities, but it wasn't until January 19, 1998, that the story received widespread national attention. That night in the midst of the burgeoning Monica Lewinsky scandal, CBS News aired an extensive story by investigative journalist Vince Gonzales. He had spent ten months researching the saga of the remains that were buried at the Tomb of the Unknown Soldier in 1984, specifically highlighting their likely association with 1LT Michael Blassie. In a subsequent interview on another network, Michael's sister, Pat, who was herself an Air Force officer, firmly stated: "If it's Michael, he is not unknown. He might be unidentified, but he's not unidentifiable. And we want to bring him home."[41]

As the sensational story slowly gained momentum, other newspapers and television networks began to pressure the Pentagon to address the perceived flaws in the designation process of the Vietnam Unknown. Still, despite the growing controversy, the idea of opening the crypt of the Unknown was an anathema to the military and was seen by many to be nothing short of sacrilegious. It would be far easier to leave the remains undisturbed and forever subject to some doubt about their true identity.

In an effort to quell the controversy, Secretary of Defense William Cohen established an investigative task force to review the original selection process for the Vietnam Unknown and the prior handling of the entombed remains. Forensic scientists were to be consulted to determine whether DNA testing could, in fact, be applied to this case to establish a positive identity. The DNA experts reported back that they were reasonably confident that by re-examining the bones and applying this new technology to the Unknown, an identity could be determined since it had already been established that only nine missing servicemen could possibly be the source of the bones in crypt.[42] Although Michael Blassie was, by far, the most likely person buried at Arlington, this extremely limited number of individuals made the success of DNA testing highly promising. For the families of the missing, the federal government had an obligation to disinter the remains to honor its sacred pledge that it would do everything possible to locate and identify the nation's MIAs.

In April, the ad hoc committee reported its findings to the Secretary of Defense. The group recommended that the military disinter the Vietnam Unknown and subject the bones to DNA analysis. Secretary Cohen accepted the panel's unprecedented proposal and he justified this decision noting that: "weighing the sanctity of the Tomb with the nation's commitment to the fullest possible accounting of service members missing in defense of this country," the remains should be exhumed.[43] He ordered the Pentagon to begin to formulate plans to open the crypt and to do so in a respectful and dignified manner. In a public press briefing following Cohen's announcement, Pentagon Spokesman Kenneth Bacon further explained the Secretary's rationale: "Scientific advances have given us identification techniques that did not exist in 1984 when the remains of an American killed in Vietnam were placed in the Tomb of the Unknowns."[44]

Arlington National Cemetery Superintendent, John "Jack" Metzler Jr., was the person on-site responsible for the actual exhuming of the remains.[45] He described the process in detail to the press utilizing several charts, illustrations, and diagrams. The actual work, Metzler explained, would take only between 24 and 36 hours. During that time, a white, plywood barrier would be constructed around the main Tomb as well as all of the crypts to conceal the work from the general public. Likewise, camouflage netting would be installed over the temporary protective barriers to shield the site from any potential aerial photography. While the work continued, the Tomb Guard sentinels would be temporarily relocated to the east memorial steps.[46]

The first stage of the disinterment began on May 13 with the removal of the stone pavers surrounding the crypt. After breaking the seal on the grave, workmen brought a portable crane onto the Memorial plaza and removed the heavy, marble crypt cover, thereby exposing the sealed casket. The Unknown's coffin was then carefully lifted out of its grave and placed upon a green shrouded bier situated on the plaza. The coffin was immediately wrapped with evidence tape by a representative from the Central Identification Laboratory. This was done to ensure the integrity of the identification process as well as to maintain a clear chain of custody.[47] Once this was finished, an American flag was draped over the casket and the marble crypt cover was returned to its original location. By the morning of May 14, the entire site had been returned its original appearance.

———————

THE UNPRECIDENTED DISINTERMENT of the Unknown had proceeded according to plans. On Sunday morning, May 24, 1998, the flag-draped casket was positioned immediately in front of the main Tomb and the now empty center crypt for brief ceremonies. At the north end of the plaza near an awaiting hearse, a joint service color guard stood at attention as several family members of missing-in-action servicemen, including the Blassie's, arrived to witnesses the historic moment.[48] When interviewed by reporters later, Patricia Blassie stated: "We are sure those remains are of Mike Blassie. Michael Blassie is not unknown, and that is why we want to bring him home to St. Louis where he belongs."[49]

Secretary of Defense Cohen delivered brief remarks. Speaking from a portable podium located in close proximity to the casket, he said: "We disturb this hallowed ground with profound reluctance. We take this step only because of our abiding commitment to account for every warrior who fought and died to preserve the freedoms that we cherish. If advances in technology can ease the lingering anguish of even one family, then our path is clear. We yield to the promise of science with the hope that the heavy burden of doubt may be lifted from a family's heart."[50] The short ceremony

(Department of Defense)

The disinterment of the Vietnam Unknown Serviceman. Secretary of Defense William Cohen ordered the exhumation in order to conduct DNA testing on the remains.

(Department of Defense)

The casket of the Vietnam Unknown is loaded onto a hearse on the plaza of the Tomb of the Unknown Soldier.

concluded with the reading of a prayer by Chaplain Colonel Leo O'Keeffe: "If it be your holy will, make known the identity of this unknown Vietnam serviceman and bring peace to an American family. But if the answer we seek is not ours to know, let us hold fast to our belief that this serviceman is known to you, O God."[51] The Army band then played a hymn as a joint service casket team moved into position. They lifted the casket of the Vietnam Unknown from its bier and carried it to the hearse parked on the plaza. The remains were driven the ten miles to the Armed Forces Institute of Pathology labs at Walter Reed in Bethesda, Maryland. There, mitochondrial DNA was successfully extracted from the bones and the samples were then sent to the Armed Forces DNA Identification Laboratory at Dover Air Force Base for further analysis.[52]

A few days later, President Bill Clinton was at Arlington National Cemetery to place a Memorial Day wreath at the Tomb of the Unknown Soldier. Afterwards, the President delivered a formal address in the Memorial Amphitheater. Clinton acknowledged that the crypt of the Vietnam Unknown Serviceman was now empty: "Eleven days ago a Vietnam veteran was removed from the Tomb of the Unknown Soldier. It was the right course of action, because science has given us a chance to restore his name and bring comfort to his family, and we had to seize it. But whatever happens, we must always remember that that stone represents the many unknown soldiers still in Vietnam and Korea, in other theaters where Americans lie far away from home, missing-in-action, still with us in spirit. They may be unaccounted for, but we must all be accountable for their memories as well. We take comfort in something Chaplain Leo Joseph O'Keeffe reminded us of at the ceremony on May 14th, that if some names are unknown to us on Earth, all names are known to God in heaven."[53]

THE ACTUAL DNA testing took several weeks to complete, but on June 30, the final results conclusively proved that the remains that had been buried at Tomb since 1984 were, in fact, those of 1LT Michael Blassie. President Bill Clinton issued a formal statement announcing that: "DNA testing positively identified the remains of the Vietnam War unknown disinterred from the Tomb of the Unknowns in May as those of the Air Force 1LT Michael J. Blassie. The Defense Department has notified the Blassie family and the other families involved in resolving this difficult case. I am pleased that one more family has finally learned the fate of a loved one, and I remain committed to seeking a full accounting of the missing in action from that conflict."[54]

Secretary of Defense Cohen issued his own press release further elaborating on the results and the identification of 1LT Blassie:

> Less than seven weeks ago, with profound reluctance, we disturbed the hallowed ground of the Tomb of the Unknowns in an effort to identify the Vietnam Unknown and ease the lingering anguish of one American family. We took that somber step only because of our abiding commitment to the fullest possible accounting for every warrior who fought and died for our nation. After successful mitochondrial DNA comparison and forensic examination using state-of-the-art technology not available in 1984, the U.S. Army Central Identification Laboratory has determined that the remains interred in 1984 as the Vietnam Unknown are those of U.S. Air Force 1st Lt. Michael Joseph Blassie.

> This morning, I conveyed that information to his mother, Mrs. George C. Blassie. The report documenting the work of the Armed Forces DNA Identification Laboratory, the U.S. Army Central Identification Laboratory, and the Defense Prisoner of War Missing Personnel Office and the resulting identification is now being reviewed independently by three outside consultants with acknowledged expertise in forensic science. Once those consultants complete

their work, the report will be conveyed to her for her review. Afterwards, the report will be forwarded to the Armed Forces Identification Review Board for the final determination.

Since the end of the war in Vietnam, the Department of Defense has identified the remains of 496 Americans. Some 2,087 Americans who died in that conflict remain unaccounted for. As we share with the Blassie family the knowledge that the remains of their loved one have been identified, I want to renew the pledge to those whose loved ones are still missing that the U. S. government and the Department of Defense will continue to search for each of the American warriors who died in foreign lands defending our nation, and whose remains have not yet been located and brought home. On behalf of the Department of Defense, I also want especially to express my appreciation to the other families whose selfless cooperation made the identification of the former Vietnam Unknown possible.

The question now before us as a nation is how best to honor the soldiers, sailors, airmen, Marines and the one Coast Guardsman who served and died in the conflict in Vietnam and have not yet been accounted for. Our commitment to the fullest possible accounting and advances in modern forensic technology have reached the point that we can now identify remains once believed to be unidentifiable. In the weeks ahead, I and other Defense Department officials will consult with the Congress, the military Services, the leadership of veterans organizations, and with the family associations in an effort to determine how best to honor our missing Vietnam veterans in the absence of a Vietnam Unknown. [55]

THE JEFFERSON BARRACKS National Cemetery is located eleven miles south of St. Louis on 331 picturesque acres overlooking the banks of the Mississippi River. Its maticulously manicured grounds are today the final resting place for over 188,000 soldiers and their families. Burials date back to 1826, when the frontier military garrison was first established just five years after Missouri had been admitted to the union as the country's 24th state. The remote, military outpost was named in honor of Thomas Jefferson, who had died earlier that year on July 4, appropriately on the fiftieth anniversary of the adoption of the Declaration of Independence. Shortly after manning the fort, the army designated some 29 acres of the grounds to serve as a military cemetery for any personnel or their families who died while serving at the frontier outpost.[56]

Jefferson Barracks served as the gateway to the western plains. It was also a staging and supply area for the various military campaigns that were then being waged against hostile Indian tribes.[57] During this early era, Robert E. Lee, Ulysses S. Grant, and Jefferson Davis were all posted at the barracks, although they did not serve there contemporaneously. In 1861, despite being a slave state, Missouri's government remained divided over the issue of secession and, as a result, its citizens fought on opposing sides during the American Civil War. After the conclusion of hostilities, the Fort Jefferson Barracks Cemetery underwent a massive expansion with the interment of over 12,000 Union soldiers as well as 1,140 Confederate prisoners-of-war. These numbers included the burial of over 3,000 unknown soldiers. In 1866, by an act of Congress, the Fort Jefferson Barracks Cemetery was officially incorporated into the national cemetery system with the mandate to: "preserve from desecration the graves of soldiers of the United States who fell in battle or died of disease…so that the resting place of the honored dead may be kept sacred forever."[58]

Over the ensuing years, the national cemetery continued to bury many of Missouri's veterans. During the second world war, the cemetery was the site of a staggering 564 military group burials.[59] The largest of these interments took place in 1952 when 123 individually unidentifiable American POW's were re-buried in 109 caskets in a mass grave located in Section 85. These men had been burned alive by retreating Japanese forces on December 14, 1944 on Palawan Island.[60] Likewise, in 1968, 41 U.S. Marines were buried in a group grave after their helicopter crashed in South Vietnam. Their commingled, mutilated remains were deemed to be individually unidentifiable.

The Jefferson Barracks National Cemetery was close to the Blassie's family home in north St. Louis. After their 26-year ordeal, they decided to bring Michael back to Missouri for his final burial. On Friday, July 10, less than two weeks after the final DNA test

(National Archives)

1LT Michael Blassie casket at Scott Air Force Base. Blassie's family requested that he be returned to his home state of Missouri for final burial.

results were made public, 1LT Michael Blassie's flagged-draped casket was taken by hearse to the flight line at Dover Air Force Base and placed onboard a C-141 Starlifter transport. His younger brother, George, accompanied the remains back to Scott Air Force Base. That evening, over 350 family and close friends gathered for a memorial service at St. Thomas the Apostle Catholic Church in Floressant, Missouri. The Catholic services were presided over by the Archbishop of St. Louis, His Excellency Justin Rigali.[61]

At 10 AM the next morning, the hearse carrying 1LT Blassie's remains arrived at the Jefferson Barracks National Cemetery. A six-man Air Force casket team carried the casket to the gravesite for the full-honors military funeral. The family had invited the general public to attend the gravesite services. Captain Patricia Blassie explained: "Although Michael is our dear mother's son and our brother, for many years he has represented so many. This is not just the Blassie family's day."[62] Also in attendance at the funeral services were Secretary of Defense, William Cohen, and Missouri Congressman, Richard Gephardt. During the Catholic committal services, four Air Force F15 jets conducted a fly-over in the missing man formation. Traditional military honors were rendered, including the 21-gun salute and a lone bugler playing "Taps." Jean Blassie, the mother who had endured years of anguish and uncertainty, approached her son's open grave and poured in a handful of dirt from Arlington National Cemetery that she had collected on the day of his disinterment. It was her final, symbolic act in bringing her son back home to Missouri.[63]

1LT Blassie's white marble government headstone had already been carved and installed at the gravesite. It was unveiled during the funeral services. On its front were inscribed Michael Blassie's name, rank, military service, his date of birth/death and the word "Vietnam." It was also engraved with a standard Christian cross and the sentiment: "Beloved Son and Brother." On the stone's reverse were listed 1LT Blassie's medals and military decorations. These included the Distinguished Flying Cross, Purple Heart, and Air Medal. Etched deep into the stone in black lettering were the

(National Archives)

An Air Force Honor guard holds the interment flag over the casket of 1LT Michael Blassie at the Jefferson Barracks National Cemetery. Blassie remains were finally identified after DNA testing.

(National Archives)
Jean Blassie and her daughter, Pat, receive the interment flag from USAF Chief of State, Michael Ryan.

words "Killed In Action" and most poignantly, a brief acknowledgement that he was the "Unknown Soldier: May 28, 1984-May 14, 1998." His gravesite at the Jefferson Barracks National Cemetery is in Section 85, Grave #1.

THERE WAS ONE final controversy that occurred after 1LT Blassie had been laid to rest in Missouri. Jean Blassie asked that her son be allowed to keep the Medal of Honor that had been awarded to him, albeit anonymously, in 1984 by President Reagan during the Amphitheater services. It had been Blassie's medal while he served as the Vietnam Unknown for 14 years. For that reason, the family requested that the medal convey even after the DNA identification. This was an extremely delicate issue for the federal government. The military fully recognized that the Blassie family had suffered through a long and terrible ordeal caused, in no small part, by the repeated mishandling of Michael's remains. The military did not want

1LT Michael Blassie's grave at the Jefferson Barracks National Cemetery. Blassie was the Vietnam Unknown Serviceman from May 28, 1984 - May 14, 1998.

to appear callous or insensitive to the family but at the same time, the Medal of Honor holds a unique position in military heraldry. It is rarely bestowed and then only for the most exceptional acts of bravery. The medals that were issued to all of the Unknowns were seen to be symbolic and not considered to be individual awards. Moreover, the American Unknowns had been awarded by several foreign governments their nation's highest military honors. The United States had reciprocated by presenting the Medal of Honor to the Unknowns of Belgium, France, Great Britain, Italy, and Romania.

All of the Unknowns' medals and decorations were on public display at either Arlington's new Visitors Center or in the Amphitheater's Trophy Room. The actual MOH citation for the Vietnam Unknown Serviceman read: "[to the] unknown American who lost his life while serving in Southeast Asa during the Vietnam Era as a member of the Armed Forces of the United States and who has been selected to lie buried in the Memorial Amphitheater of the National Cemetery at Arlington, Virginia."[64] Blassie's remains were no longer unknown nor were they buried at Arlington, effectively making the citation invalid. The military finally rejected the family's request noting that: "The award is symbolic, not personal."[65]

Undersecretary of Defense Rudy de Leon explained: "Please be assured that First Lieutenant Blassie's numerous honors and awards, to include the prestigious Silver Star recognizing his bravery in action, reflect the honorable and dedicated service he rendered to a most grateful nation." The Vietnam Unknown's medals along with the original interment flag, though, would be preserved in perpetuity as part of the historical record: "It is the department's intent to keep the Vietnam Unknown Medal of Honor on display at Arlington National Cemetery as a tribute to all who, like Michael, unselfishly gave their lives in service to our nation during the Vietnam conflict."[66]

———————————

AFTER THE IDENTIFICTION of Lieutenant Blassie's remains, the Department of Defense abandoned all efforts to inter an unknown from the Vietnam War. The military concluded that the substantive advances in medical technology had rendered the tradition of an honorary burial of an unknown soldier an anachronism, a relic of a previous era. Secretary of Defense, William Cohen, acknowledged that: "It may be that forensic science has reached a point where there will be no other unknowns in any war."[67] He promised further that: "The federal government and the department will continue to strive for the fullest possible accounting for all our servicemen who fought for our nation in the conflict and did not return."[68] It was anticipated that any American casualties from subsequent conflicts would be positively identified through the use of a newly established DNA registry that required all active duty soldiers and servicemen to submit to a DNA profile upon enlistment. This data base would be used in conjunction with the more traditional forensic methods of fingerprinting and dental record analysis as well as the recovery of personal effects.

The extensive media coverage of the recent events at Arlington gave renewed hope to many other MIA families desperate for news of their loved ones. There were still 846 unknowns from the Korean War buried at the Punchbowl in Hawaii and some Americans favored exhuming all of these remains for DNA analysis. This, however, ignored the stark reality that the bodies had already been interred for decades and could not be identified through standard methods. The Department of Defense attempted to temper the general public's unrealistic expectations for a quick resolution of unresolved missing-in-action cases. DNA technology still had significant scientific and logistical limitations; to be effective, it required that a comparison sample be taken from an individual's maternal relative to be used for verification. For DNA analysis to be a reasonable option, a body of a missing soldier had to be name-associated with a relatively small number of individuals. The hundreds of unknowns buried at the National Cemetery of the Pacific were among 8,200 servicemen that remained classified as missing-in-action from the Korean War, thus making mass DNA testing unrealistic.[69]

FOR FIFTEEN MONTHS, the crypt of the Vietnam Unknown remained empty. It no longer served as a grave, but the original crypt cover remained in place and its presence on the plaza was confusing to the many visitors to Arlington. It was possible to remove the marble stone and replace it with pavers to disguise the existing crypt but if that was done, there would be nothing to acknowledge the fact that for fourteen years an Unknown had been buried at the Tomb.

After months of consultation with members of Congress, veterans' groups, and family organizations, the Department of Defense finally decided to replace the existing crypt cover with a new stone that would acknowledge the nation's ongoing commitment to the nation's MIA's. This marker would also tacitly acknowledge the fact that the Unknown Serviceman from the Vietnam War had once been buried there.

The dedication ceremony for the new memorial was set for September 17, POW/MIA Recognition Day 1999. This commemorative holiday had been established by an act of Congress 20 years earlier as a time to remember American prisoners-of-war and those still missing from all of the nation's wars. The distinctive, black POW/MIA flag had been created by the National League of Families and bore the motto: "You are not forgotten" and represented "a symbol of our Nation's concern and commitment to resolving as fully as possible the fates of Americans still prisoner, missing and unaccounted for in Southeast Asia."[70]

Secretary of Defense William Cohen and Georgia Senator Max Cleland were the primary speakers at the unveiling ceremonies at the Tomb. Cohen noted that the DNA testing had identified 1LT Blassie, and that: "Science helped ease the sorrow and suffering of a family and returned their son to his rightful place, and science may one day help ease the weight of grief of those who wait and wonder."[71] The new marble stone covering the former grave bore the inscription: "Honoring and Keeping Faith with America's Missing Servicemen."

In his remarks at the dedication, Secretary Cohen explained: "The words that now grace the Vietnam Tomb, ... are carved in stone. Their permanence -- like our remembrance of America's fallen soldiers, sailors, airmen and Marines -- will be a measure of this nation's profound reverence and respect. And those words will always remain, eloquent in the clarity of their purpose, enduring by the dignity of their provenance."[72]

Georgia Senator Max Cleland, a Vietnam veteran, silver star recipient, and a triple amputee, also spoke: "When I come to the Tomb of the Unknowns, I am reminded of the quote from one of (the Duke of) Wellington's troops, which says, `In times of war and not before, God and soldier men adore. But in times of peace with all things righted, God is forgotten, and the soldier slighted.' We are here today to reiterate our promise to our soldiers that they will not be slighted--not now, not ever."[73] The ceremonies concluded with a flyover by several Vietnam-era Huey helicopters.

(Department of Defense)

Defense Secretary William S. Cohen and Georgia Sen. Max Cleland preside over the dedication of the new memorial stone at the Tomb of the Unknown Soldier.

(3D U.S. Infantry Regiment "The Old Guard)
A sentinel places a rose on the empty crypt of the Vietnam Unknown Serviceman.

Endnotes

1 Harry G. Summers, Jr. *Historical Atlas of the Vietnam War*. Boston: Houghton Mifflin Company, 1995, p. 178.

2 Michael Blassie (4 April 1948-11 May 1972).

3 *South Vietnam, pre-: Family Conference/Case Summary Information*. 1997. Manuscript/Mixed Material. Retrieved from the Library of Congress, available at: www.loc.gov/item/powmia/pw012854/.

4 Sarah Wagner. "The Making and Unmaking of an Unknown Soldier." *Social Studies of Science*, vol. 43, no. 5, 2013, p. 640. *JSTOR*, JSTOR, www.jstor.org/stable/43284199.

5 Eighth Special Operation Squadron report available at the Library of Congress, http://www.loc.gov.

6 Bill Thomas. "The Last Soldier buried in Tomb of the Unknowns Wasn't Unknown," *Washington Post Magazine*, 8 November 2012, available at: https://www.washingtonpost.com.

7 Vietnam U.S. Military Fatal Casualty Statistics available at: https://www.archives.gov/research/military/vietnam-war/casualty-statistics; Candice M. English. "A Noble Cause: Government Manipulation of the Vietnam Unknown Soldier." Master's Thesis, Georgia College and State University, 2011, p. 26.

8 "Intelligence/Administrative Casualty File."

9 *Ibid.*

10 *South Vietnam, pre-: Body Recovery*. 1972. Manuscript/Mixed Material. Retrieved from the Library of Congress, available at: www.loc.gov/item/powmia/pw012869/. Blassie's name was Michael Joseph Blassie.

11 "Intelligence/Administrative Casualty File."

12 Donald E. Lunday. Memorandum for the Record. 5 November 1972, *South Vietnam, pre-: Body Recovery*. 1972.

13 Mather, Paul D. *M.I.A.: Accounting for the Missing in Southeast Asia*. Washington, D.C.: National Defense University Press, 1994, p. 4.

14 *Ibid.*, pp. 10, 11.

15 *Ibid.*, pp. 12, 18.

16 *Ibid.*, p. 14.

17 *Ibid.*, p. 28.

18 Robert Poole. "The Last Unknown Soldier of the Vietnam War," *Military History Magazine*, 12 February 2018, available at: http://www.historynet.com/last-unknown-soldier-vietnam-war.htm.

19 See https://pownetwork.org/bios/s/s197.htm.

20 Michael J. Allen. "Sacrilege of a Strange, Contemporary Kind," *The Unknown Soldier and the Imagined Community after the Vietnam War.*" *History and Memory*, vol. 23, no. 2, 2011, p. 109. *JSTOR*, JSTOR, www.jstor.org/stable/10.2979/histmemo.23.2.90.

21 Poole.

22 Department of the Army, 24 April 1980. *South Vietnam, pre-: Remains Recovery/Release of documents to the next-of-kin.* 1991. Manuscript/Mixed Material. Retrieved from the Library of Congress, available at: www.loc.gov/item/powmia/pw012867/.

23 English, p. 36.

24 Bill Thomas. "Hearts and Bones, The Vietnam Soldier Who Wasn't Unknown," *Seattle Times*, 10 November 2012, available at: https://www.seattletimes.com.

25 Pentagon spokesman quoted in Allen, p. 110.

26 Johnie Webb quoted in Wagner, Sarah. "The Making and Unmaking of an Unknown Soldier." *Social Studies of Science*, vol. 43, no. 5, 2013, p. 636. *JSTOR*, JSTOR, www.jstor.org/stable/43284199.

27 Johnie Webb quoted in Poole.

28 Wagner, p. 635.

29 *South Vietnam, pre-: Field Investigation Report: Case 1853.* 1992. Manuscript/Mixed Material. Retrieved from the Library of Congress, available at: www.loc.gov/item/powmia/pw012861/.

30 *South Vietnam, pre-: Detailed Report of Investigation Report of Case 1853.* 1994. Manuscript/Mixed Material. Retrieved from the Library of Congress, available at: www.loc.gov/item/powmia/pw012858/.

31 *Ibid.*

32 *Ibid.*

33 Ted Sampley (17 July 1946-12 May 2009). Sampley was a Green Beret in Viet-

nam and received four bronze stars. He was also the founder of Rolling Thunder, the annual motorcycle rally held on Memorial Day to remember POW/MIAs.

34 Matt Schudel. "Ted Sampley, 62: Vietnam Veteran Was an Outspoken Advocate for POWs," *Washington Post*, 15 May 2009, available at: http://www.washingtonpost.com.

35 Robert Poole. "The Last Unknown Soldier of the Vietnam War," *Military History Magazine*, 12 February 2018, available at: http://www.historynet.com/last-unknown-soldier-vietnam-war.htm.

36 "Soldier in the Tomb of the Unknowns May Actually be Known," All Politics—CNN, available at: http://www.cnn.com.

37 Ted Sampley. "The Vietnam Unknown Soldier Can Be Identified," *U.S. Veterans Dispatch*, July 1994: available at: https://web.archive.org/web/20110716055742/http://www.usvetdsp.com/unknown.htm.

38 Michael's mother, Jean, wrote to the Pentagon inquiring about her son's status. Her husband, George (8 July 1919-21 January 1991), had died in 1991. Jean Blassie died on 11 June 2013 at the age of 90.

39 South Vietnam, pre-: Oral History Program OHP96-032 Report and Evaluation: Tran Nam. 1997. Manuscript/Mixed Material. Retrieved from the Library of Congress, available at: www.loc.gov/item/powmia/pw012855/.

40 *Ibid.*

41 Pat Blassie quoted in Wagner, p. 642.

42 CBS News, "Update, 'Unknown' No Longer," available at: https://www.cbsnews.com/news/update-unknown-no-longer/.

43 "Washington: Remains of the Vietnam Unknown Soldier to be Exhumed," Youtube, available at: https://youtu.be/12UdNYjyAMw.

44 "Disinterment of the Vietnam Unknown Soldier," Pentagon Briefing, 7 May 1998: available at: https://www.c-span.org.

45 Jack Metzler was the son of former Arlington Superintendent, John "Jack" Metzler, Sr. (8 May 1909--25 May 1990). After the retirement of Raymond J. Costanzo in 1990, Metzler was appointed his successor in January 1991. His 19-year tenure was marred by several controversies and charges of serious mismanagement. He was allowed to retire in 2010 after being officially reprimanded by the Secretary of the Army. See Scott N. Warner. *Gold Star Father: Honoring a Hero, Remembering a Son*. Canton, Ohio: Warner Inspirational Media, 2012.

46 Pentagon Briefing, 7 May 1998.

47 The Vietnam Unknown's casket had been sealed at the CIL-HI before the designation ceremonies and had never been opened.

48 It had been determined that there were only nine missing in action servicemen who could be the Unknown.

49 Patricia Blassie quoted in Jim Garamone. "Vietnam Unknown Disinterred," DOD News, available at: http://archive.defense.gov/news/newsarticle. aspx?id=41578.

50 Garamone.

51 *Ibid.*

52 Wagner, p. 642.

53 Bill Clinton, "Remarks at Memorial Day Ceremonies at Arlington," 25 May 1998: available at: htts://www.presidency.ucsb.edu.

54 Bill Clinton, "Statement on the Identification of Vietnam War Unknown Soldier," 30 June 1998: available at: htts://www.presidency.ucsb.edu.

55 William Cohen, Press Release, 30 June 1998, available at: http://www.arlingtoncemetery.net/unk-vn49.htm.

56 Dean W. Holt. *American Military Cemeteries*. Jefferson, N.C.: McFarland & Company, Inc., Publishers, 2010, pp.165, 166.

57 *Ibid.*, p. 166.

58 *Ibid.*, p. 167.

59 *Ibid.*, p. 168.

60 "American Prisoners of War: Massacre at Palawan," available at: http://www. historynet.com/american-prisoners-of-war-massacre-at-palawan.htm.

61 "Lieutenant Blassie Buried with Earth from Arlington National Cemetery," available at: http://www.arlingtoncemetery.net/unk-vn57.htm.

62 Pat Blassie quoted in "Lieutenant Blassie Buried."

63 "Pilot's Remains Laid to Rest Near His Home With Full Military Honors," *LA Times*, 12 July 1998, available at: http://articles.latimes.com/1998/jul/12/news/ mn-3183.

64 *The Congressional Medal of Honor: The Names and Deeds*. California: Sharp & Dunnigan, 1984, p. 494.

65 "Vietnam Unknowns Medal of Honor Transfer Denied," Department of Defense Press Release, 25 August 1998: available at: https://web.archive.org/web/20150525182046/http://www.defense.gov/news/.

66 *Ibid.*

67 William Cohen quoted in the *Washington Times*, 1 July 1998.

68 William Cohen quoted in Jim Garamone. "Vietnam Unknown Crypt at Arlington to Remain Empty," 17 June 1999, available at: http://archive.defense.gov.

69 Rudi Williams. "DNA Tests Spark Efforts to ID Korean Remains," 7 July 1999, available at: http://archive.defense.gov.

70 National League of Families POW/MIA Flag, available at: https://en.wikipedia.org.

71 "Honoring and Keeping Faith with America's Servicemen," 17 September 1998, available at: http://www.arlingtoncemetery.net/unk-vn72.htm.

72 William Cohen quoted in Jim Garamone. "Tomb Inscription Dedicated," 17 September 1999, available at: http://archive.defense.gov.

73 Max Cleland quoted in Michael Killian. "Vietnam Veterans' Crypt Rededicated to Missing," Chicago *Tribune*, 18 September 1999, available at: https://www.chicagotribune.com.

(3D U.S. Infantry Regiment "The Old Guard)
The Changing of the Guard ceremony at the Tomb of the Unknown Soldier.

Chapter VIII

The Tomb Guard

"I will never forget the times being inside the chains, on the plaza, on the mat, pacing back and forth…thanking the [Unknowns] for the freedoms I live with today. – Kevin Donovan

On Veterans Day 1991, George H.W. Bush placed the traditional presidential wreath at the Tomb of the Unknown Soldier. Following the ceremony on the plaza, the President delivered a formal address in the Memorial Amphitheater. Bush used the solemn occasion to remind the nation of the perpetual watch maintained by the Tomb Guard. "For more than 50 years," he began, "24 hours a day, a lone sentinel has kept a silent vigil aside the Tomb of the Unknowns." [1] Every day of the year, throughout the day and night, a sentry remains on duty regardless of weather, climatic conditions, global pandemics, or even terrorist attack. President Bush continued: "And recently, one of the outstanding men who guard the tomb was asked what is it like here at night, alone, in the quiet of this place. And he said he felt a kinship to the men resting here; that this was where he wanted to be, here to honor his comrades and all they represent. 'Sometimes,' this young PFC said, 'The rain streaks in your eyes or your fingers go numb from cold, but then I think about what they suffered through. And after that my duty doesn't seem hard at all.' There's a poem the honor guards learn that says

(National Archives)
President George H.W. Bush delivers a speech at the Memorial Amphitheater. In his speech, the President recognized the service of the Tomb Guard.

it all. 'You are guarding the world's most precious gifts. You, you alone, are the symbol of 250 million people who wish to show their gratitude. And you will march through the rain, the snow, and the heat to prove it.'" [2]

Since 1948, the Tomb has been under continual guard by the 3D United States Infantry, "The Old Guard." This elite unit was first established in 1784, just a few months after the end of the American Revolution. The 3D Infantry is posted at Fort Myer, (since 2005 referred to as Joint Base Myer-Henderson Hall), which is located adjacent to the western boundaries of Arlington National Cemetery. The regiment is responsible for all of the numerous ceremonial events in Washington, D.C., and serves as the official escort for the President of the United States. Members of The Old Guard are also dispatched daily to bury the nation's veterans at Arlington National Cemetery with appropriate pomp and ceremony as well as to render the final military honors at gravesite.[3] They are among the finest and most distinguished soldiers in the entire United States Army.

There are three reliefs of sentinels assigned to duty at the Tomb. Ideally, each relief consists of seven soldiers and are grouped according to height, ranging from 5'10" to 6'4" tall. Sentinels are selected from the regular ranks of the 3D United States Infantry and must volunteer for this elite duty. They undergo a rigorous, nine-month screening and training regimen which has an extremely high attrition rate. Only 20% of the "new men" will make it through the demanding process to actually post at the Tomb. The constant demands for perfection, the required professional discipline, and the need for personal improvement can be achieved only by the most motivated and dedicated soldiers.[4] Former Tomb Guard, SGT Lonny LeGrand (TGIB #249) explains: "Being a Tomb Guard is not an easy job...not everyone who tries makes it. In fact, maybe two out of every ten people that ever go to the Tomb to qualify make it past the first two weeks. You must have a deep desire and inspiration to be someone you never thought you could be."[5]

The "Sentinel's Creed," written in 1971, is prominently displayed in the Guard Quarters and is committed to memory by all members of the Tomb Guard. Beginning: "My dedication to this sacred duty is total and whole-hearted," its 99 words eloquently expresses the principles and devotion required at the Tomb.[6] Line six of the code states that a guard's "Standard Will Remain Perfection." This means that all sentinels are expected to constantly improve their performance and strive to be perfect.[7] SSG Jim Cardamon, who served with the 2nd Relief at the Tomb in 1957/58, maintains that if you successfully achieve the unit's elite standards, you are one "of the best of the best."[8] SFC David Nicholson (TGIB #254) agrees. "After seeing the guard change and the Sentinels' dedication," he writes, "I knew it would be an honor and a life-changing experience...I was truly amazed at the dedication of the soldiers I worked with and [I] did my best to perform at their level."[9]

(3D U.S. Infantry Regiment "The Old Guard")
A "new man" stands vigil at the Tomb of the Unknown Soldier. It takes nine months of rigorous study and training to earn the Tomb Guard Identification Badge.

The training for the new men who volunteer at the Tomb is constant and rigorous. The soldiers must maintain their physical fitness levels as well as fulfill all of the normal requirements for combat infantry soldiers. At the Tomb, though, the prospective sentinels must also study and master the history of Arlington National

Cemetery as well as that of the Tomb of the Unknown Soldier. In addition, they are expected to learn the precise grave locations for over 200 notables buried at the cemetery.[10] Throughout the months of intense training, the new men are constantly quizzed on their content knowledge. SP4 Kevin Donovan (TGIB #253) notes that duty at the Tomb was "hard, physically, mentally and emotionally," and that it was extremely difficult to remember "all of the knowledge, [and to] retain it, while completing [all of the] other duties."[11] Being a high profile soldier carries with it enormous responsibilities, and every soldier is expected to appreciate the significance of guarding the Tomb. They are the physical embodiment of the long and noble traditions of the United States Army as well as representations of the nation's Constitutional principles. SGT Benjamin Bell (TGIB #494) explains: "Every night hour that I was posted was yet another in an unbroken string that went back decades." When he trained new men at the Tomb, Bell took the recruits up to the Arlington House where they visited the mass grave of 2,111 Unknowns from the Civil War. Most visitors to Arlington passed by the grey, granite memorial, oblivious to its history or its significance. Yet the hundreds of men who are entombed there sacrificed their lives and their identities in a noble effort to preserve the Union. To become a Tomb Guard, Bell explained to his men, is a rare privilege and something that is attained by only a select few. Their dedication and "precise ritual" would "elevate the Unknowns and [their] military sacrifice into the conscience of the nation." [12]

While on duty, each Tomb sentinel is issued three different uniforms. It is their individual responsibility to maintain and prepare these uniforms to the Tomb's exacting standards. They are constantly evaluated on the quality of their pleats and press lines."[13] The preferred military uniform at the Tomb is the dress Army blouse. The jacket is made of wool and is worn throughout the year, including during the summer months despite Washington's legendary heat and humidity. The color of the blue blouse is reminiscent of the uniforms of the Continental Army during the American Revolution and those of Union forces during the Civil War.

(3D U.S. Infantry Regiment "The Old Guard")
Deputy Secretary of Defense Patrick Shanahan touring the Tomb Guard Quarters at Arlington. One of the sentinels shows him the steel plates on the guard's shoes.

Despite public misperception, a sentinel's blouse is not custom-tailored. Its sleek and smooth appearance is achieved by tucking all excess material into the soldier's slender, 29-inch waist belt. A sentinel will use a lighter to "burn" off any excess threads or stray snags on the fabric. All of the soldier's brass, medals, and military insignia are removable and must be highly polished and shined before being finally pinned onto a uniform. The placement of these items must be precise and accurate to within a regulation 1/16th of an inch when measured with a micrometer.[14] The uniform has to be perfect since it is, in Lonny LeGrand's words: "a direct reflection of our dedication to duty."[15] A walking sentinel's jacket, though, is devoid of military rank, in deference to the sacrifice of the Unknowns who paid the ultimate sacrifice for the nation.

The Tomb sentinel's shoes are standard military-issue, but they have been modified with extra soles to improve a soldier's posture and to protect his feet from the heat or cold on the plaza. The shoes also have metal plates (clickers) installed on the soles and heels since "heel clicks" are the primary signaling method when executing the choreographed movements of the guards. The shoe leather is shined to a high gloss using liquified polish and shoe black. This is a laborious process that takes hours of work each day to achieve perfection. The daily grind of maintaining uniforms, polishing brass, shining shoes, correcting minor errors is "the hardest part of training," according to SFC David Nicholson. Still, he maintains that: "the constant repetition and striving for perfection [is something] that we are all still striving for in our lives today."[16]

All sentinels at the Tomb are given a dispensation to wear sunglasses while on duty since the bright white marble can cause sun blindness and hinder a guard's vision.[17] The other uniforms that are regularly worn by the Tomb Guard are a raincoat for periods of inclement weather and an overcoat for when the temperatures dip below 45 degrees.

For new recruits to the Tomb, their first several weeks are spent isolated and training in the "catacombs." This off-limits area is located under the North Colonnade at the Amphitheater and was once intended to be used as burial crypts for distinguished Americans. It was, however, never used for its intended purpose and became a convenient storage area, with a portion commandeered by the Tomb Guard for training purposes.[18] It is a safe place to practice their walk and to master the manual of arms away from public scrutiny. SGT LeGrand recalls: "Weapons manual was the key—is the weapon tilted left, too high, is the butt of the weapon canted in or out, was your arm position at true 90 degrees?...All these factors played into how you were presented before the public eye."[19]

After a new man is deemed sufficiently proficient, he is permitted to do low visibility walks. These two-hour shifts take place after the cemetery is closed to public visitation and while the Tomb is a restricted military post. After further assessment and correction, the trainee is allowed to enter a relief's regular rotation but remains under constant observation and supervision. His outside performance, including his walk, timing, and precision, is continually being evaluated.[20]

The rubber mat on the plaza is 63 feet long and is positioned in front of the crypts of the World War II/Korean Unknowns and the Vietnam Memorial stone. It is changed every Memorial Day.[21] A "walker" during his assigned vigil takes 21 steps across the mat, turns and faces the Tomb for 21 seconds. This is symbolic of the twenty-one-gun salute, the highest honor rendered in the American military. The sentinel on duty carries a M-14 rifle equipped with a M-6 chrome bayonet.[22] Unlike other honor guard units, the shoulder strap on the weapon is black, symbolic of mourning.[23] The rifle is always positioned by the sentinel between the Tomb and the public, indicative of the guarding process. The Tomb Guard's primary responsibility is to enforce decorum and to ensure an atmosphere of "reverence and respect."[24]

DURING THE SUMMER months (April 1 – September 30), the new men in the Tomb Quarters twice an hour stand at attention and shout "quarter 'til."[25] This alerts the Commander of the Relief and the on-coming Tomb sentinel that they have 15 minutes to finish their preparations for the next Changing of the Guard ceremony.[26] The relief sergeant leaves the Tomb Quarters first, precisely on the half hour. He slowly makes his way down the south walkway and enters the restricted area on the plaza behind the stanchions and chains. Matching the strides of the on-duty guard on the mat, the sergeant walks slowly to a position directly in front of the Tomb. Meanwhile, the oncoming relief sentinel approaches the plaza and operates the bolt on his M-14 rifle to signal his approach.

The relief commander renders a salute to the Unknowns and then turns to address the crowd: "The ceremony you are about to witness is the 'Changing of the Guard,'" he begins. "In keeping with the dignity of this ceremony, it is requested that everyone remains silent and standing." Once the visitors have obeyed his commands, the relief commander again salutes the Unknowns, then returns to the South Plaza and to the inspection block where the new sentinel awaits. The carefully choreographed inspection begins with an examination of the guard's M-14 rifle. The sergeant looks for any

(3D U.S. Infantry Regiment "The Old Guard")
The relief sergeant conducts the inspection of a sentinel's M-14 rifle during the Changing of the Guard. Note the TGIB on the right breast pocket of his uniform.

signs of rust, dirt, or imperfections.[27] To ensure an adequate grip on the rifle, the sergeant is careful to soak his cotton gloves with water prior to leaving the Tomb Quarters. According to the Tomb Guard's rigorous standards, anyone who drops a weapon on the plaza is automatically relieved from duty. Once the rifle inspection is completed, the sentinel's uniform is carefully checked for any deficiencies. If found, the guard will be ordered back to the Tomb Quarters to make a necessary correction.

After completing the inspections, the sergeant commands both soldiers to "order arms." Using heel clicks and sounds to synchronize their timing, the two guards approach one another near the center of the plaza. They come to present arms and salute the Unknowns. The sentinel being relieved will then pass on his orders: "Post and Orders, Remain as Directed." The on-coming sentinel acknowledges these instructions and takes his post while the other sentinel is dismissed and returns to quarters.[28] The impressive ceremony lasts less than ten minutes and every single guard change and walk is meticulously logged into the permanent record books maintained in the quarters. On average, the Tomb Guard conducts over 6,000 guard changes per year.[29]

BEFORE THE MAJOR renovations of the Memorial Amphitheater in the mid-1970s, the original Tomb Quarters were located under the South Colonnade. They were spartan accommodations, consisting of just a small kitchenette, a bunk room (with two double tiered beds), an alcove containing a pressing machine, and a small waiting

(Jim Cardamon)
Tomb Guards PFC Wayne Thomas, PFC Ralph Till, PFC Pete Walters, and SP4 Jim Cardamon at the U.S.Capitol, May 1958. The men stood vigil in the Rotunda during the laying in state of the World War II and Korean Unknowns.

area with a television and bookshelves. During the 1950s, the three reliefs of sentinels were comprised of just four "walkers" and a relief commander. All of the daylight guard changes were conducted on a one-hour rotation and there were very few public wreath ceremonies.[30] This meant that the sentinel on duty would be walking the mat continually during his shift and the guards could anticipate being on the plaza for up to 8 hours per day.[31]

Prior to the post-Vietnam all volunteer army, the majority of soldiers serving with the 3D United States Infantry were draftees. Duty at the Tomb was assigned (not volunteered) to the regiment's top soldiers. Typically, these men were first assigned guard duty at the Army Chief of Staff's home, Post #1, at Fort Myer. There they would learn the basic requirements before being detailed to the Tomb.[32]

The first Tomb Guard Identification Badge (TGIB) was issued in 1958. The 2-inch, sterling silver badge depicts the East Façade of the Tomb with its allegorical figures of Peace, Victory, and Valor. An inverted, open laurel wreath surrounds the low relief engraving of the Tomb with the words: "Honor Guard" boldly written on the bottom. On February 8, 1958, MSG William E. Daniel became the first recipient of the numbered badge: TGIB #1.[33] Initially, badges were issued only for the time that a sentinel served at the Tomb. Once they returned to the regiment, the badge was given back and re-issued to a new, replacement sentinel.[34] This policy was later revised and the TGIB is now assigned as a permanent part of a soldier's orders.

Fewer than 700 Tomb Guard badges have been awarded since its inception. Only after a sentinel has honorably served for 9 months at the Tomb and has, to the satisfaction of the Sergeant of the Guard, mastered all requisite ceremonial duties, uniform requirements, and cemetery knowledge, is he presented with a badge. The TGIB is one of the least awarded badges in the United States military and is the only one that can be revoked at any time, even after a sentinel has left the military and returned to civilian life.[35] Although this happens rarely, it will occur if a guard ever brings dishonor to the Tomb.[36] The regulations read: "When the Commander of The Old Guard becomes aware of information about a current or former member of the Tomb of the Unknown Soldier who was authorized permanent wearing of the Tomb Identification Badge that suggests inappropriate conduct, including, but not limited to, acts of commission or omission for a member of that unit, or the intention to engage in inappropriate conduct," the badge is revoked.[37]

According to Kevin Donovan, becoming a badge holder is: "a tribute to my brothers on my relief" who helped him through his training to become a sentinel.[38] "It is a symbol that anything can be accomplished if you're willing to work hard and dedicate yourself to a goal."[39] SGT Benjamin Bell believes that the TGIB "brings [with it] a responsibility to bring honor to the Unknowns."[40] To honor the sacrifice of the Unknowns, the Tomb Guard collectively awarded them TGIB #175 in the 1970s.

(3D U.S. Infantry Regiment "The Old Guard")
SGT Ruth Hanks' final walk at the Tomb. Hank's became the first female relief commander and the fourth woman to earn her Tomb Guard Identification Badge.

AFTER THE VIETNAM War, the role of women greatly expanded in the nation's armed services. Today, women serve on naval vessels, fly jet aircraft and helicopters, and are deployed in combat roles. They are also eligible to volunteer for duty at the Tomb of the Unknown Soldier.

The Department of Defense transferred the 289th Military Police Company to the 3D United States Infantry at Fort Myer in 1994. This combat support unit included several women military police officers and in 1995, SGT Heather Johnsen (Wagner) became the first female to walk the mat as a Tomb sentinel.[41] The military made only one minor concession for female soldiers who wish to serve at the Tomb, which was a slight reduction in the minimum height requirement (5'8" for women vs. 5'10" for men).[42] Johnsen, like all new guards, successfully mastered the cemetery's history and learned the precise movements expected while on vigil. She maintained and perfected her uniform and was awarded badge number 423.[43] SGT Johnsen served with distinction at the Tomb through December 1996. She maintained that: "There is no higher honor, there is no greater honor. I can't think of anything else I'd rather do for my country than to guard the unknowns.[44]

Since SGT Johnsen, there have been three other women who have also earned their TGIBs: SGT Danyell E. Wilson (TGIB 439), SSG Tonya D. Bell (TGIB 463), and SGT Ruth Hanks (TGIB 643). SGT Hanks holds the distinction of being the first female assistant relief commander and was responsible for conducting the guard change.

Ruth Hanks had been a varsity soccer goalie at Birmingham-Southern College prior to joining the army in 2011. She became a military police officer and was deployed to Afghanistan. There, she met a former Tomb Guard and badge holder and developed an interest in serving at Arlington. She reported for duty at the Tomb in September 2015 and served there for two years. About her service at the Tomb, SGT Hanks notes: "The motto of the tomb guard is 'Soldiers never die until they are forgotten. Tomb guards never forget.' That's what we have to keep doing...The three soldiers whose tombs we guard gave everything. Even their names."[45]

IT WAS A beautiful, late summer day on September 11, 2001 in the Washington, D.C. area. The post-Labor Day crowds at Arlington were noticeably smaller with the approach of fall, but it appeared to be a typical day at the cemetery. There was a full slate of military funerals scheduled throughout the day; Superintendent Jack Metzler was preparing to leave for Capitol Hill where he was scheduled to testify before Congress on land acquisitions and cemetery expansion; the Tomb Guard were maintaining their vigil and were still on the 30-minute rotation for the Changing of the Guard.[46] Shortly after the conclusion of 9:30 AM change, the deafening roar of a low flying jetliner interrupted Arlington's solemnity. The jet noise was followed instantaneously by the sound of an immense explosion that rattled the doors of the Administration building and shook the windows at the Visitors Center. Dark smoke was seen billowing into the blue sky from massive fires burning at the Pentagon. The nation's capital, for the first time since the War of 1812, was under attack.

American Airlines Flight 77 had taken off from Washington's Dulles Airport at 8:20 AM, en route to Los Angeles. The Boeing 757 airliner was 33% full, carrying just 58 passengers and a crew of six.[47] Captain Charles Burlingame, a Naval Academy graduate and reserve officer, was the pilot of the flight. He was assisted in the cockpit by First Officer David Charlebois. After the plane had reached altitude, it was hijacked over southern Ohio by Islamic terrorists. Once the extremists had commandeered the plane, they turned it around and headed back towards Washington, D.C. At 9:37 AM, the plane flew low over the southern portion of Arlington National Cemetery at an estimated speed of 530 miles per hour. It slammed into the west block of the Pentagon, disintegrating upon impact and instantly killing all on board as well as 125 military and civilian workers in the building. Earlier that day, two other planes

ADAM LYNN
DICKMYER
SSG US ARMY
AFGHANISTAN
FEB 2 1984
OCT 28 2010
BRONZE STAR
PURPLE HEART
TOMB SENTINEL
BADGE 528

(Philip Bigler)
The grave of SSG Adam Dickmyer in Section 60. SSG Dickmyer was killed while serving in Afghanistan. He was the third Tomb Guard to die in combat, the first since the Vietnam War.

had been hijacked and deliberately crashed into the twin towers at the New York World Trade Center. The United States lost 2,993 people in the attacks, a death toll that exceeded that of Pearl Harbor. The nation was once again at war, although now with a new state-less enemy.

As the Pentagon was burning, Superintendent Metzler ordered Arlington closed to public visitation. Families who had funerals scheduled that day, though, were given the option of continuing with the services despite the surrounding chaos, albeit with greatly reduced military participation.[48] All of the Tomb sentinels, including those who were off duty, were summoned to the cemetery. The Tomb was declared to be a restricted military post and the ceremonial guard duty was suspended. Instead, sentinel SGT Benjamin Bell and another sentry took up positions on the plaza in their battle dress uniforms (BDU's) to continue the guard, while: "a security perimeter was set up around the Tomb as well."[49]

F-14 fighter planes began combat air patrols over Washington, D.C., while all civilian and commercial flights were grounded nationwide. Fire and police rescue operations continued at the Pentagon and a mobile triage area was established near the impact site to treat and evacuate the wounded. Soldiers from the 3D United States Infantry were dispatched to the area to support civilian rescue efforts as well as to assist in force protection and to begin recovery operations. Over the next several days, several Tomb sentinels were detailed to help look for any survivors, or when needed, to serve, as body bearers for the dead. Throughout the crisis "the Tomb was continuously guarded." [50]

President George W. Bush launched a major military response against terrorist sanctuaries in both Afghanistan and Iraq. Over the ensuing years, many of the Tomb Guard earned their combat infantry badge with units engaged in the nation's global war on terror. SSG Adam Dickmyer (TGIB #528) served at the Tomb of the Unknown Soldier from April 2004 through September 2007. After his tour of duty at Arlington, he joined the 101st Airborne and was deployed to Kandahar, Afghanistan as part of Operation Enduring Freedom. [51] While on patrol in 2010, SSG Dickmyer was killed by a vehicle-borne improvised explosive device (IED); he became the third Tomb Guard to die in combat. SSG Dickmyer was buried with full military honors at Arlington National Cemetery in Section 60. A replica of his Tomb Guard Identification Badge is attached to his government issued headstone. One of his fellow sentinels remembered: "[SSG. Dickmyer] always showed respect and carried himself like a Tomb Guard from day one." [52]

———

THE STANDARD MILITARY sidearm since mid-1980s had been the 9mm Beretta M9 handgun. In 2017, in an effort to modernize, the government initiated a competitive bid process for a replacement weapon. Eventually, a contract for over 200,000 pistols was awarded to the arms manufacturer Sig Sauer. With the Centennial commemorations for the Tomb's anniversary approaching, the company created four commemorative M17 pistols for the Tomb Guard.

Each gun had a special serial number and customized hand grips made from wood taken from the USS *Olympia*, the cruiser that had carried the World War I Unknown from France to America in 1921. Each of the pistols was individually engraved with the Roman Numerals XXI in acknowledgement of the 21-steps that each sentinel takes across the mat while guarding the Tomb. On the sight plate is an etching of the figures of "Peace, Victory, and Valor" from the east façade of the Tomb. The four pistols are individually named "Silence," "Respect," "Dignity," and "Perseverance."[53]

(3D U.S. Infantry Regiment "The Old Guard")
The new, commemorative M17 pistol made for the Tomb Guard by Sig Sauer.

Endnotes

1 George W. Bush. "Remarks at the Tomb of the Unknown Soldier," 11 November 1991: available at: htts://www.presidency.ucsb.edu.

2 *Ibid.*

3 "About the 3rd Infantry Unit," available at: https://www.oldguard.mdw.army.mil/regiment.

4 *The Unknowns: Duty, Honor, Sacrifice.* DVD. Produced by Ethan Morse, Neal Schrodetzki, and Matthew Little. Time To Kill Productions, 2016.

5 SGT Lonny LeGrand. (TGIB #249). Written Interview. 7 November 2018.

6 Sentinel's Creed available at: https://tombguard.org.

7 *Ibid.*

8 SSG James Cardamon. Written Interview. 21 October 2018.

9 SFC David Nicholson (TGIB #254). Written Interview. 12 October 2018.

10 *The Unknowns.*

11 SP4 Kevin Donovan (TGIB #253). Written Interview. 22 October 2018.

12 SGT Benjamin S. Bell (TGIB #494). Written Interview. 28 October 2018.

13 *The Unknowns.*

14 *Ibid.*

15 LeGrand.

16 SFC David Nicholson (TGIB 254). Written Interview. 12 October 2018.

17 Military Police and aviators are also allowed to wear sunglasses even though they are not part of a regulation military uniform. Philip Bigler. I*n Honored Glory: Arlington National Cemetery, the Final Post.* St. Petersburg, Fl.: Vandamere Press, 2010, p. 65.

18 The original design for the Memorial Amphitheater included 48 crypts to be used as graves for famous individuals from each of the states. The plan was abandoned early on due to the difficulties in establishing appropriate protocols for interment. As a result, the crypts were never used and became convenient storage facilities. Several have been destroyed in subsequent renovations. The first Tomb Quarters was built where a few crypts had existed on the south portion of the building. After the 1976 renovations and the construction of the new and current

Tomb Quarters, this area was converted into handicapped bathroom facilities and a special elevator was installed so that people could enter the Amphitheater without climbing steps.

19 LeGrand.

20 Bigler, p. 62.

21 The old rubber mat is taken down to the catacombs after being replaced each Memorial Day. It is then used for the training of the new men.

22 The sentinel also wears a M8A1 scabbard on his waist belt.

23 Traditional honor guard straps are white.

24 *The Unknowns.*

25 The guard change is every thirty minutes during the summer hours. During the winter months, October 1 – March 31, the change is every hour.

26 The Relief Commander is a non-commissioned officer (NCO).

27 The M14 rifle weighs 9.2 pounds and was a standard-issue weapon for the United States military after World War II. It was replaced by the M-16 during the Vietnam War. Today it is used primarily as an honor guard rifle.

28 The Changing of the Guard ceremony can be seen at: https://www.youtube.com/watch?v=MgoZWQ1opDE.

29 SFC Paul Basso (TGIB #487) recorded that in 2015, the Tomb Guard conducted 5,647 walks, 6,022 Guard Changes, 2,550 wreath ceremonies, and 745 historical briefings.

30 Anyone can lay a wreath at the Tomb with prior written permission. During the summer months, a wreath ceremony is conducted between almost every guard change. See: https://www.arlingtoncemetery.mil/Visit/Events-and-Ceremonies/Request-a-Ceremony.

31 James Cardamon. Telephone Interview. 25 October 2018.

32 *Ibid.*

33 William Daniel served at the Tomb from February 1957 through June 1960. The TGIB has since been made retroactive to sentinels who served prior to 1958, although these badges are not numbered. MSG William Daniel (24 Dec. 1924-30 Jan. 2009), Sect. 35, #218. His grave is located near the Memorial Amphitheater.

34 *Ibid.*

35 The astronaut badge is the least awarded badge in the American military; the TGIB is the second.

36 Society of the Honor Guard available at: https://tombguard.org/society/faq/.

37 Guard, Tomb of the Unknown Soldier Identification Badge, Code of Federal Regulations: Title 32-National Defense, Section 578.110.

38 Donovan.

39 *Ibid.*

40 Bell.

41 Marylou Tousignant. "A New Era for the Old Guard," *Washington Post*, 23 March 1996, available at: http:www.washingtonpost.com.

42 Heather Johnsen was 5'11" tall and did not need this dispensation.

43 Tousignant; Also see the Society of the Honor Guard's website, available at: http://www.tombguard.org.

44 See the Arlington National Cemetery website at: http://www.arlingtoncemetery.net/heather-johnsen.htm.

45 Ruth Hanks quoted in Martha Koester. "4th Female Sentinel Proud to Revere Tomb's Unknown Soldiers," *NCO Journal*, 22 February 2017, available at: http://ncojournal.dodlive.mil/tag/sgt-ruth-hanks/.

46 Bigler, p. 113.

47 The plane's capacity was 188 passengers. There were actually 69 people on-board the plane; five of these were the hijackers. The terrorists are intentionally not being included in the totals out of respect for the innocent victims. *The 9-11 Commission Report.* Washington, D.C.: National Commission on Terrorists Attacks Upon the United States, 2004, p. 8.

48 Bigler, p. 114.

49 Bell.

50 *Ibid.*

51 Adam Dickmyer (2 February 1984-28 October 2010), Section 60, #9396.

52 Nathan Lunman quoted at: https://tombguard.org/column/2015.

53 "Sig Sauer Presents Ceremonial M17 Pistols."

Epilogue

[The Tomb's] beauty is the symbol of our national pride in their heroism; our gratitude for their supreme devotion. – Herbert Hoover

The United States continues to maintain its steadfast commitment to locating and identifying all of the nation's missing soldiers and servicemen, regardless of their military rank or the time that has elapsed or the expenses involved. As LTC Oliver North explains: "No country devotes more time and treasure to bring their fallen home as does the United States."[1] These efforts were initiated shortly after the end of World War II. Soldiers from the Graves Registration Service began a methodical search looking for the lost remains of the thousands of missing American sailors and GIs. In 1947, the Central Identification Laboratory was established in Honolulu in conjunction with these ongoing efforts. The CIL-HI attempted to employ the latest scientific methods to help identify all newly recovered remains.

After the subsequent Korean and Vietnam Wars, the Defense POW/MIA Accounting Agency (DPAA) was created to: "continue the mission to recover our fallen," and to do so even during times of peace.[2] Today, years after the end of the last of America's twentieth century wars, the DPAA maintains its global efforts to locate old crash sites and burial locations which could potentially contain the remains of American military personnel. Their work even includes overwater crash sites and sunken ships. These aquatic locations, once identified, are first explored by scuba divers and then are thoroughly excavated by skilled underwater archaeologists.

Before any DPAA recovery teams are ever sent to a region, historians conduct extensive archival research, examining military records, after-action reports, and eyewitness statements. Once the researchers have determined a promising location, an excavation team is dispatched. These expeditions are comprised of skilled scientists, engineers, medical experts, anthropologists, and archaeologists. A military ordnance expert usually accompanies the team on-site since unexploded grenades, unstable explosives, and lethal ammunition are frequently discovered in untended graves. Most of the unexplored areas that are now being discovered are in remote, desolate regions. Before any excavation can take place, the area has to be cleared of jungle and underbrush by support personnel using chainsaws, machetes, and shovels. The recovery team will first conduct a survey of the location and then begin a thorough grid search.

(Department of Defense)
U.S. Army SFC Roy Rodriguez and members of the Joint POW/MIA Accounting Command conduct a search for the remains of an American missing serviceman in Houaphan Province, Laos.

Every team member has been specifically trained to identify bone fragments as well as any other grave artifacts. These items have usually decomposed and been reduced to remnants after having been buried for decades.[3]

Any human remains that are recovered are handled with honor and the utmost respect, since they could be those of an American serviceman who paid the ultimate sacrifice for the nation. A special repatriation ceremony is conducted when the remains are finally transported back to Hawaii. There, the recovered materials and remains will undergo further laboratory examination and analysis conducted by skilled scientific experts. The use of modern technology and procedures, including x-rays, facial overlays, and forensic odontology, have proven to be remarkably successful in identifying thousands of recovered remains. Still, DNA testing is often used to confirm a positive identity. The ultimate goal of the DPAA is to bring closure to MIA families by returning a missing veteran to the United States for an appropriate burial with full military honors.[4] According to a recent report issued by the Defense POW/MIA Accounting Agency, 40% (1,052 men) of all missing American servicemen from the Vietnam War have been recovered and identified since 1972. Currently, 1,592 servicemen still remain classified as MIA from the war as the search continues.[5]

The major advances in forensic technology has meant that it is now possible to identify many of the soldiers, sailors, and servicemen from World War II who were previously buried as unknowns in mass graves. The most ambitious identification project has been an effort to identify the remains of the sailors and Marines who died while serving onboard the USS *Oklahoma*. During the Japanese attack on Pearl Harbor, the battleship was sunk after sustaining several torpedo strikes. The ship capsized at its mooring dock, trapping hundreds of sailors below its decks. Navy rescue teams desperately attempted to cut holes through the overturned ship's hull and successfully saved the lives of 32 sailors who had been trapped inside.[6] Another 429 crew members, however, perished in the sinking. From December 1941 through June 1944, salvage efforts successfully re-

(Philip Bigler)

The USS Oklahoma *Memorial on Ford Island. The ship was sunk during the attack on Pearl Harbor on December 7, 1941. The Unknown dead were eventually buried at the Punch Bowl in Honolulu.*

covered the remains of over 400 entombed sailors, but only 35 individuals could be positively identified and buried in marked graves. The remaining sailors were individually unknown, and eventually were interred as a crew in 46 plots at the National Memorial Cemetery of the Pacific in Honolulu.[7]

In 2003, 58 years after the *Oklahoma* had been sunk, the military authorized the disinterment of the ship's dead in order to conduct DNA testing on the commingled remains. Brigadier General Mark Spindler noted: "We must work as hard as we can to restore their names."[8] Although this ambitious project is ongoing and expected to take years to complete, it is hoped that 80% of the recovered *Oklahoma* dead will eventually be positively identified and returned to surviving family members for proper burial. In December 2017, the DPAA reached a significant milestone when the 100th

(Department of Defense)
An unknown sailor's remains from the USS Oklahoma *are disinterred from the National Memorial Cemetery of the Pacific. Over 100 sailors have been identified using DNA technology.*

(National Archives)
The reinterment ceremony for S2C Warren Hickock. Hickock was killed at Pearl Harbor and was once buried as "X-2 Unknown sailor" unitil his identification in 2005.

Oklahoma sailor was positively identified.[9] These men who were once "unknown but to God," have at last had their lost identities finally restored.

THE FIRST MINOR cracks in the marble die block of the Tomb of the Unknown Soldier were noticed during the Truman administration. These insignificant, physical blemishes were of little immediate concern and were not seen as a threat to the monument's structural integrity or beauty. No one, however, could determine what had caused the initial damage. It was speculated that there probably had been a slight flaw in the uncarved stone which went undetected during the quarrying process. Over time, this imperfection worsened and finally became apparent.

By 1963, the cracks had noticeably expanded. It was decided to conduct a photographic survey of the Tomb to establish an accurate benchmark by which to gauge any further deterioration.[10] Some twelve years later, the fissures on the die block had increased significantly and were beginning to adversely affect the aesthetics of the monument. This led to the first efforts to make some cosmetic repairs to the monument by patching and caulking the cracks.[11]

By 2003, the cracks had worsened and become so large and numerous that Arlington Cemetery Superintendent Jack Metzler supported replacing the die block with an entirely new stone. Furthermore, the once sharp, well-defined features of the allegorical figures of "Peace, Victory, and Valor" on the East Façade of the Tomb, had become worn and indistinct from years of wind, rain, and snow damage. Metzler maintained that the visiting public wanted to see a pristine memorial, not one that was marred by obvious physical flaws. He further cautioned that the existing cracks could eventually lead to a catastrophic structural failure. In an interview with the *New York Times*, Metzler explained that: "We know this is not a stagnant thing. This thing is continuing to move."[12] The Deputy Superintendent of Arlington, Thurmond Higginbotham, went further, claiming that: "I would rather see us do the right thing so that

(Philip Bigler)

The two major cracks in the Tomb of the Unknown Soldier and the environmentally damaged allegorical figures. The cracks have continued to enlarge and may someday threaten the structural integrity of the Tomb.

someday when we have 10,000 people watching the changing of the guard, we won't have a piece of marble fall off."[13]

Metzler initially estimated that the cost of a replacing the original die stone would be close to one million dollars. When an appropriate replacement stone had been found and carved, the actual work on the plaza could be completed within a two-week time frame.[14] Metzler recommended that once removed, the damaged die stone be placed on exhibit in a museum as a historical artifact.

After hearing about Arlington's plight, John Haines, a Colorado businessman, took it upon himself to locate a suitable replacement stone for the Tomb. He personally financed the quarrying of a new die block from the same Yule mine that had been the source of the Tomb's original stone.[15] The U.S. Geological Service concluded that the Haines stone "was found to be remarkably similar in quality to the existing monument in Arlington National Cemetery."[16]

Haines attempted to donate the new Yule block to the federal government, even offering to finance all of the related expenses involved in its transportation to Arlington. But he soon ran into a series of frustrating bureaucratic obstacles. The government insisted that it could not accept a private donation since all federal contracts had to go through a rigorous competitive bidding process. Arlington's Deputy Superintendent, Thurmond Higginbotham, explained: "It's not doable. A citizen can't just give us any piece of marble and say, 'This is what we'll use to replace the tomb.'"[17] As a result, the Haines replacement block was never accepted and remains in perpetual limbo. It currently sits outside of the old Yule Marble Quarry as an unfinished curiosity for visiting tourists.

Metzler's enthusiasm for replacing the existing Tomb, though, was not unanimous. Indeed, the National Trust for Historic Preservation opposed any plans for replacing the die block. The organization's president, Richard Moe, argued that: "[The Tomb] has served since 1932 for Americans to come and grieve for their lost loved ones, and there is absolutely no reason for it to be replaced. Even though there are cracks in the marble, they are purely cosmetic and can easily be repaired."[18] He elaborated further: "This is arguably the nation's most important war memorial, and we are working to insure that it is preserved, not replaced."[19] Amy Hollis, an Architectural Conservator, agreed, stating: "As a preservationist,

I certainly understand the need to retain this original material and honor the sculptor, and the architect, and the original intent of this site as well."[20]

The existing Tomb of the Unknown Soldier is, indisputably, a national treasure and a cherished historical monument. It is the actual shrine that was first envisioned and designed by Lorimer Rich and Thomas Hudson Jones. The current die stone is the original marble block that was carved and shaped on the plaza by the Piccirilli Brothers. The Tomb is the exact same memorial that has been visited by American presidents while in office, including President John F. Kennedy, who stood before the monument on November 11, 1963, just eleven days before his assassination. To remove and replace the existing stone would be, in essence, destroying a significant part of American history and once a replacement is made, it can never be undone.

Congress intervened in the contentious debate and placed a moratorium on any efforts to replace the current die stone. As Virginia Senator Jim Webb, explained: "Though cracked, this monument represents the patriotic spirit of all of the brave unidentified men and women who have fought and died in America's wars."[21] National Trust President, Richard Moe, celebrated the Congressional intercession, claiming: "This is a victory for all Americans who cherish the authentic Monument at the Tomb, just as we love the tattered Star-Spangled Banner and the cracked Liberty Bell."[22]

With all efforts to replace the stone placed on hold, in 2010 initial work began to clean and patch the cracks on the Tomb by conservationists from the Architectural Preservation Services. The largest crack measured 11.3 feet, and ran the entire length of the Tomb, while a secondary fissure was slightly smaller at 8.5 feet. There were several other less prominent cracks also visible. All of these imperfections and fractures had to be covered using a special mixture of lime, cement, and crushed marble to prevent further deterioration by water and debris. The repairs had to blend into the original marble so that the patching was inconspicuous.[23]

All of the conservation work at the Tomb was supervised by the Army Corps of Engineers and had to be done under strict logistical limitations. The repairs had to be completed at night between the hours of 8 PM and 3 AM, a time when the cemetery was closed to the public. Moreover, all evidence of the work had to removed by the end of each shift. Preservationists were also restricted from walking near the crypts of the World War II and Korean Unknowns, due to the sacred nature of the site. [24]

The current conservation is only a temporary fix and has done nothing to address the serious structural issues involving the cracks on the die stone. The ultimate resolution of the issue remains mired in political controversy and Congressional impasse.

DURING THE PELOPONNESIAN War, the great Greek statesmen, Pericles, stood before the Athenian war dead to recognize their supreme sacrifice in the war against Sparta. He charged his fellow citizens to always remember these noble soldiers, eulogizing: "The sacrifice which they collectively made was individually repaid to them; for they received again each one for himself a praise which grows not old, and the noblest of all tombs, I speak not of that in which their remains are laid, but of that in which their glory survives, and is proclaimed always and on every fitting occasion both in word and deed. For the whole earth is the tomb of famous men; not only are they commemorated by columns and inscriptions in their own country, but in foreign lands there dwells also an unwritten memorial of them, graven not on stone but in the hearts of men."[25]

So, too, for the last century, the Tomb of the Unknown Soldier has served as America's enduring monument to the sacrifice and dedication of the nation's millions of soldiers and servicemen who have gallantly served their country during times of peril. The perpetual guard at the Tomb is an inspiring tribute to those citizen-soldiers who have sacrificed their lives for the nation's beliefs and ideals.

Arlington National Cemetery is hallowed ground, a place to relive history. Each headstone represents a biography, a story to be remembered in the continuing chronicle of America. Since 1921, 17 presidents have visited the Tomb to place a wreath in honor of the nation's Unknown Soldiers. The same pilgrimage to the Tomb is repeated each day by the countless visitors to Arlington National Cemetery who come to remember, to honor, and to learn.

On Veterans Day, 1961, John F. Kennedy placed the presidential wreath at the Tomb of the Unknown Soldier. He then delivered a formal address in the Memorial Amphitheater. "On this day of remembrance," the President observed, "let us pray in the name of those who have fought in this country's wars...that there will be no veterans of any further wars—not because all shall have perished but because all shall have learned to live together in peace. And to the dead here in this cemetery, we say: They are the race—they are the race immortal."[26] While the President was speaking, a short distance away on the plaza, a lone sentinel was maintaining the vigil, eternally guarding and protecting America's Tomb of the Unknown Soldier. And so it continues today and every day at Arlington National Cemetery.

Endnotes

1 "Leave No One Behind," *War Stories with Oliver North*, Fox News, broadcast 8 December 2010.

2 Johnie Webb presentation to the VFW, 24 July 2016, available at http://www.dpass.mil.

3 "Leave No One Behind."

4 "The Last B-24," *NOVA*, PBS, Season 45, Episode 16, broadcast 7 November 2018.

5 This statistic is current toOctober 2018. The Defense POW/MIA Accounting Agency updates their statistics monthly and can be viewed at: http://www.dpaa.mil/.

6 Vice Admiral Homer N. Wallin. Pearl Harbor: *Why, How, Fleet Salvage and Final Approval*. Washington, D.C.: Government Printing Office, 1968, p. 177.

7 SFC Kristen Duss. "DPAA Reaches Milestone in USS *Oklahoma* Identification," Defense POW/MIA Accounting Agency available at http://www.dpaa.mil.

8 Brigadier General Mark Spindler quoted in SSG Kathrine Dodd. "USS *Oklahoma* Disinterments Complete," Defense POW/MIA Accounting Agency available at http://www.dpaa.mil.

9 SSG Kathrine Dodd. "USS *Oklahoma* Disinterments Complete," Defense POW/MIA Accounting Agency available at http://www.dpaa.mil.

10 Amy Hollis. "Conserving the Nation's Gravesite: Treatment of the Tomb of the Unknowns at Arlington National Cemetery," available at the National Center for Preservation and Training, NPS and at: http://youtu.be/zhi02VXKPTs.

11 *Ibid*.

12 "Cracks May Force Replacement of Tomb, 2 August 2006, available at: https://www.nytimes.com/2006/08/02/us/02tomb.html.

13 Thurmond Higginbotham quoted in Nancy Lofholm. "Marble for Unknowns Tomb Just Sits," Denver *Post*, 27 August 2008.

14 "Cracks May Force Replacement."

15 V.G. Mossotti, 2014. Comments on the Yule Marble Haines Block—Potential Replacement, Tomb of the Unknown Soldier, Arlington National Cemetery U.S. Geological Survey Open-File Report, available at: http://dx.doi.org, p. 1.

16 *Ibid.*, p. 2.

17 Thurmond Higginbotham quoted in Loftholm.

18 Richard Moe quoted in Sarah Abruzzese. "For a Memorial With Cracks, Fix or Replace?" New York Times, 12 November 2007.

19 Richard Moe quoted in Michael E. Ruane. "Bid to Replace Tomb Stalls," Washington *Post*, 30 January 2008, available at: http://www.washingtonpost.com.

20 Hollis.

21 Jim Webb quoted in Ruane.

22 Richard Moe quoted in "Tomb of the Unknown Soldier Cracked: Repair vs.replacement," Civil War Talk, available at: https://civilwartalk.com.

23 "Work to Repair Tomb of the Unknown begins tonight," 14 September 2011, available at: https://www.youtube.com/watch?v=5LhD9e2LEB4

24 Hollis.

25 Pericles' speech was quoted in Thucydides History of the Peloponnesian War, available at: http://hrlibrary.umn.edu/education/thucydides.html.

26 John F. Kennedy. Veterans Day Speech at the Memorial Amphitheater. 11 November 1961, available at: https://www.presidency.ucsb.edu/.

(National Archives)

A contemporary aerial photograph of the Memorial Amphitheater and the Tomb of the Unknown Soldier.

Appendix A

The Establishment of Decoration Day

HEADQUARTERS GRAND ARMY OF THE REPUBLIC
General Orders No.11, WASHINGTON, D.C., May 5, 1868

The 30th day of May, 1868, is designated for the purpose of strewing with flowers or otherwise decorating the graves of comrades who died in defense of their country during the late rebellion, and whose bodies now lie in almost every city, village, and hamlet church-yard in the land. In this observance no form of ceremony is prescribed, but posts and comrades will in their own way arrange such fitting services and testimonials of respect as circumstances may permit.

We are organized, comrades, as our regulations tell us, for the purpose among other things, "of preserving and strengthening those kind and fraternal feelings which have bound together the soldiers, sailors, and marines who united to suppress the late rebellion." What can aid more to assure this result than cherishing tenderly the memory of our heroic dead, who made their breasts a barricade between our country and its foes? Their soldier lives were the reveille of freedom to a race in chains, and their deaths the tattoo of rebellious tyranny in arms. We should guard their graves with sacred vigilance. All that the consecrated wealth and taste of the nation can add to their adornment and security is but a fitting tribute to the memory of her slain defenders. Let no wanton foot tread rudely on such hallowed grounds. Let pleasant paths invite the coming and going of reverent visitors and fond mourners. Let no vandalism of avarice or neglect, no ravages of time testify to the present or to the coming generations that we have forgotten as a people the cost of a free and undivided republic.

If other eyes grow dull, other hands slack, and other hearts cold in the solemn trust, ours shall keep it well as long as the light and warmth of life remain to us.

Let us, then, at the time appointed gather around their sacred remains and garland the passionless mounds above them with the choicest flowers of spring-time; let us raise above them the dear old flag they saved from his honor; let us in this solemn presence renew our pledges to aid and assist those whom they have left among us a sacred charge upon a nation's gratitude, the soldier's and sailor's widow and orphan.

It is the purpose of the Commander-in-Chief to inaugurate this observance with the hope that it will be kept up from year to year, while a survivor of the war remains to honor the memory of his departed comrades. He earnestly desires the public press to lend its friendly aid in bringing to the notice of comrades in all parts of the country in time for simultaneous compliance therewith.

Department commanders will use efforts to make this order effective.

By order of

JOHN A. LOGAN
Commander-in-Chief

Appendix B

Inscriptions on the
Memorial Amphitheater

The Memorial Amphitheater was constructed between 1915 and 1920. All of the inscriptions listing battles and military leaders pre-date American entry into World War I.

Stage Area

George Washington: *"When we assumed the soldier we did not lay asside the citizen."*

Abraham Lincoln: *"Let us here highly resolve that these dead shall not have died in vain."*

Army Commanders (14)	Navy Commanders (14)
Washington	Jones
Greene	Truxtun
Wayne	Preble
Jackson	Hull
Scott	Decatur
Taylor	Perry
Grant	Macdonough
Sherman	Stewart
Thomas	Farragut
Sheridan	Porter
McClellan	Foote
Meade	Worden
Shafter	Dewey
Merritt	Sampson

Colonnade

War of Independence (10)	War of 1812 (6)	Mexican War (7)
Lexington	Lake Erie	Buena Vista
Bunker Hill	Lake Champlain	Resaca
Ticonderoga	Chippewa	Monterey
Guilford Court House	Lundy's Lane	Contreras
Saratoga	Plattsburg	Churubusco
Trenton	New Orleans	Chapultepec
Monmouth		Molino del Rey
Stoney Point		
King's Mountain		
Yorktown		

War Between the States (19)	Spanish-American War (2)
	Santiago de Cuba
Fort Sumter	Manila
Donelson	
Antietam	
Cedar Creek	
Shiloh	
Gettysburg	
Vicksburg	
Malvern Hill	
Chickamauga	
Franklin	
Nashville	
Knoxville	
Atlanta	
Winchester	
The Wilderness	
Petersburg	
Appomatox	
Mobile Bay	

Appendix C

President Warren G. Harding: Remarks on the Burial of the Unknown Soldier from the Great War

November 11, 1921

Mr. Secretary of War and Ladies and Gentlemen:

We are met today to pay the impersonal tribute. The name of him whose body lies before us took flight with his imperishable soul. We know not whence he came, but only that his death marks him with the everlasting glory of an American dying for his country.

He might have come from any one of millions of American homes.

Some mother gave him in her love and tenderness, and with him her most cherished hopes. Hundreds of mothers are wondering today, finding a touch of solace in the possibility that the nation bows in grief over the body of one she bore to live and die, if need be, for the Republic. If we give rein to fancy, a score of sympathetic chords are touched, for in this body there once glowed the soul of an American, with the aspirations and ambitions of a citizen who cherished life and its opportunities. He may have been a native or an adopted son; that matters little, because they glorified the same loyalty, they sacrificed alike.

We do not know his station in life, because from every station came the patriotic response of the five millions. I recall the days of creating armies, and the departing of caravels which braved the murderous seas to reach the battle lines for maintained nationality and preserved civilization. The service flag marked mansion and cottage alike, and riches were common to all homes in the consciousness of service to country.

We do not know the eminence of his birth, but we do know the glory of his death. He died for his country, and greater devotion hath no man than this. He died unquestioning, uncomplaining, with faith in his heart and hope on his lips, that his country should triumph and its civilization survive. As a typical soldier of this representative democracy, he fought and died, believing in the indisputable justice of his country's cause. Conscious of the world's upheaval, appraising the magnitude of a war the like of which had never horrified humanity before, perhaps he believed his to be a service destined to change the tide of human affairs.

In the death gloom of gas, the bursting of shells and rain of bullets, men face more intimately the great God over all, their souls are aflame, and consciousness expands and hearts are searched. With the din of battle, the glow of conflict, and the supreme trial of courage, come involuntarily the hurried appraisal of life and the contemplation of death's great mystery. On the threshold of eternity, many a soldier, I can well believe, wondered how his ebbing blood would color the stream of human life, flowing on after his sacrifice. His patriotism was none less if he craved more than triumph of country; rather, it was greater if he hoped for a victory for all human kind. Indeed, I revere that citizen whose confidence in the righteousness of his country inspired belief that its triumph is the victory of humanity.

This American soldier went forth to battle with no hatred for any people in the world, but hating war and hating the purpose of every war for conquest. He cherished our national rights, and abhorred the threat of armed domination; and in the maelstrom of destruction and suffering and death he fired his shot for liberation of the captive conscience of the world. In advancing toward his objective was somewhere a thought of a world awakened; and we are here to testify undying gratitude and reverence for that thought of a wider freedom.

On such an occasion as this, amid such a scene, our thoughts alternate between defenders living and defenders dead. A grateful Republic will be worthy of them both. Our part is to atone for the losses of heroic dead by making a better Republic for the living.

Sleeping in these hallowed grounds are thousands of Americans who have given their blood for the baptism of freedom and its maintenance, armed exponents of the nation's conscience. It is better and nobler for their deeds. Burial here is rather more than a sign of the Government's favor, it is a suggestion of a tomb in the heart of the nation, sorrowing for its noble dead.

Today's ceremonies proclaim that the hero unknown is not unhonored. We gather him to the nation's breast, within the shadow of the Capitol, of the towering shaft that honors Washington, the great father, and of the exquisite monument to Lincoln, the martyred savior. Here the inspirations of yesterday and the conscience of today forever unite to make the Republic worthy of his death for flag and country.

Ours are lofty resolutions today, as with tribute to the dead we consecrate ourselves to a better order for the living. With all my heart, I wish we might say to the defenders who survive, to mothers who sorrow, to widows and children who mourn, that no such sacrifice shall be asked again.

It was my fortune recently to see a demonstration of modern warfare. It is no longer a conflict in chivalry, no more a test of militant manhood. It is only cruel, deliberate, scientific destruction. There was no contending enemy, only the theoretical defense of a hypothetic objective. But the attack was made with all the relentless methods of modern destruction. There was the rain of ruin from the aircraft, the thunder of artillery, followed by the unspeakable devastation wrought by bursting shells; there were mortars belching their bombs of desolation; machine guns concentrating their leaden storms; there was the infantry, advancing, firing, and falling—like men with souls sacrificing for the decision. The flying missiles were revealed by illuminating tracers, so that we could note their flight and appraise their deadliness. The air was streaked with tiny flames marking the flight of massed destruction; while the effectiveness of the theoretical defense was impressed by the simulation of dead and wounded among those going forward, undaunted and unheeding. As this panorama of unutterable destruction visualized the horrors of modern conflict, there grew on me the sense of the failure of a civilization which can leave its problems to such cruel arbitrament. Surely no one in authority, with human attributes and a full appraisal of the patriotic loyalty of his countrymen, could ask the manhood of kingdom, empire, or republic to make such sacrifice until all reason had failed, until appeal to justice through understanding had been denied, until every effort of love and consideration for fellow men had been exhausted, until freedom itself and inviolate honor had been brutally threatened.

I speak not as a pacifist fearing war, but as one who loves justice and hates war. I speak as one who believes the highest function of government is to give its citizens the security of peace, the opportunity to achieve, and the pursuit of happiness.

The loftiest tribute we can bestow today—the heroically earned tribute—fashioned in deliberate conviction, out of unclouded thought, neither shadowed by remorse nor made vain by fancies, is the commitment of this Republic to an advancement never made before. If American achievement is a cherished pride at home, if our unselfishness among nations is all we wish it to be, and ours is a helpful example in the world, then let us give of our influence and strength, yea, of our aspirations and convictions, to put mankind on a little higher plane, exulting and exalting, with war's distressing and depressing tragedies barred from the stage of righteous civilization.

There have been a thousand defenses justly and patriotically made; a thousand offenses which reason and righteousness ought to have stayed. Let us beseech all men to join us in seeking the rule under which reason and righteousness shall prevail.

Standing today on hallowed ground, conscious that all America has halted to share in the tribute of heart and mind and soul to this fellow American, and knowing that the world is noting this expression of the Republic's mindfulness, it is fitting to say that his sacrifice, and that of the millions dead, shall not be in vain. There must be, there shall be, the commanding voice of a conscious civilization against armed warfare.

As we return this poor clay to its mother soil, garlanded by love and covered with the decorations that only nations can bestow, I can sense the prayers of our people, of all peoples, that this Armistice Day shall mark the beginning of a new and lasting era of peace on earth, good will among men. Let me join in that prayer.

(National Archives)

President Warren G. Harding speaking at the internment ceremonies for the Unknown Soldier of the Great War. The Unknown was buried on the plaza of the new Memorial Amphitheater at Arlington National Cemetery.

Appendix D

Information Paper: Dept. of the Army

Subject: Unknown Soldier from the Vietnam Era

March 21, 1977

PURPOSE: In view of increasing Congressional interest in the interment of a Vietnam Unknown at the Tomb of the Unknown Soldier in Arlington National Cemetery, this paper explains the various facets of this project and its current status.

BACKGROUND:

a. As a result of the Civil War, 75 national cemeteries had been established by 1873 which contained the graves of 170,162 known and 147,800 unknown Union soldiers. After the Spanish-American War and the China (Boxer) Expedition, the policy of returning American dead to the United States for final interment was initiated.

b. Of the 78,111 remains recovered after World War I, 97.8% were identified. One Unknown was selected from the unidentifiable remains, returned to the United States and interred at the Tomb of the Unknown Soldier on 11 November 1921.

c. Authority for memorialization of an Unknown from World War II was approved by Congress in 1946. However, events in Korea resulted in a Presidential recommendation that the interment of a World War II Unknown be delayed. Legislation approved in 1956 provided for the burial of an Unknown from Korea in conjunction with a World War II Unknown to take place on Memorial Day in 1958. In 1973 Public Law 93-43 was approved which provided for the interment of a Vietnam Unknown. A crypt has been completed at the Tomb to receive the Unknown.

CRITERIA:

The following criteria for the selection of an Unknown were established by the Army Quartermaster General based upon experience gained in the section of the World War I Unknown and were used to screen 8,532 unidentifiable candidates for the selection of a World War II Unknown and 643 unidentifiables for the Unknown from the Korean War. Of primary importance, the remains selected must be those of a member of the Armed Forces of the United States. In addition, to insure that the bodies are those of Americans and will remain unidentifiable is established as follows:

a. Automatic elimination of any remains recovered without clothing, personal effects, and/or other media which would effectively serve to establish nationality.

b. The remains must be nearly complete.

c. Cremated remains are eliminated.

d. There must be no identifying clues with the remains, such as initials on a ring.

e. The Unknown must not have been part of comingled remains from which a residual Unknown may result.

f. There must be no clues to pinpoint the Unknown as a member of a small unit such as a company.

g. Geographic location of recovery, race, dental charts, and/or other physical characteristics must be without significance insofar as screening is concerned.

VIETNAM SITUATION:

a. Approximately 57,453 servicemen lost their lives as the result of the hostilities of the Vietnam Era. Of this number approximately 55,105 remains have been recovered, identified, and returned to the next of kin. Approximately 2,348 United States military personnel and 94 civilians have not been accounted for.

b. Active search and recovery operations for Vietnam had to be discontinued after the withdrawal of American Forces. It is hoped that the current negotiations with representatives of the Socialist Republic of Vietnam will result in authority to reinstitute search and recovery operations.

c. Modern techniques employed by the U.S. Army Central Identification Laboratory, Hawaii (CIL), have resulted in a high percentage of identification of the remains recovered to date. Techniques include dental charting, examination of bones to detect healed fractures or anomalies, analysis of bone and hair samples to determine blood type, and other examination of remains which results in information that is compared against health and dental records of missing or believed-to-be persons. The superimposition of a transparency of the skull over photographic portraits is also employed. Prior to the return this past weekend of the 12 remains from Vietnam, there were only six unidentified remains in the CIL. Three remains recovered between 1970 and 1974 had been recently identified. Of the six unidentified, four have been name associated. That is, circumstances surrounding the recovery of the remains provide good indication as to identity, but a comparison of the remains with health and dental records has not established proof beyond any reasonable doubt. The remaining two cannot be confirmed to be American military personnel.

(National Archives)
President Gerald Ford places a wreath at the Tomb of the Unknown Soldier. He is standing on the empty, center crypt for a Vietnam Unknown Serviceman which has been covered with granite pavers.

Appendix E

President Ronald Reagan: Remarks on the Burial of the Vietnam Unknown Soldier

May 28, 1984

My fellow Americans, Memorial Day is a day of ceremonies and speeches. Throughout America today, we honor the dead of our wars. We recall their valor and their sacrifices. We remember they gave their lives so that others might live.

We're also gathered here for a special event—the national funeral for an unknown soldier who will today join the heroes of three other wars.

When he spoke at a ceremony at Gettysburg in 1863, President Lincoln reminded us that through their deeds, the dead had spoken more eloquently for themselves than any of the living ever could, and that we living could only honor them by rededicating ourselves to the cause for which they so willingly gave a last full measure of devotion.

Well, this is especially so today, for in our minds and hearts is the memory of Vietnam and all that that conflict meant for those who sacrificed on the field of battle and for their loved ones who suffered here at home.

Not long ago, when a memorial was dedicated here in Washington to our Vietnam veterans, the events surrounding that dedication were a stirring reminder of America's resilience, of how our nation could learn and grow and transcend the tragedies of the past.

During the dedication ceremonies, the rolls of those who died and are still missing were read for 3 days in a candlelight ceremony at the National Cathedral. And the veterans of Vietnam who were never welcomed home with speeches and bands,

345

but who were never defeated in battle and were heroes as surely as any who have ever fought in a noble cause, staged their own parade on Constitution Avenue. As America watched them—some in wheelchairs, all of them proud—there was a feeling that this nation—that as a nation we were coming together again and that we had, at long last, welcomed the boys home.

"A lot of healing went on," said one combat veteran who helped organize support for the memorial. And then there was this newspaper account that appeared after the ceremonies. I'd like to read it to you. "Yesterday, crowds returned to the Memorial. Among them was Herbie Petit, a machinist and former marine from New Orleans. 'Last night,' he said, standing near the wall, 'I went out to dinner with some other ex-marines. There was also a group of college students in the restaurant. We started talking to each other. And before we left, they stood up and cheered us. The whole week,' Petit said, his eyes red, 'it was worth it just for that.'"

It has been worth it. We Americans have learned to listen to each other and to trust each other again. We've learned that government owes the people an explanation and needs their support for its actions at home and abroad. And we have learned, and I pray this time for good, the most valuable lesson of all—the preciousness of human freedom.

It has been a lesson relearned not just by Americans but by all the people of the world. Yet, while the experience of Vietnam has given us a stark lesson that ultimately must move the conscience of the world, we must remember that we cannot today, as much as some might want to, close this chapter in our history, for the war in Southeast Asia still haunts a small but brave group of Americans—the families of those still missing in the Vietnam conflict.

They live day and night with uncertainty, with an emptiness, with a void that we cannot fathom. Today some sit among you. Their feelings are a mixture of pride and fear. They're proud of their sons or husbands, fathers or brothers who bravely and nobly answered the call of their country. But some of them fear that this ceremony writes a final chapter, leaving those they love forgotten.

Well, today then, one way to honor those who served or may still be serving in Vietnam is to gather here and rededicate ourselves to securing the answers for the families of those missing in action. I ask the Members of Congress, the leaders of veterans groups, and the citizens of an entire nation present or listening, to give these families your help and your support, for they still sacrifice and suffer.

Vietnam is not over for them. They cannot rest until they know the fate of those they loved and watched march off to serve their country. Our dedication to their cause must be strengthened with these events today. We write no last chapters. We close no books. We put away no final memories. An end to America's involvement in Vietnam cannot come before we've achieved the fullest possible accounting of those missing in action.

This can only happen when their families know with certainty that this nation discharged her duty to those who served nobly and well. Today a united people call upon Hanoi with one voice: Heal the sorest wound of this conflict. Return our sons to America. End the grief of those who are innocent and undeserving of any retribution.

The Unknown Soldier who is returned to us today and whom we lay to rest is symbolic of all our missing sons, and we will present him with the Congressional Medal of Honor, the highest military decoration that we can bestow.

About him we may well wonder, as others have: As a child, did he play on some street in a great American city? Or did he work beside his father on a farm out in America's heartland? Did he marry? Did he have children? Did he look expectantly to return to a bride?

We'll never know the answers to these questions about his life. We do know, though, why he died. He saw the horrors of war but bravely faced them, certain his own cause and his country's cause was a noble one; that he was fighting for human dignity, for free men everywhere. Today we pause to embrace him and all who served us so well in a war whose end offered no parades, no flags, and so little thanks. We can be worthy of the values and ideals for which our sons sacrificed—worthy of their courage in the face of a fear that few of us will ever experience—by honoring their commitment and devotion to duty and country.

Many veterans of Vietnam still serve in the Armed Forces, work in our offices, on our farms, and in our factories. Most have kept their experiences private, but most have been strengthened by their call to duty. A grateful nation opens her heart today in gratitude for their sacrifice, for their courage, and for their noble service. Let us, if we must, debate the lessons learned at some other time. Today, we simply say with pride, "Thank you, dear son. May God cradle you in His loving arms."

We present to you our nation's highest award, the Congressional Medal of Honor, for service above and beyond the call of duty in action with the enemy during the Vietnam era.

Thank you.

(National Archives)
President Ronald Reagan presents the Medal of Honor to the Vietnam Unknown during Memorial Day Services at Arlington National Cemetery, 1984.

Appendix F

Military Cemeteries Abroad

There are 26 permanent American military cemeteries located on foreign soil. Nine of these cemeteries are from World War I while 14 are from World War II. Families in both world wars were offered the option of returning the remains of loved ones killed in action to the United States after a cessation of hostilities and 70% opted to do so.

There were over 4,400 soldiers whose bodies were not identified after World War I. Currently, some 73,000 American sailors and servicemen from World War II remains are still unidentified or unaccountable while 8,209 were declared missing from the Korean War. In 1973, 2,600 soldiers were still missing in action from the Vietnam War but through ongoing recovery and identification efforts, that number has since been reduced to just over 1,600.

The Defense POW/MIA Accounting Agency (http://www.dpaa.mil/) continues its efforts to recover and identify the remains of all American service personnel. By using the latest DNA technology, the military has been able to identify many previously unknown soldiers. Notably, this has included the disinterment of the commingled remains of some 388 previously unknown sailors who perished on board the USS *Oklahoma* at Pearl Harbor. To date, over 30 have been positively identified.

Cemeteries and Memorials. American Battle and Monuments Commission available at: https://www.abmc.gov/.

"Commemorative Sites Booklet." Washington, D.C.: American Battle and Monuments Commission.

World War I

Belgium
Flanders Field American Cemetery
368 burials; 43 missing in action

England
Brookwood American Cemetery
458 burials; 563 missing in action

France
Aisne-Marne American Cemetery
2,289 burials; 1,060 missing in action

Lafayette Escadrille Memorial Cemetery
51 burials; 5 missing in action

Meuse-Argonne American Cemetery
14,246 burials; 954 missing in action

Oise-Aisne American Cemetery
6,023 burials; 241 missing in action

Somme American Cemetery
1,844 burials; 333 missing in action

St. Mihiel American Cemetery
4,153 burials; 284 missing in action

Suresnes American Cemetery
1,565 burials; 974 missing in action

A total of 1,652 unknown soldiers are buried in the eight World War I cemeteries.

World War II

Belgium

Ardennes American Cemetery
5,321 burials; 463 missing in action

Henri-Chapelle American Cemetery
7,992 burials; 450 missing in action

France

Brittany American Cemetery
4,409 burials; 500 missing in action

Epinal American Cemetery
5,254 burials; 424 missing in action

Lorraine American Cemetery
10,489 burials; 444 missing in action

Normandy American Cemetery
9,387 burials; 1,557 missing in action

Rhone American Cemetery
860 burials; 294 missing in action

Italy

Florence American Cemetery
4,401 burials; 1,409 missing in action

Sicily-Rome American Cemetery
7,861 burials; 3,095 missing in action

Luxembourg

Lorraine American Cemetery
5,076 burials; 371 missing in action

Netherlands

Netherlands American Cemetery
8,301 burials; 1,722 missing in action

Philippines

Manila American Cemetery
17,191 burials; 36,286 missing in action

Tunisia

North Africa American Cemetery
2,841 burials; 3,724 missing in action

United Kingdom

Cambridge American Cemetery
3,812 burials; 5,127 missing in action

A total of 6,514 unknown soldiers are buried in the 14 World War II cemeteries.

(Philip Bigler)

The Henri-Chapelle American Cemetery in Hombourg, Belgium. The 57-acre cemetery contains the graves of 7,992 American soldiers including 94 unknowns. It is one of 14 American cemeteries abroad and is maintained by the American Battle Monuments Commission.

Appendix G

Sentinel's Creed

My dedication to this sacred duty is total and wholehearted.
In the responsibility bestowed on me, never will I falter.
And with dignity and perseverance
My standard will remain perfection.
Through the years of diligence
And the discomfort of the elements,
I will walk my tour in humble reverence to the best of my ability.
It is he who commands the respect I protect,
his bravery that made us so proud.
Surrounded by well-meaning crowds by day,
alone in the thoughtful peace of night,
this Soldier in honored glory rest under my eternal vigilance.

(John F. Kennedy Library)

Private First Class Dwight H. Findley
on duty at the Tomb of the Unknown Soldier, 1961.

Bibliography

"137 American Lives Lost; U.S. Demands Explanation," *The Evening World*, 8 May 1915, p. 1.

"Activities of the Graves Registration Service in France, 1919-1920." National Archives and Records Service. RG-111, available online at: https://catalog.archives.gov/id/24713.

"The Actual Unknown Soldier—Remembrance Day, World War I," *YouTube*, 13 June 2018, https://youtu.be/v=cvOI4RPe8v0.

Allen, Michael J. "Sacrilege of a Strange, Contemporary Kind," *The Unknown Soldier and the Imagined Community after the Vietnam War.*" *History and Memory*, vol. 23, no. 2, 2011, pp. 90–131. *JSTOR*, JSTOR, www.jstor.org/stable/10.2979/histmemo.23.2.90.

_____. *Until the Last Man Comes Home: POWs, MIAs, and the Unending Vietnam War*. Chapel Hill: University of North Carolina Press, 2009

Anders, Steven E. "With All Due Honors: A History of the Quartermaster Graves Registration Mission" available at: http://old.qmfound.com/grave.htm.

"Arlington Cornerstone Services to Draw Veterans," *The Evening Star*, 30 Sept. 1915, p. 17.

"Arlington Swept by Terrific Thunderstorm," *The Evening Star*, 5 June 1914, p. 3.

Bailey, Ron. *The Colorado Yule Marble Quarry: Our National Treasure*. DVD, 2009.

Bell, SGT Benjamin S. (TGIB #494). Written Interview. 28 October 2018.

Bigler, Philip. *In Honored Glory: Arlington National Cemetery, the Final Post*. St. Petersburg, Fl.: Vandamere Press, 2010.

Bowie, Beverley M. "Known But to God," *National Geographic Magazine*, November 1958, pp. 593-605.

Brands, H.W. *Woodrow Wilson*. New York: Time Books, 2003.

Budreau, Lisa M. *Bodies of War: World War I and the Politics of Commemoration in America, 1919 – 1933*. New York: New York University Press, 2010.

"Capital Honors GAR," *The Washington Times*, 29 Sept. 1915, p. 1.

Cardamon, SSG James. Written Interview. 21 October 2018.

_____. Telephone Interview. 25 October 2018.

"Care Taken to Protect Papers in Memorial Corner Stone," *The Evening Star*, 13 Oct. 1915, p. 10.

Cemeteries and Memorials. American Battle and Monuments Commission, available at: https://www.abmc.gov/.

Chang, Iris. *The Rape of Nanking: The Forgotten Holocaust of World War II*. New York: Basic Books, 1997.

Chase, Enoch A. "Fame's Eternal Camping Ground: Beautiful Arlington, Burial Place of America's Illustrious Dead," *National Geographic Magazine*, 1928, pp. 621-638.

"Chief of Nation Aids in Honoring Memory of Dead," *The Evening Star*, 13 Oct. 1915, p. 1.

Clark, Thurston. *Pearl Harbor Ghosts: A Journey to Hawaii Then and Now*. New York: William Morrow and Company, Inc., 1991.

"Commemorative Sites Booklet." Washington, D.C.: American Battle and Monuments Commission.

"Conditions Due to War Halt Amphitheater," *The Evening Star*, 10 April 1918, p. 18.

The Congressional Medal of Honor: The Names, the Deeds. Forest Ranch, CA.: Sharp & Dunnigan, 1984.

"Coolidge Favors Armed Guard at Tomb of the Unknown Soldier when Told of Disrespect," *The Evening Star*, 8 March 1926, p. 1.

Cooling, Benjamin Franklin. *USS* Olympia. Annapolis: Naval Institute Press, 2000.

Crane, David. *Empires of the Dead: How One Man's Vision Led to the Creation of WWI's War Graves*. London: William Collins, 2013.

"Dedication of Maine Monument: A Feature of Memorial Day Celebration at Arlington," *The Evening Star*, 30 May 1915, p. 27.

"Designs for Tomb Competition Asked," *The Evening Star*, 12 Jan. 1928, p. 38.

"The Distressing Truth Revealed Why It is Not Possible to Properly Bury Soldier Dead from the Torn Battlefields and How the Undertakers are Pressing the Scheme for Business Reasons," *The Washington Times*, 8 February 1920, p. 2.

Donovan, SP4 Kevin (TGIB #253). Written Interview. 22 October 2018.

Echoes of the Great War: American Experiences of World War I. Washington, D.C.: The Library of Congress, 2017.

English, Candice M. "A Noble Cause: Government Manipulation of the Vietnam Unknown Soldier." Masters Thesis, Georgia College and State University, 2011.

"Funeral of the Unknown Soldier," *YouTube*, 14 June 2018, https://youtube/C9O0U-g2VSk.

Gavaghan, Michael. *The Story of the Unknown Warrior: 11 November 1920*. London: M. and L. Publications, 1995.

"German Official Note to U.S. To-Day Insists Blame Rests with England; Sorry American Lives were Lost," *The Evening World*, 10 May 1915, p. 1.

Gilbert, Martin. *The First World War: A Complete History*. New York: Henry Holt and Company, 1994.

Green, Constance McLaughlin. *Washington: Capital City 1879-1950*. Princeton: Princeton University Press, 1963.

"Ground is Broken for Amphitheater," *The Evening Star*, 1 March 1915, p. 2.

Grubb, Evelyn and Carole Jose. *You Are Not Forgotten: A Family's Quest for Truth and the Founding of the National League of Families*. St. Petersburg, FL.: Vandamere Press, 2008.

"Guard Disapproved at Unknown's Tomb," *The Evening Star*, 24 Oct. 1925, p. 26.

"Guns along the Meuse Roar Grand Finale of Eleventh Hour," Stars and Stripes, 15 September 1918, p. 1.

Hammond, William M. *The Unknown Serviceman of the Vietnam Era*. Washington, D.C.: Center of Military History, 1985.

Hanson, Neil. *The Unknown Soldier: The Story of the Missing of the Great War*. London: Transworld Publishers, 2005.

Harding, Warren G. "The Unknown American Soldier." Washington, D.C.: Government Printing Office, 1921. Available at: https://archive.org/details/unknownamericans00hard.

Hawaii At War. Honolulu: *Honolulu Star Bulletin*, 1942.

"Heroes Live Again in Memory of American People," *The Evening Star*, 31 May 1915, p. 1.

"Heroism Recalled as Tribute is Paid to Confederate Dead," *The Evening Star,* 4 June 1914, pp. 1-2.

Holmes, Richard. *Tommy: The British Soldier on the Western Front 1914-1918*. London: Harper/Collins Publishers, 2014.

Honaker, Charles W. *The Dead Were Mine*. Charles W. Honaker, 2014.

"Honor Confederate Dead," *The Sunday Star*. 31 May 1914, p. 15.

Holt, Dean W. *American Military Cemeteries*. Jefferson, N.C.: McFarland & Company, Inc., Publishers, 2010.

Inaugural Addresses of the Presidents of the United States from George Washington 1789 to George Bush 1989. Washington, D.C.: United States Government Printing Office, 1989.

Inglis, K.S. "Entombing Unknown Soldiers from London and Paris to Baghdad," *History and Memory*, vol. 5, no. 2, 1993, pp. 7-31. *JSTOR*, JSTOR, www.jstor.org/stable/256-18650.

"'Is All Heroes Day,' Says Mr. Daniels at Memorial Dedication," *The Evening Star*, 15 May 1920, p. 4.

"Judge Kimbell is Claimed by Death," *The Evening Star*, 15 May 1916, p. 4.

Keene, Judith. "Bodily Matters Above and Below Ground: The Treatment of American Remains from the Korean War." *The Public Historian*, vol. 32, no. 1, 2010, pp. 59–78. *JSTOR*, JSTOR, www.jstor.org/stable/10.1525/tph.2010.32.1.59.

Larson, Eric. *Dead Wake: The Last Crossing of the Lusitania.* New York: Crown Publishers, 2015.

"Lee Ignored: Dixie Roiled," *The Washington Times*, 9 May 1920, p. 1.

Letters to Brigadier General Elwood Richard Quesada. Dwight D. Eisenhower Library: Papers 1920-1967, Box 1.

LeGrand, SGT Lonny. (TGIB #249). Written Interview. 7 November 2018.

Logan, John. "General Orders #11." Lane Memorial Library available at: http://www.hampton.lib.nh.us.

Long Shadow: Remembering and Understanding. Directed by Russell Bames, historian David Reynolds, Clearstory, 2014. *Netflix,* https://www.netflix.com/browse?jbv=80109639&jbp=0&jbr=1.

Long Shadow: Us and Them. Directed by Russell Bames, historian David Reynolds, Clearstory, 2014. *Netflix,* https://www.netflix.com/browse?jbv=80109639&jbp=0&jbr=1.

MacArthur, Douglas. *Reminiscences.* McGraw-Hill Book Company, 1964.

Mather, Paul D. *MIA: Accounting for the Missing in Southeast Asia.* Washington, D.C.: National Defense University Press, 1994.

McElya, Micki. *The Politics of Mourning: Death and Honor in Arlington National Cemetery.* Cambridge: Harvard University Press, 2016.

The Congressional Medal of Honor: The Names and Deeds. California: Sharp & Dunnigan, 1984.

Memorial Amphitheater. Arlington National Cemetery available at: http://www.arlingtoncemetery.mil/Explore/Memorial-Amphitheater.

Merridale, Catherine. *Lenin on the Train.* New York: Metropolitan Books, 2017.

Metzler, John C. "The Arlington National Cemetery." *Records of the Columbia Historical Society, Washington, D.C.*, 60/62, 1960, pp. 224–230. *JSTOR*, JSTOR, www.jstor.org/stable/40067227.

Miglorie, Catherine. *Vermont's Marble Industry: Images of America.* Charleston, S.C.: Arcadia Publishing, 2013.

"Mines Destroy Five Ships; 95 Perish," *The Washington Times*, 18 Nov. 1915, p. 1.

Mossman, B.C. and M.W. Stark. *The Last Salute: Civil and Military Funerals 1921-1969.* Washington, D.C.: Department of the Army, 1971.

"Mrs. Wilson Dies at White House," *The Evening Star*, 7 August 1914, p. 1.

"Murder, Lust, Pillage, Prevailed in Belgium," *The Washington Herald*, 13 May 1915, p. 2.

"New Amphitheater to be America's Westminster Abbey," *The Evening Star*, 27 May 1917, p. 6.

Nicholson, SFC David (TGIB #254). Written Interview. 12 October 2018.

Nixon, Richard M. *The Memoirs of Richard Nixon.* New York: Grosset & Dunlap, 1978

O'Donnell, Patrick K. *The Unknowns: The Untold Story of America's Unknown Soldier and WWI's Most Decorated Heroes Who Brought Him Home.* New York: Atlantic Monthly Press, 2018.

"Pacifists Attack Senator Lodge in Capitol Corridor," *The Evening Star*, 2 April 1917, p. 1.

"Pacifists Besiege Capitol but Fail to Gain Entrance," *The Evening Star*, 2 April 1917, p. 2.

Poole, Robert M. *On Hallowed Ground: The Story of Arlington National Cemetery.* New York: Walker & Company, 2009.

"President and Mrs. Galt Wed in Presence of the Families: Honeymoon at Hot Springs, VA.," *The Evening Star*, 19 Dec. 1915.

"President Lauds Heroes of Nation," *The Sunday Star*, 31 May 1914, pp. 1, 15.

Presidential Elections 1789 – 2004. Washington, D.C.: Congressional Quarterly, Inc., 2005.

"President's Tribute to Men Who Fought," *The Evening Star*, 15 May 1920, p. 1.

"President Wilson's War Proclamation," *The Washington Times*, 6 April 1917.

Program of the ceremonies at the dedication of the Arlington Memorial Amphitheater, National Cemetery, Arlington, Virginia, May 15, 1920, available at: https://lccn.loc.gov/20011537.

"Reports of Desecration Lead Davis to Order Guard," *The Evening Star*, 24 March 1926, p. 2.

Report of the Quartermaster General, U.S. Army to the Secretary of War. Washington, D.C.: Government Printing Office, 1919.

"Secretary Daniels Predicts Memorial Bridge Will Join Arlington and the Capital," *The Evening Star*, 13 Oct. 1915, p. 11.

Sherman, John Dickinson. "The Unknown Dead," *Fulton County Tribune*, 31 Dec. 1920, p. 2.

"Shrine to Heroes Opened to Nation," *The Evening Star*, 16 May 1920, p. 2.

Shoman, Joseph. *Crosses in the Wind: Graves Registration Service in the Second World War*. New York: Stanford House, Inc. 1947.

Simpson, Kirke Larue. *The Unknown Soldier*. New York: Service Bulletin of the Associate Press, December 1921.

Smith, Jeremy Gordon. *Photographing the Fallen: A War Graves Photographer on the Western Front, 1915-1919*. East Yorkshire: Pen and Sword Ltd., 2017.

Stauffer, Alvin P. *The Quartermaster Corps Operations in the War Against Japan*. Washington, D.C.: Center of Military History, 2004.

Steere, Edward and Thayer M. Boardman. *Final Disposition of World War II Dead:1945-1951*. Washington, D.C.: Office of the Quartermaster General, 1951.

"Story of the Tomb of the Unknown Warrior," *YouTube*, 13 June 2018, https://youtu.be/tN-6NctDdTa.

"Stricken Belgians Rejoice over Food," *The Evening Star*, 14 Nov. 1914, p. 4.

"Stricken Belgium Again Seeks Aid," *The Evening Star*, 18 Nov. 1914, p. 9.

"Tribute is Paid to Sailor Dead at Maine Memorial Services at Arlington Cemetery," *The Evening Star*, 01 June 1915, p. 7.

Summers, Harry G., Jr. *Historical Atlas of the Vietnam War*. Boston: Houghton Mifflin Company, 1995.

Thomas, Bill. "The Last Soldier buried in Tomb of the Unknowns Wasn't Unknown," *Washington Post Magazine*, 8 November 2012, available at: https://www.washingtonpost.com.

The Unknowns: Duty, Honor, Sacrifice. DVD. Produced by Ethan Morse, Neal Schrodetzki, and Matthew Little. Time To Kill Productions, 2016.

"Unknown's Tomb Finishing Urged," *The Evening Star*, 15 April 1927, p. 1.

"USS Maine Memorial." Arlington National Cemetery available at: http://www. arlingtoncemetery.mil/Explore/Monuments-and-Memorials/USS-Maine-Mast-Memorial.

Voices From the Tomb. DVD. Directed by Tom Denne. Montgomery College Television Production, 2004.

Wagner, Burt. "Opposes Any Addition to Tomb of Unknown," *The Evening Star*, 29 April 1927, p. 8.

Wagner, Margaret E. *American and the Great War.* New York: Bloomsbury Press, 2017.

Wagner, Sarah. "The Making and Unmaking of an Unknown Soldier." *Social Studies of Science*, vol. 43, no. 5, 2013, pp. 631–656. *JSTOR*, JSTOR, www.jstor.org/stable/43284199.

Waldman, Michael, ed. *My Fellow Americans: The Most Important Speeches of America's Presidents from George Washington to George W. Bush.* Naperville, Ill.: Sourcebooks, Inc., 2003.

Wallen, Homer N. *Pearl Harbor: Why, How, Fleet Salvage and Final Appraisal.* Washington, D.C.: Government Printing Office, 1968.

"War Congress is Besieged by Pacifist: Wilson May Go to Capitol Late Today; Hostile Constituent Attacks Lodge," *The Washington Times*, 2 April 1917, p. 1.

"Wars' Veterans Join in Dedication of Amphitheater," *The Evening Star*, 15 May 1920, pp. 1, 4.

"Whole Nation Joins Wilson In His Tribute to Hero Dead," *The Washington Times*, 31 May 2015, p. 1, 3.

"Wilson Allays G.A.R. Feelings: His Belated Acceptance to Speak Not Entirely Satisfactory, However," *The Washington Herald*, 31 May 1914, p. 1.

"Wilson Gives in to G.A.R.'s Protest," *The New York Tribune*, p. 4.

"Wilson to Follow Saturday Custom," *The Evening Star*, 29 May 1914, p. 1.

Wilson, Woodrow. Memorial Day Address at Arlington National Cemetery, May 30, 1914. The American Presidency Project available at: http://www. presidency.ucsb.edu/ws/index.php?pid=65378

Wilson, Woodrow. President Wilson's Declaration of Neutrality, 19 August 1914. Teaching American History available at: http://teachingamericanhistory. org/library/document/president-wilsons-declaration-of-neutrality/.

World War I Remembered. Washington, D.C.: The National Park Service, 2017.

Younger, Edward F. "I Chose the Unknown Soldier," *The Evening Star:* This Week, 8 November 1936, p. 2.

Index

Acknowledgments

Arlington National Cemetery is a special, sacred place. In October 1982, my wife and I were married on the portico of the Arlington House mansion on a beautiful, autumn day. One year later, almost to the day, I received a civil service appointment to serve as one of the cemetery's historians. Each day that I went to work was inspiring. I was able to witness and experience history through the lives and stories of our nation's military veterans. After two years, I returned to my teaching career. In 1986, I wrote a history of Arlington entitled: *In Honored Glory: Arlington National Cemetery, the Final Post*. At that time, my book was the only current history of the cemetery. Today, it remains on sale at Arlington's bookstore after having gone through four editions and 23 printings. Both of my parents have since been buried at Arlington. Their grave is located in Section 7A, adjacent to the great Jimmy Doolittle and just a short distance below the Tomb of the Unknown Soldier. My in-laws are likewise buried nearby in Section 7.

This book's genesis began with the approach of the Amphitheater's and Tomb's centennials. It has been an eventful 100 years and it was a story that needed to be documented and told in a focused narrative. Conducting research for me is exciting and inspiring. A historian is, in many ways, a sleuth of the past engaged in an unending quest for facts and the unadulterated truth. It is always a fascinating journey. I spent several days and countless hours at the National Archives going through boxes of original documents, military reports, commission reports, letters, and photographs. I was also fortunate to work at the Commission of Fine Arts in Washington, D.C. The Commission is the main protector of our nation's memorial history and there, historian Kay Fanning provided me with access to their many files and meeting minutes. For her efforts, I am especially thankful. During the writing of this book, I had the opportunity to visit the Eisenhower Library in Abilene, Kansas. Valoise Armstrong and Kathleen Strauss were extremely supportive and made that visit productive. Several former Tomb Guards have graciously shared with me their experiences and views about the Tomb. Kevin Donovan has been particularly supportive and encouraging in this project. I would also like to thank sentinels Dave Nicholson,

Lonny LeGrand, Jim Cardamon, and Benjamin Bell for their assistance. Lastly, I am indebted to the dozens of other historians and scholars whose numerous books and insightful research have aided me in compiling this history of the Tomb.

My wife, Linda, has remained my most supportive partner in this endeavor. Her insights and suggestions have enhanced this book immeasurably. To all of these individuals, named and unnamed, I extend my most heartfelt thanks.

Praise for Philip Bigler's book:
Tomb of the Unknown Soldier

"A comprehensive account about one of our nation's most sacred monuments... Expertly written by the utmost knowledgeable source, Philip Bigler... A compelling, poignant read...I highly recommend this book!"

Stacy Lee Carroll

"By far, this is the most complete and comprehensive book on the origin and continuing history of our nation's most sacred shrine. A must for all and should be mandatory reading for all who wears the uniform of an American Service-member."

Reggie Mason, TGIB #239

Contact & Booking Information

info@appleridgepublishers.com